The First Marx

ALSO AVAILABLE FROM BLOOMSBURY

The First Marx

A Philosophical Introduction

**DOUGLAS BURNHAM AND
PETER LAMB**

BLOOMSBURY ACADEMIC
LONDON • NEW YORK • OXFORD • NEW DELHI • SYDNEY

BLOOMSBURY ACADEMIC
Bloomsbury Publishing Plc
50 Bedford Square, London, WC1B 3DP, UK
1385 Broadway, New York, NY 10018, USA

BLOOMSBURY, BLOOMSBURY ACADEMIC and the Diana logo are trademarks of
Bloomsbury Publishing Plc

First published in Great Britain 2019

A catalogue record for this book is available from the British Library.

A catalog record for this book is available from the Library of Congress.

ISBN: HB: 978-1-3500-2686-5
PB: 978-1-3500-2961-3
ePDF: 978-1-3500-2685-8
eBook: 978-1-3500-2687-2

Typeset by Newgen KnowledgeWorks Pvt. Ltd., Chennai, India
Printed and bound in Great Britain

To Catherine, Eleanor and Val

CONTENTS

PREFACE

Karl Marx was born on 5 May 1818. We finished the manuscript for this book two months before the day of his bicentennial anniversary. The first Marx with whom we are concerned in the book actually began to emerge in the 1830s when his voracious reading led him to discover Kant, Hegel and the thinkers who became known as the Young Hegelians. He soon became very critical, although to different degrees, of all these philosophers along with many others of his own times and before. By the late 1840s, Marx had begun to undergo the process of metamorphosis by which he gradually became quite a different thinker – albeit one who never entirely abandoned many of his earlier ideas, even though he voiced some of them in quite different terms.

We are not concerned in what follows with the later Marx, tempting as it is in some places to compare and contrast him with the first Marx. Instead we have identified ways in which the first Marx's many various writings, along with some of those of Engels with whom he had had already by 1844 begun to work closely, can together be reconstructed to form a coherent, radical social and political philosophy. Marx at times indicated that he intended to do something like this. Once, however, he had abandoned the manuscript of *The German Ideology* to the mice, philosophy had taken a back seat as he was concerned primarily with actually changing the world. We hope our reconstruction makes a worthwhile contribution to the early project which he never finished.

Douglas Burnham and Peter Lamb
March 2018

ACKNOWLEDGEMENTS

We would like to thank everybody at Bloomsbury, especially Frankie Mace and Liza Thompson, for being so understanding about the unfortunate and unavoidable delay in submitting our manuscript. We are also very grateful to the staff of the National Health Service for making the completion of this book possible.

Thanks go to Staffordshire University for allowing us the time to work on the book and to our colleagues at the University who have been very helpful in many ways. We also acknowledge the invitation we accepted to present our ideas on the first Marx in the Royal Institute of Philosophy lecture series at Keele University. We received some very helpful questions and other feedback from the audience at our lecture.

Finally, it almost goes without saying that we thank Val, Catherine, Eleanor, others in our families, our colleagues and our friends for all their help over the course of a very difficult period.

A NOTE ON REFERENCING

For secondary sources, we use the (author, date: page[s]) method in the text, with a list of references at the end of the book. The references also include Marx and Engels' *Collected Works*, 50 volumes. To help readers trace items referenced from the *Collected Works*, these items are inserted in brackets in the text in the following style: (EPM, CW3: p[pp] ... .). Please see Table 1.

TABLE 1 Items in Marx and Engels' *Collected Works* (CW)

Reference in Text	Author and Title
C1, CW35	Marx, *Capital, Volume One*
CAAZ, CW1	Marx, 'Communism and the *Augsburg Allgemeine Zeitung*'
CCHPL, CW3	Marx, *Contribution to the Critique of Hegel's Philosophy of Law*
CCHPLI, CW3	Marx, *Contribution to the Critique of Hegel's Philosophy of Law. Introduction*
CE, CW3	Engels, 'The Condition of England'
CJM, CW3	Marx, 'Comments on James Mill, *Élémens d'économie politique*'
CMN, CW3	Marx, 'Critical Marginal Notes on the Article "The King of Prussia and Social Reform by a Prussian"'
CPE, CW29	Marx, *A Contribution to the Critique of Political Economy*
CQG, CW6	Engels, 'The Constitutional Question in Germany'
CWCE, CW4	Engels, *Condition of the Working Class in England*
DAKG, CW6	Marx, 'Declaration Against Karl Grün'
DD, CW1	Marx, *Doctoral Dissertation: Difference Between the Democritean and Epicurean Philosophy of Nature*
DLTW, CW1	Marx, 'Debates on the Law on Thefts of Wood'

Reference in Text	Author and Title
EPM, CW3	Marx, *Economic and Philosophic Manuscripts of 1844*
FNL, CW6	Engels, 'The Festival of Nations in London'
GI, CW5	Marx and Engels, *The German Ideology*
HF, CW4	Marx and Engels, *The Holy Family, or Critique of Critical Criticism*
JCFM, CW1	Marx, 'Justification of the Correspondent from the Mosel'
LA28/12/1846, CW38	Marx, 'Letter to Annenkov 28/12/1846'
LA179, CW1	Marx, 'Leading Article 179 in the *Kölnische Zeitung*'
LB, CW49	Engels, 'Letter to Bloch, 21–22/9/1890'
LDFJ, CW3	Marx, 'Letters from *Deutsch-Französische Jahrbücher*'
LF 3/10/1843, CW3	Marx, 'Letter to Feuerbach, 3/10/1843'
LF 11/8/1844, CW3	Marx, 'Letter to Feuerbach, 11/8/1844'
LM 19/11/1844, CW38	Engels, 'Letter to Marx, 19/11/1844'
LM 28/9/1892, CW49	Engels, 'Letter to Mehring, 28/9/1892'
LMFT, CW1	Marx, 'Letter from Marx to His Father in Trier'
LR 13/3/1843, CW1	Marx, 'Letter to Arnold Ruge, 13/3/1843'
MCP, CW6	Marx and Engels, *Manifesto of the Communist Party*
OCPE, CW3	Engels, *Outlines of a Critique of Political Economy*
OJQ, CW3	Marx, *On the Jewish Question*
PP, CW6	Marx, *The Poverty of Philosophy*
Pr, CW1	Editors, 'Preface'
RBBA-C, CW5	Marx and Engels, 'A Reply to Bruno Bauer's Anti-Critique'
RYM, CW1	Marx, 'Reflections of a Young Man on the Choice of a Profession'
SFEA, CW3	Marx, 'Summary of Frederick Engels' Article "Outlines of a Critique of Political Economy" Published in *Deutsch–Fronzösiche Jahbücher*'
SR, CW2	Engels, *Schelling and Revelation*
TF, CW5	Marx, *Theses on Feuerbach*

CHAPTER ONE

Introduction

In the early to mid-1840s, Karl Marx produced a wide and varied range of writings which, when considered together, comprise a coherent and cogent political philosophy. Beginning with the doctoral dissertation (DD, CW1) he submitted in the spring of 1841, and spanning the next five years until he and Friedrich Engels wrote *The German Ideology* (GI, CW5) in 1845 and 1846, the building blocks of this philosophy emerged in an untidy assortment of books, journalistic pieces, letters, drafts and various other documents. The majority of these items were never published in Marx's lifetime and the fragments of the philosophy embedded in this assortment have yet to be satisfactorily pieced together.

The Marx one finds in the fragments is generally seen not as a political philosopher in his own right, but as merely a prologue or anticipation of his later work. This book challenges that view. It should perhaps be stressed from the outset that we are not suggesting that the philosophy assembled in its chapters will somehow enlighten readers with very broad truths about the world. Indeed, as Jonathan Wolff suggests in his introductory book *Why Read Marx Today?* such truths are rarely considered to be the main concern one has in mind when suggesting that the work of a long-deceased philosopher is worth reading again. As Wolff (2002: 101) puts it, 'we value the work of the greatest philosophers for their power, rigour, depth, inventiveness, insight, originality, systematic vision, and, no doubt, other virtues too'. He comments briefly on such virtues as can be found in Marx's early writings. We hope that by piecing the different parts of those writings together in a more detailed study, such virtues will be very clear to see. Although we broadly sympathize with much of what Marx had to say in this early work, the intention is certainly not to put him on a pedestal as some kind of prophet. Echoing what Terry Eagleton (2011: x) has recently said of Marx's work more generally, this book suggests that the early ideas may be presented 'not as perfect but as plausible'. In other words, there is a middle ground between idolizing a historical thinker as our 'contemporary' and treating him or her as of mere historical interest. Of course, there is nothing wrong with being of historical interest, but the coherence of the topic matters little in that case. Eagleton calls this middle ground 'plausible', but we prefer the term 'fertile'. That is to say, there are ideas and analyses in the early Marx that merit our attention, and implications or extensions that have not been pursued to their fullest extent. Indeed, since, as we have claimed, this period of Marx's work has not yet received *sustained treatment on its own terms*, this fertility might prove greater than anyone expects.

The doctoral dissertation and *The German Ideology* were among the early works that were published only posthumously. While these two items may be identified as marking imprecise boundaries of the period in question, they should not be considered as strictly prescribed outer limits that the present study should not cross. Occasionally, indeed, some of his very early writings warrant attention. The same can be said regarding some of his later ones, insofar as they may shed illumination upon the period in question. Nevertheless, as the earlier writings were written in his youth and the later ones when his main interests had changed, one can find in the period on which we concentrate the political philosopher to whom we might refer as the *first Marx*. In what follows, we identify and analyse a self-contained, coherent, plausible and indeed fertile philosophical account of human being, production, alienation, exploitation, change and emancipation in works including the dissertation published in 1841, *The German Ideology* which Engels and he completed early in 1846 and various writings in between.

The identification of *The German Ideology* as marking the end of the period of the first Marx may surprise some readers. It is, indeed, traditionally considered as a text in which Marx had abandoned the concern with the nature and alienation of the human being and began instead to focus on what later came to be known as the materialist conception of history – a conception based on a scientific analysis of society and economics which charts a historical trajectory. While we agree with Robert Tucker's suggestion in his *Philosophy and Myth in Karl Marx* that alienation was not abandoned but rather had 'gone underground' (Tucker, 1961: 176) in the later period, we argue that *The German Ideology*, while indeed a transitional study, included enough of the first Marx as to warrant the last major study of the early period rather than the first of the so-called mature Marx. Although he and Engels focused in that study on the division of labour rather than the alienated human being, the concern with the latter remained. Marx and Engels argued that upon the abolition of the division of labour, communism would be built. Human nature would change, traits such as greed and envy would diminish, and humans would flourish in a communal, cooperative society in which they would not be tied to the drudgery of an unrewarding occupation (Lamb, 2010: 862–3). This notion of human nature will be an important theme in the present study.

Although after *The German Ideology* he did not suddenly change his mind about humanity, Marx began to believe that this should not be his concern. In a letter to the Russian intellectual Pavel Annenkov in December 1846, Marx criticized Pierre-Joseph Proudhon for using 'high-sounding words' such as 'Universal Reason' and 'God', and thus showing a misunderstanding of the historical development of humanity, which meant economic development. The 'social history of man', Marx stressed, was 'never anything else than the history of his individual development, whether he is conscious of this or not'. The material relations at the base of all relations between humans were, however, 'only the necessary forms in which their material and individual activity is realised' (LA, 28/12/1846, CW38: 96). Marx's concern was clearly now with systemic relations of humans in their society, rather than with the nature of those humans. In his *The Poverty of Philosophy* – a critical study of Proudhon's *The Philosophy of Poverty* – which he wrote over the winter of 1846–47, Marx ridiculed Proudhon as follows for reviving (as had Marx in the foreword to his doctoral dissertation six years earlier: DD, CW1: 30–1) the mythical emancipatory Prometheus to argue for an egalitarian economy.

What then, ultimately, is this Prometheus resuscitated by M. Proudhon? It is society, social relations based on class antagonisms. These are not relations between individual and individual, but between worker and capitalist, between farmer and landlord, etc. Wipe out these relations and you annihilate all society, and your Prometheus is nothing but a ghost without arms or legs. (PP, CW6: 159)

One finds discussions of relations among workers, capitalists, farmers, landlords and so on in Marx's earlier works, but after *The German Ideology* he was not merely unconcerned with, but also dismissive of, the significance of human nature for the understanding of society.

The task of this book

Of course, the very fact that some of the most significant of Marx's manuscripts of the period, including *The German Ideology*, remained unpublished in Marx's lifetime indicates that, in order to construct the political philosophy of the first Marx, extensive work is needed to knit together the key ideas of the various fragments. That, indeed, is the task of this book. Immediately our description of this task may provoke objections that, if such construction needs to be done at all, the result will be a concoction, putting words into Marx's mouth to which he never intended to give voice. This objection can be met with a two-staged reply. First, although after 1846 he basically lost interest in this political philosophy as his mind turned to other political and intellectual projects, this does not mean that the collection of fragments he abandoned was incoherent, but only that for reasons that seemed at the time to him compelling, he happened to move in a different direction. Second, as this book will show, there are enough synergies in the writings to indicate that he *was* aware of connections between his analyses of the period.

That a process of construction is needed reflects the fact that Marx did not intentionally set out with such a single, finished product already in mind. Nevertheless, in that intensely enquiring mind many of the fragments were, to some degree consciously but in some cases less so, connected with one another. Occasionally Marx acknowledged that there were such connections. In the preface to what, as will be seen in the following chapters, is perhaps the most important of the fragments – *The Economic and Philosophic Manuscripts of 1844* – he was quite clear about this. He noted that while this was primarily a work of political economy, he had 'already announced in the *Deutsch-Französische Jahrbücher* the critique of jurisprudence and political science in the form of a critique of the *Hegelian philosophy of Law*' (EPM, CW3: 231). He was referring to the *Contribution to the Critique of Hegel's Philosophy of Law. Introduction* (CCHPLI, CW3) which, written earlier that year, had been intended to cover a rich and diverse array of subjects. He now realized that this array 'could have been compressed into *one* work only in a purely aphoristic style' and that this 'would have given the impression of arbitrary systematism'. 'I shall,' he went on (EPM, CW3: 231), 'therefore publish the critique of law, ethics, politics, etc., in a series of distinct, independent pamphlets, and afterwards try in a special work to present them again as a connected whole, showing the interrelationship of the separate parts, and lastly attempt a critique of the speculative elaboration of that material.' The 'critique' mentioned would be a comprehensive critique of the work of Georg Wilhelm Friedrich Hegel and his later followers, which would also be a comprehensive statement of Marx's own philosophy. Marx's early work is replete with such announcements, providing at least prima facie indication of the approach mentioned earlier.

Had he gone on to complete the project, there are indications that the earlier ideas would not have been compartmentalized and forgotten. For example, in his article *On the Jewish Question* published the previous year, he had discussed political and ethical issues, criticizing Hegel's view of the roles of state and civil society in the defence of property rights (OJQ, CW3: 163). This would appear to be material that would have fitted into one of the pamphlets and also the specially connected whole. In the *Economic and Philosophic Manuscripts* he wrote in Paris in 1844 (referred to hereafter as *Paris Manuscripts*), moreover, Marx criticized Hegel's theory of self-consciousness and the view of alienation that it entailed (EPM, CW3: 326–46). Marx had criticized self-consciousness as an abstract principle in his doctoral dissertation (DD, CW1: 73), and one gets a fuller picture of his view on this concept by reading both the dissertation which had been finished in the spring of 1841 and the *Paris Manuscripts* of 1844. These are just two examples of ideas that, sometimes in revised forms, were retrieved and revived in Marx's early writings, influencing others that emerged against the backdrop of his intellectual, political and social environment in a period characterized by rapid change. Often, as his interests changed, the revised ideas, those that they influenced, and yet others that thereby emerged dialectically were also put to one side rather than published, but his statement being in the *Paris Manuscripts* about independent pamphlets and a connected whole gives a clue that those revised ideas were being stored, or finding their place in a revised whole, rather than discarded.

Although the ideas of the first Marx began to take shape from 1837, when he expressed some of his youthful views of the world and his role in it, two very relevant landmarks were, as mentioned earlier, his doctoral thesis and *The German Ideology*. The dissertation was his first major piece of work, and over the course of the few years that followed, he developed some of the ideas further. After *The German Ideology* of 1845–46, the focus and emphasis of his work changed. He began to follow his own well-known mantra, stated in his *Theses on Feuerbach* of 1845, that: 'The philosophers have only interpreted the world, in various ways; the point, however, is to change it' (TF, CW5: 5). Philosophy began to be relegated in his mind to a position of less importance than political struggle and political economy. Such was the waning of his and co-author Engels' enthusiasm for political philosophy that, as Marx recalled in 1859, when the publishing deal fell through for the completed manuscript, they abandoned *The German Ideology* 'to the gnawing criticism of the mice all the more willingly as we had achieved our main purpose – self clarification' (CPE, CW29: 264).

'Self-clarification' is a hugely significant term in this context. It indicates that he moved away from the early political philosophy onto new projects *not* because he thought the earlier work was of no value or that it was fundamentally flawed, but because, on the contrary, he was reasonably content with what he had written, even though he felt no pressing urgency to spell it out for other people to read. There was thus now no reason at this point, if ever, to complete the project he had mentioned in the *Paris Manuscripts* of 1844. What we aim to do in this book is precisely to spell out what the project would likely have been. Even though Marx lost interest – and again not because he felt the project was inadequate in some way, but rather because other more pressing concerns confronted him – one finds, by completing the project, a political philosophy of the first order that stands the test of time as an account of human nature and the extant and immanent human condition.

It is worth adding that the famous comment on the Young Hegelian thinker Ludwig Feuerbach quoted earlier did not emerge from the sky like a thunderbolt and rapidly render political philosophy impotent: echoes of this observation can be found much earlier, and indeed are of a piece with the criticisms of Hegel on abstraction one finds in the preface to the *Paris Manuscripts*. In an article in the *Kölnische Zeitung* of 1842 he had insisted that German philosophy had always had an urge for isolation and systematic exclusion, but that 'the time must come when philosophy not only internally by its content, but also externally through its form, comes into contact and interaction with the real world of its day' (LA179, CW1: 195). In the preface to the *Paris Manuscripts*, thinking of the Young Hegelians in general and Bruno Bauer in particular, Marx (EPM, CW3: 231–4) criticized 'theologians' whose critique of Hegel failed to escape abstraction. In that preface Marx was more sympathetic to the ideas of Feuerbach, but nevertheless indicated that even the latter thinker had not gone far enough in his critique of Hegel. We will have of course much more to say on this matter later, and of the significance of the Young Hegelians, but for the moment notice the exact wording: Marx writes that the philosophers have only understood the world, not that they *cannot do otherwise*. The problem is not with philosophy but with philosophers. After all, the overcoming of the distinction between theory and practice is already found in Feuerbach, for example, in his 'The Necessity of a Reform of Philosophy' (2012: 151), and precisely with respect to the impotence of existing philosophy regarding the political order. In turn, this means that the rejection of Feuerbach implied not a simple rejection of philosophy, but rather an indication that it has achieved all that it could achieve while remaining a merely theoretical enterprise. What is raised here by Marx is the question of whether there could be a political philosophy that is *also* a political praxis. Whether Marx, with some important input from Engels, achieved such a combination is one of the issues to be addressed in this book.

As was mentioned earlier, Marx wrote *The German Ideology* with Engels as co-author. As Terrell Carver stated in his book on the intellectual relationship between the two authors: '*The German Ideology* was a true collaboration by Marx and Engels, in that they seem genuinely to have written it together' (Carver, 1983: 69). Furthermore, as Carver (2010) has emphasized more recently, this collaboration was very much one of experimentation with their ideas, rather than the polished political philosophy as which it might be perceived following its posthumous publication several decades after its authors' deaths. A question this may raise is that of how and why we can attribute views expressed in that book to Marx, rather than Engels. To answer this question, it is useful to note that, in fact, the entire period of the early to mid-1840s was, for Marx, one of experimentation of ideas. What can be done with *The German Ideology* is to identify points that clearly relate to some of Marx's earlier works. Some of the points in those earlier works were themselves influenced by Engels' very early writings. Although, however, the first Engels was one of the thinkers who influenced some of the ideas that can be constructed as the project of the first Marx, the latter thinker did not simply reject everything he had said beforehand. Some of the political philosophy he produced before he was influenced by Engels was entirely consistent with the new ideas he began thereafter to express. In light of such details, we should at this point discuss briefly the way that the task of constructing something like the connected whole that he mentioned in the *Paris Manuscripts* will be accomplished.

The way the task will be undertaken

In piecing together components from his various writings into the coherent political philosophy of the first Marx, there will, necessarily, be some interpretation of his ideas. For several recent decades the influential Cambridge school of historians of political thought discouraged any interpretation other than that of the authors being studied. This, in their view, was because in order to grasp and understand the writings of authors from the past, one must focus on authorial intention and illocutionary force (or in other words what the author was actually doing by means of their writing), bearing in mind linguistic context and convention (Bevir, 2011; Edwards and Townshend, 2002: 2–5). To be sure, context – especially intellectual – was important, but *subsequent* interpretations much less so and anachronistic interpretations entirely distorting. Although the Cambridge line was very influential in the late twentieth century, there were various sorts of dissent. Analytical philosophers argued that the texts themselves should be studied, not their intellectual environment. Others stressed that more important than authorial intention was the intellectual, political and social impact that the ideas had and the ways they were used. In each case interpretation was a factor.

In this book, authorial intention and linguistic convention are indeed taken into consideration; otherwise, one can be wholly mistaken about a piece of political philosophy. Mistaking a particular use of a word for another can lead to a fundamental misunderstanding of a key argument. This is especially important with a writer such as Marx. After all, he often needed to use some terms in very different ways to the traditions in which they were employed by thinkers such as Hegel and Feuerbach. Authorial intent thus becomes an all-important brake on overenthusiastic or careless interpretation. In addition and more positively, we also claim here that the young Marx *did* have an overarching conception of what his political philosophy was, albeit perhaps only sketchily. So, our task of construction here must be understood as, in part, an attempt to build up from fragmentary traces precisely what was Marx's authorial intent. What we must not do, however, is build that intent by relying upon what Marx and Engels said *later*, which here must count as subsequent or anachronistic interpretation. As we have suggested, the early Marx is too often seen merely as the proto-Marx, as interesting only because of its anticipations of the far more famous and influential work to come. We see our task as allowing the early Marx to emerge on his own terms.

We are, however, not restricted to the faithful adherence to authorial intention and to doing nothing else with the ideas one finds in Marx's work. All philosophers, including of course Marx, are themselves influenced by the ideas of earlier thinkers. Political philosophers use and develop previously used concepts. A particular thinker is writing for or against something – whether that be a long-established tradition or a contemporary debate – and moreover, in writing they are addressing and presenting themselves to their contemporaries. As Terence Ball (1995: 10) has insisted, 'all interpretations are, in a word, interest-laden'. Texts are complex communications received by readers over time. Readers today interpret the texts, just as the authors of those texts have interpreted previous ones. All interpretation, he elaborates, involves appraisal and reappraisal. This has two particularly acute implications for us. First, we suggest, with respect to Marx, that there are some ideas that are so much part of the atmosphere of European thought in the period that Marx hardly needed to mention them and thus, strictly speaking, they are not a part of his fully conscious intent. Some notions key to German Idealism such as consciousness, activity or freedom are good examples – thus part of our account of the first Marx will be sketching in this background. Second, we find ourselves in the highly curious situation of reading early works by a thinker whose later work is the very reason anyone finds him interesting, but trying to read him without reference to that later work. A professional contortionist might grimace at such a position. Although for example it is Marx's later accounts of history and class that make him a thinker with whom one must engage, nevertheless here we must not assume without careful critical analysis that references in early Marx to 'history' or 'class' have anything like the same meaning.

It is worth pointing out that literary criticism has gone through the same debates as historians of political thought, and through the same arguments and counterarguments, concerning what is or is not admissible evidence in interpretation. In other words, the concept of interpretation of texts is one that can be illuminated if not conclusively solved by interdisciplinary appraisal. Here, in brief, we take a 'liberal' approach to interpretation, one not uncommon in literary studies today: *everything counts*, provided only it can show itself significant in extracting coherent meaning from the texts. So, influences, biography, texts of all types, literary mode (Marx and Engels wrote much of their early collaborations in the mode of vicious satire), language and of course political and intellectual context – all of these *can* be of use.

As indicated at the beginning of this introduction, in line with authors like Wolff and Eagleton we want to show how the ideas of the first Marx can have value in at least throwing light on problems that human beings continue to experience more than a century and a half after Marx wrote them. The piecing together of the various ideas in his early writings involves appraisal. Otherwise, one would not be able to determine whether the ideas that are selected for inclusion should indeed be selected. For example, the *Paris Manuscripts* of 1844 contain long passages that work largely on the basis of Feuerbach's account of the sensuous. Should these be included? The principle is simple: we include ideas and analyses that cohere with the emerging 'bigger picture'. Indeed, considering that we are suggesting that the ideas can be brought into a coherent political philosophy we are, in fact, *reappraising*. We will always try to make clear to our readers where we are explicating the texts themselves, and where we are as sympathetically, as plausibly and as carefully as possible seeking to fill in gaps, that is, where we are interpreting and appraising.

Were this book to be five times its current length, we could easily imagine a comprehensive re-evaluation of this period of Marx's work. Such a book would appraise any relevance this work holds for more recent cultural or political issues – and this is something we very tentatively do already in the Conclusion. Such a book would also look at its relationship to the more famous later writings, and other developments (philosophical, economic and otherwise) that have appeared since. Likewise, it would be unwise to exclude any discussion of the relation that the first Marx might have to later political forms and events over the past 150 years. Finally, this project would appraise the validity of all those philosophers who have used or argued with this period of Marx's work. Five times might be a severe underestimate! Here, though, our aim is something much more moderate: to present the first Marx in his own terms. As far as possible, we have sought to suspend the question of the relation of this period to any subsequent period, event or idea; we have strived not to be anachronistic. Our title, significantly, is *The First Marx* and not, for example, *The Early Marx*. (There are a small number of known exceptions, where a philosophical concept from later intellectual history just seemed so useful and non-distorting – for example, our usage of the type/token distinction.) While we have depended a great deal on recent scholarship concerning Marx, we have tried to employ only that which is intrinsically historically defensible, and to filter out that which depends upon later ideas or values. For example, many readers might expect the work of Louis Althusser (2006) to feature prominently in this study, for Althusser is a pivotal figure with respect to two questions which concern our period: first, is there any meaningful continuity between the work of the early 1840s and Marx's later writings? And second, is this early work of any philosophical or political value? Althusser answers 'no' and 'no', and his appraisal has been enormously influential. However, in our judgement, Althusser's assessment relies on at least two later intellectual developments, namely psychoanalysis and structuralism. Importantly, Althusser does not feature in this book not because we consider him wrong, or because we hold that psychoanalysis and structuralism are wrong, but because to a first order approximation they simply are not relevant to the reconstruction of the first Marx, on his own terms. (Althusserians of course would dispute this, arguing that there is nothing anachronistic about using psychoanalysis to identify and understand 'symptoms' in a historical figure. If we ever write that really big book imagined earlier, we will return to such problems.) Similarly, we are uninterested in anachronistic evaluations of Marx's 'humanism'. That the first Marx was a humanist, albeit not conventionally so, is undeniable (and yes, even in *The German Ideology*). That this humanism makes this work more or less valuable, or more or less defensible, is a relevant question for us here only insofar as the discussion occurs within the horizon of the intellectual debate contemporary to Marx.

The political philosophy of the first Marx is retrieved in the following five main thematic chapters, leading to a conclusion in which the key features of his early political philosophy are spelled out. The themes are production, alienation, exploitation, change and emancipation. As the network of ideas is produced in the course of this series of chapters the links between these themes will become evident. The first of these chapters is on production. It outlines and discusses what one might call Marx's philosophical anthropology, which inverts the Hegelian image of humanity as a vehicle for the history of spirit, and instead understands human 'species-being' as essentially *concrete*, *social* and *self-producing*.

The chapter on production is followed by one on alienation. It discusses Marx's appropriation of the various precedents for his concept of alienation, such as the ideas of Hegel (including the master–slave dialectic), and the Feuerbachian account of religion. From early on, however, Marx sees alienation in terms of labour and commodity production and thus rejects earlier idealist and passive accounts. Moreover, alienation is also individuation and thus alienation from the 'species-being'. The larger context of alienation consists of the social and economic systems that feed off and in turn produce it. This means there is a close, organizational link between alienation and exploitation.

The chapter on exploitation examines Marx's analysis of the state and political economy as such an exploitative organization. For him, the state develops as a pseudo-community attempting to reconcile the range of interests in what is portrayed as a 'natural society', when in reality there is a division of labour and private capital. The chapter continues by showing how the early Marx included within his account scarcity, competition and monopoly.

Moving on, the chapter on change shows that Marx provided a general account of the nature of change in dialectic. This, for example, is the core thought of his doctoral dissertation on Epicureanism and continues with his analyses of the contradictions arising in various political economies. However, because it is materialist, and essentially related to Marx's account of the species-being of the human as self-productive, this dialectic is an inverted Hegelianism. The dialectic is both an account of the philosophy of history (especially the advent of capitalism from feudalism) and a philosophy of 'revolutionary praxis' – that is, the conditions under which the exploited (eventually identified as the proletariat) forms itself as an immediate and universal expression of human being.

As a philosopher of praxis Marx sought to find the path to human emancipation. There is, hence, in this book a chapter on emancipation. Significant in this respect is Marx and Engels' early treatment of what they sometimes called communism. Communism is a concept that long predates the 1840s, and Marx and Engels will be seen to have arrived at their own account of emancipated humanity by means of a critique of earlier communisms, specifically how those theories remain trapped within the inhuman situation that is alienation and exploitation. The conclusion briefly sketches out the full philosophical treatment that the book has discovered, before turning to address a series of implications, where we briefly address the relevance of the first Marx to contemporary political issues.

A thread that is woven through these chapters is that of human nature. As mentioned earlier, in the early writings covered by this book Marx offers his understanding of human beings as, naturally, creative producers. Not only that, however, he saw humans as communitarian beings. Unlike other such beings humans were so, in his view, self-consciously, or at least they would be were it not for alienation (Berry, 1986: 4–5 and 41). As Marx thus believed that it was necessary to understand human beings both in the context of their communities and in respect of their individual thoughts and motives, it is important to recognize that he engaged in different levels of analysis – the individual and social levels – in an approach that can be considered anti-reductionist. In order to make this clear, at various places in the chapter that follow, we employ a type-token distinction.

The structure and thread just outlined indicate that his book differs from the existing full-length studies of the Marx of the early to late 1840s. The early works of Marx, and his early collaborations with Engels, have, since the mid-twentieth century been increasingly well known and widely available. They have also been discussed extensively in print – although less often in monograph form. However, what marks out *The First Marx* as genuinely unique is that we refuse to read this early material only from the perspective of the later writings. Instead, our argument is that it presents a coherent and at least partially fleshed-out philosophical analysis, which bears scrutiny and deserves attention in its own right.

Why write this book?

Although the analysis of Marx's work in this book is not primarily concerned with the long-term development of Marx's ideas, it is worthwhile at this point to say briefly where it fits into a debate that has been prominent in the broader study of Marx for many years. The debate in the literature concerns the question whether there is a clear break between the young Marx and a mature Marx. A relatively recent book that takes the continuity line is Michael Löwy's *The Theory of Revolution in the Young Marx* (2005). As the title suggests, Löwy argues that the roots of Marx's later revolutionary writings can be found in the early work. While once again we do not oppose the view that there is continuity in this respect, our main concern is different. We argue that arguments regarding revolutionary change, contradiction and other topics such as production, alienation and emancipation contribute to a powerful argument in the early works of Marx, even though this is distributed among a range of books, papers and other writings, when *taken on their own* without asking if they are 'continuous' or not with the later work. 'Continuity' would seem to assume that what happened later has the *final* say in our image of Marx, *even of early Marx*. Circa 1844, Marx certainly did not think of himself as 'immature', wondering whether he would still hold these ideas to be valuable when he 'grew up'.

A substantial and very readable account of the early Marx is that of David McLellan in his book *Marx Before Marxism* (1972). He too expresses the continuity thesis. His book has a very broad scope, combining history, biography and political philosophy. Our book will similarly combine history of political thought with political philosophy when this helps substantiate and clarify the latter. Nevertheless, it is the political philosophy that is the main concern of our study. In this respect, a very important way in which our book differs from that of McLellan is that we will be drawing on the various early writings in order to construct a political philosophical theory that Marx seems to have been building, even though he eventually decided to move on as his interests changed, rather than piece it all together in a single substantial tract. In this respect also our study differs from that of John Maguire's *Marx's Paris Writings: An Analysis*. Arguing that the works Marx wrote from his base in Paris in 1843 and 1844 comprise a body of work with intrinsic merits, Maguire (1972: xix–xxii), nevertheless, suggests that all of Marx's works, including his later, major study *Capital*, can be considered as part of a single whole, because some works elaborate on issues that are presented only briefly in his other writings. Be this as it may (and we do offer a few examples of continuity), the parts of any such comprehensive whole would probably be only very loosely constructible. By way of contrast, the writings up to and including *The German Ideology* would, as the following chapters seek to illustrate, contribute to a surprisingly tight and cohesive social and political philosophy.

The possibility that one may find in Marx's early work the ingredients of such a major philosophical thesis is hinted at by Lucio Colletti in his substantial introduction to the Penguin edition of Marx's *Early Writings* (1975). Colletti also acknowledges briefly that in the early 1840s Marx worked with and developed the ideas of Feuerbach, rather than simply imbibing them. Colletti, however, is mainly concerned in his introduction to offer a sophisticated contribution to the continuity thesis. While we lean towards that thesis, although not unreservedly, the purpose of this book is again the very different one of showing that there is a coherent and well-rounded political philosophy in the early work up to 1846.

An earlier book that does suggest that Marx's early writings can be seen to comprise a political philosophy is *The Young Marx*, written by Bernard Delfgaauw (1967). Delfgaauw's study is essentially, and overtly, a work of Christian criticism of that political philosophy. Rather than offer a substantial Christian argument in response to Marx's ideas, Delfgaauw does not really go much further than suggest that Marx was mistaken in his philosophical views on topics such as materialism, alienation and religion because those views conflicted with Christianity. The irony is not lost on Delfgaauw that Marx's early work emerged on the field of a group of Young Hegelians one of whose primary concerns was to offer a critique of Christianity.

Several studies have focused on Marx's intellectual relationship with other thinkers who, like he, were associated with the Young Hegelian intellectual movement. The movement began to emerge after Hegel's death in 1832 among thinkers who supported his idea of the historical advancement of the human understanding of the world but argued that the Hegelian doctrine needed to be further developed. They disagreed with the right-Hegelians' dominant conservative interpretation of Hegel's philosophy. In various ways they criticized the religious element of Hegel's philosophy and argued for it to be demystified. The term 'Young Hegelians' did not refer to a formal organization with signed up members; hence there is not a clearly identifiable set of thinkers who should be categorized as such. David Strauss, who is usually included in the category, offered a different set of categories of Hegelian: left, centre and right depending on the extent to which they were prepared to move away from Hegel's reconciliation of philosophy and religion, or in other words how radical they were prepared to be (McLellan, 1969: 3–4). Radicals among the Young Hegelians stressed that the present society was no more than one of the phases in the dialectical process. They insisted that the progress of reason was far from complete, and that greater attention needed to be paid to such progress as it manifested itself in the real world and actual societies. Marx's sympathy for the ideas of the radical Young Hegelians is evident from a passage in a note on a chapter in his dissertation that is now unfortunately missing. The note itself is hugely important, arguing that a division, and opposition, could be drawn in early nineteenth-century German philosophy between what he called a liberal party, by which he meant those thinkers who became known as the Young Hegelians, and positive philosophy on the other side. 'The act of the first side,' he suggested, 'is critique, hence precisely that turning-towards-the-outside of philosophy; the act of the second is the attempt to philosophise, hence the turning-in-towards-itself of philosophy' (DD, CW1: 86). Philosophy needed to concern itself with the real world. Only the first side, he argued, achieved any progress. Five years later the analysis would not change, except to add that even critique itself did not sufficiently 'turn-towards-the-outside', but remained within the fold of philosophy.

An early example of work on the Young Hegelians and the early Marx's work in this context is *The Young Hegelians and Karl Marx*, in which McLellan (1969) focuses on the influence of Marx's early contemporaries in the school upon his own ideas. A more recent book by Warren Breckman (1999), *Marx, the Young Hegelians, and the Origins of Radical Social Theory*, has a similar theme. In the last main chapter of the book, Breckman (1999: 258–97) focuses on Marx, while the earlier chapters discuss themes from and thinkers within the school. In his Introduction, Breckman

(1999: 1–19) alerts his readers, to the scope of his book. As part of a study of the Young Hegelian philosophical movement, his short account of the early Marx covers the period starting with his doctoral studies until 1843. This restriction means that for the purposes of the present study Breckman's chapter on Marx, while certainly useful, omits some very significant material. While taking into consideration the influence of a lengthier temporal intellectual environment, the chapters that follow in *The First Marx* are also concerned primarily with the broader political philosophy which this influence helped shape, both in the early period focused on by Breckman and also three more years after it.

A very significant contribution to the literature on the political ideas of the early Marx is David Leopold's *The Young Karl Marx: German Philosophy, Modern Politics, and Human Flourishing*, published in 2007. This is another study that is concerned with a relatively short time span. Leopold is concerned with the political thought that Marx expressed in writing produced between March 1843 and September 1845. Political thought itself is, moreover, defined narrowly as 'his account of the emergence, the character, and the (future) replacement of the modern state' (Leopold, 2007: 11). He is, he adds, concerned with the clear and consistent thread one can find in the relations between this narrow conception of politics and Marx's conception of human nature. Like Leopold, we suggest that Marx was concerned with what the modern state had achieved, its failings and the unrealized possibilities of human flourishing. We, too, argue that this is a part – indeed a significant part – of the political philosophy of the first Marx. Our study, however, interprets politics and its significance more broadly than does Leopold, to include cultural, social, economic, technological and historical factors. The state, although of course guiding or inhibiting production in certain ways, is a product of human historical life, and this must be borne in mind throughout. Moreover, as indicated at the beginning of this introduction, we consider some of his earlier work such as his doctoral dissertation to be hugely significant and also deem *The German Ideology*, which he and Engels wrote just outside Leopold's time frame, to be likewise of importance to the self-contained philosophy we are reconstructing.

The German Ideology is also excluded by Lawrence Wilde in his short, concise and informative chapter in an edited book on political thinkers. As Wilde suggests (2003: 406), written in the winter of 1845–46 and left unpublished, this was a book which 'is regarded as a significant breakthrough, as it sets down for the first time his general theory of historical development and resolves on a more empirical approach towards understanding the origins and structure of socio-economic power'. While Wilde is making an important observation, we argue that there is, nevertheless, material in *The German Ideology* that can usefully contribute to the construction of the political philosophy of the first Marx. The *German Ideology* is clearly a transitional book, and must be dealt with carefully for that reason, but to exclude it from offering insight into the early Marx is absurd. *The German Ideology* represents a change, to be sure, but not by rejecting, instead by assuming and radicalizing in the sphere of praxis the earlier thought.

In the previous few paragraphs readers will have noticed brief mentions of the intellectual context in which Marx wrote in the early to mid-1840s. As was discussed earlier in this introductory chapter, such contextual detail is of course important. Hence, in order to prepare for the chapters that follow, the next section offers a more detailed, albeit still very brief, outline of the environment in which the first Marx worked. Our aim here is to introduce some of the major issues that were in the air, and how Marx responded to them. In later chapters we will have occasion to return to some of these contextual matters in greater detail than is appropriate here (e.g. the discussion of Kantian practical philosophy as a philosophy of production, found in the chapter that follows this introduction).

The first Marx's intellectual environment

The time frame of Marx's early writings fell within the final years of the period that Eric Hobsbawm (1962: ix) famously called the period of 'dual revolution'. The term 'dual' refers to the political and industrial aspects of rapid change that characterized much of Europe from the outbreak of revolution in France in 1789 until the failed uprisings in a number of European cities in 1848. Marx started work in the later stages of this period and certainly was concerned with the achievements and failures of the revolution in France that marked its beginning (Seed, 2010: 21–4).

The French old order had been overthrown at the beginning of the period of dual revolution. But nevertheless the communist groups which (unlike their critic Marx a few decades later, we must note) called for absolute equality, crude social levelling and austerity were marginalized and suppressed (Smaldone, 2014: 9–13). The economic strength of the industrial upper middle classes (or bourgeoisie) and those who lived off interest grew, and on that basis a significant degree of political power passed to this class (Callinicos, 1995: 52–5). As Marx (MCP, CW6: 486) interpreted the situation in the *Communist Manifesto* of 1848, this enabled the bourgeoisie to enjoy exclusive political sway in the modern representative state. Whether or not the extent of 'sway' was as exclusive as Marx suggested, the socio-economic conditions of European countries including France, Germany and the United Kingdom were one of stress for the majority of people, thus creating a climate which Marx and other radicals considered to be conducive to revolution (Levin, 1998).

The political aspect of the dual revolution finally petered out with the unsuccessful uprisings of 1848. This marked the end of the period when, just as the bourgeoisie had benefited from political activity from the beginning, there was hope in some circles that the revolution would eventually help emancipate those in society who were still oppressed and exploited (Smaldone, 2014: 13–17). This hope had been around from the beginning, influenced by the ideas of thinkers such as Thomas Paine and Antoine-Nicolas de Condorcet. However, in fact, the working classes and peasantry benefited very little from what was being portrayed as progress. For many, indeed, life got significantly worse. In the 1830s constitutional reforms in several European countries had really only benefited the middle class (Herres, 2015: 15–16). The French Revolution had promised liberty and equality for humanity, but doubts that the gains of the bourgeoisie would be shared with others in society spread. Dissatisfaction thus began to stir in Europe (Smaldone, 2014: 4–8). The political revolutionary atmosphere that had begun to be felt in 1789 continued to influence liberal thinkers in the first few decades of the eighteenth century, but the uprisings of 1848 frightened many liberals who began to support the counter-revolutionary actions of their states (Arblaster, 1984: 203–23). In fact, this had happened in the German states a decade earlier. In any case, the end of the period of dual revolution was thus marked with reaction. Nevertheless, what is significant is that those uprisings reflected the view that had begun to emerge among radicals over the previous few years that if a new revolution were to help emancipate the most oppressed and exploited, it would need to be very different than any that had gone before. Marx was the key figure among those radicals (Herres, 2015).

As it was crucial to the emergence of the broader intellectual environment in Europe during the early nineteenth century, the French revolution of 1789 contributed to the development of events in Prussia which were having profound effects on the narrower German milieu. Hegel was the dominant philosophical figure in the German speaking world during the first third of the nineteenth century. The importance of Hegel for the young Marx cannot be overemphasized – Marx's first ventures into political philosophy addressed themselves in large part or in their entirety to Hegel. Hegel admired the ideals of the Revolution, especially constitutional government, but opposed the Jacobin element that came to dominate. The Jacobin group, led by Maximilien Robespierre, came to control the revolutionary government from June 1893 until they were overthrown in July the following year. Originally inspired by egalitarianism and the belief that humans were fundamentally good, they attempted to build a republic of virtue in which citizens would be liberated from their moral corruption and thus purified. They defended their use of despotism and terror as a necessary means to such purification. Hegel's view was that the Jacobins failed because they attempted to impose a false and abstract conception of freedom that did not take into account the cultures and civil societies of particular communities (Higonnet, 1998: 120–1). Hegel also became increasingly disenchanted with the revolution's democratic implications. Hegel initially welcomed Napoleon's victory at the battle of Jena and the subsequent restoration of order; a code of rights was introduced in Prussia.

A problem, for Hegel, was that Napoleon *also* ignored national dispositions, and instead imposed abstract universal forms of right and governance regardless of the environment. Hegel therefore decided that the best form of government was constitutional monarchy. These political views were linked to Hegel's communitarian belief in the dialectical progress of spirit, whereby a community would advance towards freedom. The state embodied spirit and thus the appropriate constitutional arrangements would facilitate that progress, that is, the reconciliation of the contradictions at the level of civil society (Avineri, 1972: 62–72; Cullen, 1979: 14–16; Plant, 1983: 72–3 and 119–20). Hegel's early assessment of the French Revolution thus helped him formulate his distinctive political contribution to the German Idealist philosophical tradition which held that individual will could achieve freedom by means of the direction of an objective, rational idea, found in the state, which transcended the arbitrariness and particularism of actual ways of life. Hegel came to argue that constitutional monarchy was the most appropriate political system to accommodate the progress of the universal spirit in guiding individual wills. Individual interests would be represented, but the representatives would not be mandated; rather they would think from a viewpoint of all and thus bring subjective individual views into mutual recognition. The monarch's purpose in the system would be to help bring about social cohesion (Redding, 2011). The underlying German Idealist view of will being guided by ideas abstracted from the actual world in progress towards freedom would, as will become evident in the chapters which follow, be considered by Marx to be fundamentally wrong.

By the 1840s, philosophers such as Marx were experiencing increasing hostility. After the defeat of Napoleon in 1815, censorship of the press, which had been relaxed in the period of occupation, was re-introduced to different degrees in the states of the German Confederation. The backlash against progressivism of all sorts that was common in Europe after 1848 was experienced much earlier in Germany. In Prussia, including the capital Berlin, the newspapers were published with particular caution with one eye on the censors (Fetscher, 1980: 377–80). Nevertheless, in the 1830s and 1840s, intellectuals did not face the same level of legal restriction as mainstream journalists; works of more than 20 pages in length were not subjected to such stringent censorship as shorter pieces that were likely to reach a wider readership (Green, 2001: 158–60). In reality, however, the situation was less relaxed than the legal situation might have indicated in the post-Napoleonic period. By 1830, indirect pressure to conform was being felt. Hegel had been appointed as professor at the University of Berlin in 1818, a position he held until his death in 1831. Throughout this period, Hegelianism became the *de facto* official state philosophy of Prussia. To achieve academic success intellectuals had to impress the influential specialists of their discipline in a period when the influence of the recently deceased Hegel's thought had become so pervasive that nearly every chair of philosophy in the universities was held by Hegelians. These, however, were conservative (or 'old' or 'right') Hegelians (Turner, 1971: 166–76). In other words, intellectual life was dominated not just by Hegelianism, but by a particular species of Hegelianism: an interpretative tradition that took Hegel's political philosophy as a defence of the existing political arrangements in Prussia, and thus entailed the intellectual incoherence and political dangerousness of any progressive or revolutionary thought.

By 1840, a number of distinct voices in German political philosophy had emerged, competing for the title of the genuine philosophical opposition to this conservative Hegelian status quo. Some of these figures were content to work within the broad Hegelian tradition, but interpreting his work in a much less conservative manner – among them Bauer, August von Cieszkowski and to a lesser extent Strauss. Others such as Feuerbach were much more upfront in their criticism of Hegel. Even the latter, though, had to accept Hegel as their intellectual environment; it was the only philosophical language available to them, the only point of departure. Thus both these trends are often grouped under the heading of 'left' Hegelians. It was this group which became known as the Young Hegelians, mentioned several times earlier.

For the young Marx, chief among these younger philosophers was Feuerbach. Feuerbach had been publishing books, mostly on the history of modern thought, throughout the 1830s, with increasingly anti-Hegelian overtones derived from an underlying materialist outlook. In 1841, he published *The Essence of Christianity*, which was something of a scandal and best seller across Europe. He argued that the basic principles ascribed to the divine by Christians were in fact the essence of human beings, and by projecting them into the beyond, human beings were alienating – indeed poisoning – themselves. Human existence had to be understood materialistically, not idealistically or theologically – that is, not as something merely finite and determined with respect to an absolute. Consequently, philosophy now had the task of reunifying the human being that religion had split asunder, a schism that the modern political state unwittingly was perpetuating. Just as we said earlier that the importance of Hegel for Marx cannot be overestimated, so likewise for Feuerbach; indeed, looking at the table of contents of the book you are now reading, the chapter titles could have been lifted from plausible books about either Marx or Feuerbach! Feuerbach was just what Marx needed to help him find an effective and radical critique of Hegel and of the whole movement of Hegelianism, one that had powerful (if largely only potential) political implications. However, although both Marx and Engels deeply admired Feuerbach, they were never simply devotees. From the beginning, as we shall see, Marx felt unsettled by Feuerbach's somewhat limp political edge, his never fully historical materialism and most famously by his account of the role of philosophy with respect to the political domain. Feuerbach, he commented in a letter to another of the radical Young Hegelians, Arnold Ruge, in 1843, 'refers too much to nature and too little to politics' (LR 13/3/1843, CW1: 400). One needed to consider the actions of states and other political actors, rather than assuming things happened by nature.

Since the French revolution of 1789 the civil service and the rest of the bureaucracy in Prussia had been consolidating its autonomy and power. After the defeat of Napoleon in 1815 the political authorities of most units of the new German Confederation including the dominant state within it, Prussia, had begun to turn their backs on modern political arrangements. The bureaucracy retained a strong position until around 1830, when reaction really gained traction (Gillis, 1968). In the 1830s support began to grow for the view that even the conservative Hegelianism which accepted the status quo was too progressive – a view prompted in part by the popularity of works by those of the Young Hegelians who saw their thought as the true interpretation of Hegel. The monarchies which held power in much of the Confederation sought to restore *feudal* society and politics. Prussia in particular actively discouraged modern political developments throughout the Confederation. By the time the staunchly anti-Hegelian Frederick William IV ascended the throne of Prussia in 1840, the country and indeed most other states of the German Confederation had, in political terms, regressed still further. The new king reaffirmed his opposition to Hegelianism, announced his intention to restore Christianity and promised to 'slay the dragon of revolution' (Hahn, 1977: 879–80). The king's early appointments served to confirm the reactionary nature of the regime. The new minister of education and religious affairs Johann Albrecht Eichhorn implemented the king's policies zealously; for example, academics who opposed those policies were removed from their posts and replaced with supporters of the regime (Hahn, 1977: 880). Furthermore, Frederick William installed the staunchly anti-Hegelian philosopher F. W. J. Schelling into a senior position in the University of Berlin in the spring of 1841. There was intense speculation in Prussia and elsewhere in the Federation about what direction this appointment would push Prussian intellectual life, until Schelling confirmed in November, to the disappointment of progressive thinkers, that he saw the duties of the appointment in terms of German salvation by means of philosophy and culture (Olesen, 2007: 234; Toews, 2004: 1–3).

Frederick William IV was ultraconservative not only in educational terms but also regarding religious and political issues. Although individualism and self-interest continued to be unquestioned in Prussian civil society, as soon as he took the throne he accelerated the reaction against such individualist ideas and principles as might challenge hierarchical control, and also against bureaucratic power, demanding that he and the estates should be the holders of religious and political power. He encouraged the estates to challenge such power. His goal was to revive the political system of medieval Germany, based on group rights and the corporate power and authority of the estates (Jensen, 1974: 149–50). His domain was thus hardly the place in which radicalism would be well received. Hence, before moving on to study his early political philosophy in detail in the chapters that follow, it remains to look very briefly at Marx's entry into and position within this distinctly unreceptive intellectual environment.

The first Marx in his intellectual environment

The brief sketch of Marx's activities offered in this final section of the introduction is by no means adequate to readers who are interested in the detail of Marx's life and times until the mid-1840s. Such readers are, however, thankfully well-served by some excellent fairly recently published biographies (McLellan, 2006; Sperber, 2013; Stedman Jones, 2016; Thomas, 2012; Wheen, 1999). The intention of this sketch is simply to provide a picture that will help readers to put the political philosophy into the context of their author's circumstances.

Born in Trier in the Rhineland of Germany, Marx experienced a humanist upbringing and education. His father Heschel was from an influential Jewish family but converted to Protestantism when the Rhineland passed back into the hands of the Prussian monarchy upon the demise of the Napoleonic occupation. The Prussian regime increased restrictions on the career paths open to Jews, leading the humanist Heschel to change his Jewish name to Heinrich (Stedman Jones, 2016: 18). Heinrich went on to convert pragmatically to Protestantism so that he would be able to continue practicing as a lawyer (Stedman Jones, 2016: 22–3). As an enthusiast for the rationalist and liberal ideas of the Enlightenment, he sent Karl to a humanist school. Karl Marx took to this education very well (McLellan, 2006: 1–13). He was subsequently sent by his father to the university in Bonn. Concerned, however, that Marx was not taking his studies seriously enough there, his father withdrew him after only one year and transferred him to Berlin University in October 1936 (McLellan, 2006: 13–15; Wheen, 1999: 14–17). As a student in Berlin, Marx developed an interest in the philosophy of Hegel. Having previously read fragments of Hegel's work, he declared in a letter to his father in December 1837 that, in a period of illness, he 'got to know Hegel from beginning to end, together with most of his disciples' (LMFT, CW1: 19). Having not until then cared for Hegel's philosophy, he now became somewhat of an enthusiast. However, this was not to last. He became increasingly critical, and in his involvement with the Young Hegelians his scepticism for Hegel's philosophy grew (Sperber, 2013: 48–70). Marx decided to pursue an academic career and hoped his studies for a doctoral thesis at the University of Berlin would help him to reach this goal (Wheen, 1999: 31).

The arrival of Schelling at Berlin, and the king's enthusiasm for the work of this now reactionary philosopher, led Marx to see the full political significance of his doctoral dissertation. (See the very pointed comments about Schelling falling away from his earlier radical views, which Marx appended to his dissertation in 1841 (DD, CW1, 103).) He submitted it to the University of Jena, rather than to Berlin where he had studied, mindful that it would not be received at all enthusiastically by the latter institution. Moreover, as soon as he had submitted the thesis he left Berlin. He was not alone. Ruge, who was by then a prominent Young Hegelian thinker, was among the other radicals who decided to move away from the city. As the *Halle Yearbooks* of which Ruge was the editor became increasingly radical, he decided to relocate to Dresden, hoping in this way to avoid the worst of the censors; this effort to evade censorship was successful for less than two years and the *Yearbooks* was suppressed in 1843 (Spies, 1996: 322).

After graduating in 1841, the hostility in authoritarian Prussia to radical philosophy all but ruled out Marx's chances of gaining an academic post, and certainly a secure one. He therefore began to earn a living from journalism. As a radical journalist editor and writer for the *Rheinische Zeitung* newspaper, however, he attracted the attention of the censors. He made the decision to leave Prussia for Paris in order to be able to write more freely (Stedman Jones, 2016: 104–22). Ruge would do the same. First though, Marx hurriedly drafted the article *On the Jewish Question* in preparation for publication in a short-lived German-language newspaper, *Deutsch-Französische Jahrbücher*, based in Paris. This article (OJQ, CW3: 146–68) made the significant argument that the source of the most fundamental problem of modern society economics was not politics or religion but, rather, economics. The article, so titled, was a critique of the work of Bruno Bauer who not only disapproved of the Christian state for its restrictions on the rights of Jews, but also criticized Jews themselves for expecting the enjoyment of civil rights without renouncing their own religion. Marx argued that the problem was neither the Jewish faith nor the Christian state in particular but, rather, the modern state itself. As mentioned earlier in this introduction, for Marx the real problem was that the state focused on political rights. This allowed individualism to flourish in civil society, and this in turn meant that social rights were not considered at all. The predominantly egoistic character of human beings was not natural or foundational, as it was commonly presented (as famously in Thomas Hobbes, and then within a more narrowly economic framework, taken as a basic principle by thinkers such as Adam Smith). Rather, this egoism was a product of and cultivated in capitalist society. Furthermore, the root of human alienation was not at its foundation religious or philosophical doctrine – as Feuerbach had suggested only as recently as 1841 – but rather economic life, and this fundamental point was disguised. Money had become the greatest barrier to human freedom. People who suffered alienation could not fulfil their natural role as community-oriented species beings. To appreciate the significance of these views of Marx within his intellectual environment one should perhaps note that he was thus offering an argument radically opposed to the state of the art in economic theory of the period. Having emerged in the previous century in the work of Adam Smith, such liberal economic theory as presented by

James Mill, Thomas Malthus, and David Ricardo among others assumed that there should be strict limits to political intervention, as the operation of self-interest in the market will indirectly serve the general good of society far more reliably and efficiently than good intentioned private or governmental action (Arblaster, 1984: 237–53).

Marx presented his notion of alienation in greater detail in the *Paris Manuscripts* of 1844 (EPM, CW3: 270–82). In the meantime, however, he published another important article in the *Deutsch-Französische Jahrbücher*. This was the *Contribution to the Critique of Hegel's Philosophy of Law. Introduction*, which was originally intended to be an introduction to a far larger critique of Hegel's *Philosophy of Law*. (The German word in Hegel's title is 'Recht'. Some translators render this as 'law', some as 'right'. We will stick with 'law' because that is how the title is presented in Marx's *Collected Works*. 'Right' is more literal, but does not capture the fact that much of Hegel's book is about both legal and constitutional frameworks.) It represented an important development of Marx's thought in that he wrote clearly about the possibility of proletarian revolution and its proliferation. At this point he suggested that, by liberating itself, the German proletariat could emancipate other spheres of society in Germany, where capitalism was relatively undeveloped. This could develop into broader human emancipation. In turn this broader process of emancipation would be required for the maintenance of the narrower emancipation which would have sparked it (CCHPLI, CW3: 183–7). *The Deutsch-Französische Jahrbücher* was suppressed in Prussia after the first double issue and did not have sufficient readers in France to make it a viable publication. By March 1844, it had therefore ceased production. Nevertheless, as we saw earlier, in the *Paris Manuscripts* of 1844 he acknowledged that he would continue to bear in mind many of the ideas expressed in his earlier writings and perhaps at some point (a point that never came) put them together with others into a more general statement of his philosophy.

By the time he wrote the *Paris Manuscripts* Marx's intellectual development had led him into collaboration with Engels. Born in 1820 to a wealthy, protestant businessman, Engels was brought up in the German Rhineland town of Barmen (now part of Wuppertal) before going to work for his father's company, thus gaining direct experience of capitalism. He also participated in debating clubs and wrote some radical journalistic articles which were published in some of the more progressive regional newspapers. He came to reject religion and to take an interest in radical interpretations of the ideas of Hegel, especially the latter thinker's philosophy of the dialectic (Hunt, 2010: 12–77). In September 1841 he volunteered to take the year of military service expected of him in Berlin, and while residing in the city, he attended Schelling's early reactionary and anti-Hegelian lectures with great interest (Hunt, 2010: 45–50). Hence, Engels had come to be concerned with the implications of Schelling's arrival at Berlin and the anti-Hegelian campaign just a few months after Marx had seen that he could neither submit his doctoral dissertation to the University of Berlin, nor indeed stay in that city any longer. Engels expressed this concern in the pamphlet *Schelling and Revelation* (SR, CW2), which was published the following year. In this sharp critique of Schelling, Engels made very clear his sympathies with the Young Hegelians and his enthusiasm for the work of Feuerbach. As 1842 progressed he rapidly became disillusioned with the broadly liberal line of the Young Hegelians (Hunt, 2010: 77). The ideas of Marx and Engels were thus already beginning to bear distinct similarities. Nevertheless, at their first meeting in November that year, Engels was not greeted enthusiastically by Marx, whose trust he had yet to gain (Hunt, 2010: 66).

Engels' approval of Feuerbach's philosophy at this stage amounted in effect to stepping outside Hegelianism rather than extending it. He was beginning to draw on this Young Hegelian's ideas while being conscious that something important was still being overlooked. Hence, the belief in a dialectical process of history had become securely lodged in Engels' own thought. Philosophy was not, however, the only thing which cultivated in his mind the ideas that would inspire him to work with Marx. As mentioned earlier, he gained first-hand experience of working within the capitalist system. When he moved to England in the early 1840s to work for his father's business in Manchester, he saw with his own eyes the poverty, misery and desperate living and working conditions of ordinary people. These conditions were, he judged, the direct consequences of capitalism. The industrial working class that sold its labour for a wage – the proletariat – had been created artificially by the capitalist system and would, he predicted in accordance with his conception of historical development, eventually lead the movement to replace it with a better society. He published the result of his study of working-class life in *The Condition of the Working Class in England* (CWCE, CW4) in 1845. Like Marx, he had thus begun to combine his philosophy with political economy, most notably in his *Outlines of a Critique of Political Economy* (OCPE, CW3) which, written in 1843, was published as a journal article the following year. The 'basic elements' of the *Paris Manuscripts*, Marx (EPM, CW3: 232) conceded in the preface, had 'been indicated to me in a very general way' by Engels' article. Engels' argument was that political economy, including the work of the liberals such as Smith, Ricardo, Malthus and Mill, was basically a means to legitimate wholesale swindling in society. The first sentence announced this argument in stark terms: 'Political economy came into being as a natural result of the expansion of trade, and with it its appearance elementary, unscientific huckstering was replaced by a developed system of licensed fraud, an entire science of enrichment' (OCPE, CW3: 418). The liberal economists had introduced generalizations including 'natural wealth', but 'natural wealth' was meaningless while private property was still in existence (OCPE, CW3: 421). Labour, Engels stressed, was the main factor of production and the source of wealth. A problem with the economic system legitimated by political economy was that the product of labour confronted labour as wages, thus giving the impression that labour and its product were separate from one another. The abolition of private property would mean that 'the true significance of the wages of labour, hitherto alienated, comes to light – namely, the significance of labour for the determination of the production costs of a thing' (OCPE, CW3: 431). Marx seized upon these ideas and in 1844 offered a far more sustained and substantial argument that private property was in fact the result of alienation (EPM, CW3: 72). As will be discussed in the second main chapter of the present study, this was a crucial part of his political philosophy.

In August 1844 Engels visited Marx in Paris. Unlike their previous meeting, this one, in which they engaged in intense discussion for 10 days, resulted in a professional and personal friendship that would last until Marx's death in 1883. In 1844 they jointly authored a pamphlet with the rather unusual title *The Holy Family*, which was published in February the following year. The title is a satirical dig at Bruno Bauer and his intellectual circle, accusing them of a godlike arrogance and also of still being caught in theological ways of thinking – the heavily satirical tone is carried on throughout the book. Marx and Engels criticized Bauer for persisting with the argument that spirit is the progressive force in history. They stressed that it was the proletarian movement, and particularly the communist-minded workers, which constituted the progressive force. This movement would take shape when the people who comprised the proletariat were able to overcome the alienation and dehumanization that resulted from the system of private property (HF, CW4: 24–54). A chapter defending the work of the socialist/anarchist thinker Pierre-Joseph Proudhon from the 'circle' is significant. It was only three years after Proudhon's hugely influential argument that property was theft that Engels wrote his critique of private property and political economy in his essay *Outlines of a Critique of Political Economy*. While in the *Paris Manuscripts* of 1844 he acknowledged the influence of Engels' essay and attributed the institution of private property to alienation, Marx criticized Proudhon directly for demanding the equality of wages. It was only because of private property that wages became an issue. Hence, wages and private property were 'identical' (EPM, CW3: 280). Marx often criticized the anarchist Proudhon, who opposed revolutionary communism and indeed any organized political action as authoritarian (Thomas, 1980: 175–248). Marx and Engels would make their distaste for what they saw as this 'bourgeois' opposition loud and clear in the *Communist Manifesto* of 1848 (MCP, CW6: 513). Nevertheless, their defence of Proudhon in *The Holy Family* indicates that in the mid-1840s they still considered Proudhon's work as important as 'an advance which revolutionises political economy' (HF, CW4: 32).

By the time *The Holy Family* went to press in early 1845, Marx's journalistic work had begun to alarm the Prussian government. He had in the summer of 1844 accepted the opportunity to write in the communist periodical *Vorwärts!*, which was the only uncensored German-language radical journal. The Prussian authorities were alerted to Marx's work and complained to the French king who demanded that the paper cease publication in January 1845. The authorities in Paris went a step further and expelled Marx from France. From there he went to the Belgian capital Brussels (Wheen, 1999: 66–7 and 90–1). In an important step in their growing intellectual relationship, Engels decided to go to Belgium for a period of work with Marx (Hunt, 2010: 128). Together, they began to write *The German Ideology*.

By the end of Hobsbawm's period of dual revolution, and in part because of increasingly reactionary regimes in Prussia and elsewhere, the view began to spread that any progress that had begun in 1789 was fading away. In this environment socialist and communist ideas had been conceived and propagated. There were various earlier notions of communism, most notably that of Francois-Noel Babeuf and Sylvain Marechal in revolutionary France, following the fall of the Jacobin government in 1794 (Babeuf and Marechal, 1997: 49–52). This and the communist visions it inspired were republican, egalitarian and authoritarian. While the socialists of the early nineteenth century likewise wanted social and political change for the benefit of ordinary people, they tended to be less radical and egalitarian and more concerned with association and cooperation (Lichtheim, 1975: 28, 37–8, 58 and 60–63). By the 1840s, the distinction was narrowing in the thought of some radicals, such as Moses Hess, who argued that a moral revolution would bring about a social revolution and thus communism. This was communism for humanity – communism as humanism – rather than communism for the proletariat. Socialism and communism were as one in the thought of Hess (Hook, 1994: 188–200).

Socialists and Communists of various types perceived possibilities for far more fundamental social and political change than even the drafters of the French revolutionary bill of rights had demanded. Marx and Engels became prominent among those who grasped and built on this brewing radicalism. By the mid-1840s they had begun to give increasingly full consideration to the likelihood that the proletarian class would need to plan and execute its own revolution in order to build a communist society. Before he began to make this argument, Marx was more concerned to offer a philosophical critique than argue for and encourage revolution, or at least saw a thorough philosophical critique of the intellectual backdrop of the modern political economy as a necessary feature of such a revolution. In the last few years approaching 1848 he combined this philosophy with the political economy and revolutionary activism that were coming to dominate his thought. He and Engels criticized early radical communism for its austerity as well as what had come to be considered as the more respectable and moderate socialism. They were particularly hostile to German socialists such as Karl Grün for accommodating aristocratic criticism of capitalism, and thus playing into the hands of the nobility and thus the government and bureaucracy. The problem was that these socialists attempted to extrapolate French and English radical thought to a more general theory applicable to Germany, without recognizing that German social, political and economic conditions were very different from the countries in which the theories they borrowed were written. The clearest and most concise attack of this nature on these German socialists, who styled themselves as true socialists, was a piece Engels wrote in March/April 1847 which, intended as a pamphlet (but not published in Engels' lifetime), is now known as 'The Constitutional Question in Germany'. According to Engels, the true socialists even included some who were considered by themselves, but not by Engels, as communists. Their literature was so tame that it was ignored by the censors. 'Even the German police,' he teased, 'find in it little to take exception to.' This was for him proof that it belonged 'not to the progressive, revolutionary elements but to the stale, reactionary elements in German literature' (CQG, CW6: 75). The actual German communists should, he insisted, disavow the reactionary 'true' socialists (CQG, CW6: 78). At the same time that Engels was working on his piece Marx (DAKG, CW6: 73) was writing a short article, published on 8 April 1847, in which he claimed that he had, the previous year, attacked Grün's true socialism in a review that was presented as an appendix to his and Engels' unprinted book *The German Ideology*. Actually, the review formed part of the main text of the version of *The German Ideology* published in 1932 (GI, CW5: 484–530).

Marx and Engels sought to establish a new form of communism as a predominantly proletarian movement with considerable autonomy from other classes (Leopold, 2015: 34–5; Thomas, 2012: 94–7). As radical thinkers in this environment Marx and Engels became key figures in the Communist League in 1847 and, on the basis of Engels' drafts, Marx wrote the *Communist Manifesto*. In the *Manifesto* Marx and Engels (MCP, CW6: 507–13) criticized a range of socialist theories including those he described as Utopian for their schemes to build socialist communities, conservative or bourgeois socialism which sought merely to address social grievances and reactionary socialism such as that of the German theorists such as Grün. Each of these types of socialism failed to understand the necessity for revolutionary class struggle and the social conditions that were developing, which were making that struggle both necessary and winnable. In his criticism of his opponents Marx can be considered a theorist of modernity.

The condition of modernity clearly permeated the *Communist Manifesto* (Lamb, 2015: 16–19; Osborne, 2005: 84–5). Published in 1848, the *Manifesto* expresses Marx's belief that the new capitalist society and its political order were as equally implausible as had been the *ancien régime* (Dunne, 1993: 89–90), that is, the regime in France prior to the revolution of 1789. The epoch of the bourgeoisie had nevertheless brought about advancements in industry, science, navigation, transportation and other practices that could be utilized to bring about further progress. Although not as assertively as in the *Manifesto*, and without the flair of that famous pamphlet, this belief can also be detected in the work of the first Marx. In the *Manifesto* he expressed confidently a view that the working class could take action to shape their own future and that of their descendants. Although by the mid-1840s he had begun to envisage the communist workers at the forefront of the proletariat in the struggle against their oppressors and exploiters, he had yet to posit the full revolutionary potential of the proletariat. The conviction that capitalism must soon be replaced with a better society is missing from the writings he produced earlier in that decade. Nevertheless, these early writings are characterized by their own modern optimism, suggesting that radical reform of political and social structures could achieve much for human emancipation. In the early years of the decade he wrote that *human*, rather than political or class, emancipation (OJQ, CW3) and revolutionary change would be necessary to bring this about (CCHPLI, CW3); or, where class was discussed, class emancipation was part of human emancipation. This emphasis explains why the early Marx is often portrayed as a 'humanist'. Importantly, although Germany was politically underdeveloped, philosophically it was very advanced and could catch up and overtake other countries with regard to the progress stimulated by the upheaval of 1789 (Levine, 2002: 230–2). The revolution could indeed begin in Germany because of this philosophical maturity. When the authorities in Prussia and in Germany more generally got wind of these radical views, they began to sit up and take them very seriously.

Even in the early 1840s, Marx, indeed, stood out from the many intellectuals, especially those in the broadly Hegelian tradition, who tried to reconcile a German cultural identity with the modernity that the French Revolution had fostered. Within this circle, optimism had begun to wane in the early 1840s, especially as the Prussian regime was becoming increasingly authoritarian. The view began to spread that, as Harold Mah (1990: 6) has put it, 'Germany was deeply and intractably resistant to modernity.' Marx had never held that German cultural identity was compatible with progress, for precisely these reasons; he believed that although the revolution could start in Germany because of its philosophical sophistication, this would require the repudiation of the German past and present (Mah, 1990: 16–19). The revolution must, therefore, secure human emancipation, rather than German emancipation.

It can thus be discerned that, during the 1840s, there was in Marx's thought an intersection of two phases of modernity. In the first phase, which encompassed the early to middle years of that decade, he recognized that progress had been made and was offering his views on the social, economic and political changes that would be needed and the reasons why this was so, in order to make further progress towards human emancipation. The second phase emerged in Marx's radical political thought when, in the second half of the 1840s, he became the pre-eminent theorist of proletarian revolution. Continuity is certainly in evidence as he moved from the first phase into the second. Indeed, he needed to go through the early, distinctly philosophical phase to reach the later one in which he saw the role of revolutionary activist and strategist to be the far more important one. We suggest in what follows that whatever the strengths and weaknesses of the later phase (which is not our concern in this book), his early work is, for the reason mentioned at the beginning of this introduction, of far greater lasting significance than he envisaged when he abandoned *The German Ideology* to the mice.

CHAPTER TWO

Production

Any study of the early or later work of Marx should focus closely on his understanding of production, which is undeniably central. There are two dangers here that interpretation must avoid. The first danger is the least likely to happen: to not take the notion of production seriously enough, not seeing it as a central problem. More troubling is the second danger, which is to underestimate the *scope* of the concept. To be sure, Marx's materialist outlook rests on the view that by nature humans produce cooperatively in their community. When this cooperative production either does not happen or takes place in a way that is imposed upon people, then this becomes an unnatural situation (indeed, in the language we will pursue in our next chapter, they are in a condition of 'alienation'). The situation in Europe that Marx observed – industrial capitalism – was, on his analysis, characterized by just such unnaturalness, and Marx's political philosophy centred upon this analysis.

As yet, though, we have still restricted too far the scope of the concept of production. For Marx is not merely talking about industrial or agricultural production of a familiar type. Likewise, despite its obvious importance, Marx is not thinking about production just in any narrow economic sense. Instead, he insists that cooperative production is the basis of *all* human physical and mental activity: so, for example, in the domain of the family, the production of children; in the domain of thought, the production of science and philosophy. Indeed, this amounts to the view he expressed in the *Paris Manuscripts* of 1844 (EPM, CW3: 333) that to consciously produce as such, and to do so cooperatively, is what makes human beings into a species (see also a less direct statement to this effect in Marx's and Engels' ridiculing of Max Stirner's (Sancho's) views to the contrary in *The German Ideology* (GI, CW5: 77 and 420–7). This does not mean that people stop being human beings under the condition of modern capitalism, but that they are not functioning properly or fully as humans. This point of view is actually illustrated very well by a passage from a journalistic article that Marx published in August 1844, which refers to working people who are unable, because of their circumstances, to engage in cooperative production:

> The community from which the worker is isolated by *his own labour* is *life* itself, physical and mental life, human morality, human activity, human enjoyment, *human* nature. *Human nature* is the *true community* of men. The disastrous isolation from this essential nature is incomparably more universal, more intolerable, more dreadful, and more contradictory, than isolation from the political community. (CMN, CW4: 204–5)

In the passage just quoted, Marx refers specifically to 'the worker'. As will be gathered from the opening paragraph of the present chapter, he was particularly concerned with the producing worker who, as he put it in the *Paris Manuscripts*, 'can create nothing without nature, without the sensuous external world' (EPM, CW3: 273). In capitalism, 'the worker' provides the most universal instance of productive activity, and thus also of alienation – and this tempts one to a too narrow restriction on the concept of production. In the next chapter, alienation as the main predicament in which human beings find themselves in societies characterized by the institution of private property will be discussed. In order to grasp that predicament properly it will be necessary to examine his view that productive activity is the key factor in the mediation of humans with nature. As István Mészáros (2005: 79) suggests, this is an absolute ontological factor 'because the human mode of existence is', for Marx, 'inconceivable without the transformations of nature accomplished by productive activity'.

Alex Callinicos has summarized very well the importance of production to Marx's theory of human nature. Referring to Marx's view of the human activity of material production by means of transforming elements of a pregiven environment, he noted that this meant that humans by nature shape the material world by means of their labour, which was undertaken consciously by cooperating humans and was thus a social practice. 'This conception of human nature as constituted by an active, redirective, transformative relationship to nature through the labour process is', as Callinicos (1983: 40) argues, 'fundamental to Marx's thought'. The consciously guided practice of production was a vital feature of this relationship.

Even now, however, we have not yet sufficiently widened the scope of the concept of production. The common sense view – that production means industrial or agricultural output, and thus the producer is always the 'worker' – has been surpassed in thinking that all human activities are to be understood as production, and thus also that the essential nature of the human as a species is production. Marx goes one radical step further. If, as he suggests, the nature of humans involves cooperative work which they themselves perform, human beings can be said to contribute collectively to their essence. In Marx's view humans produced not only material objects, intellectual efforts or artworks, but also their own social and political institutions with their inherent ideas and values, and thereby also *produce their own nature* (Kitching, 1988: 21). In other words, the key factor in the positive essence (i.e. specific content) of the human is that of cooperative production; without this key factor the human is significantly undeveloped and produces *itself* as undeveloped. As Andrew Chitty (1997: 91–4) suggests, Marx's view can be described as a productionist one. 'Production', although most commonly a translation of the Latinate German word *Produktion*, is better understood as a concept underlying Marx's use of a set of terms which may carry slightly different contextual meanings, such as 'create', 'make', 'practical activity', 'build' and so on.

For Marx, other features of the species which enable each member of it to flourish are *products* of cooperation. Thus, to take only the most obviously pertinent example, those philosophers who claim that selfishness or egoism is an inherent characteristic of human beings, and thus a genuinely socialist society is impossible, are only in a limited sense correct: This is true only for the human as it has been produced under the historically contingent circumstances of capitalism. Humans can be otherwise, if they consciously and cooperatively produce themselves otherwise. This view of the importance of cooperation to bring about change can be observed in the Introduction to the *Contribution to the Critique of Hegel's Philosophy of Law* which Marx wrote at the end of 1843. By demanding the negation of private property and proclaiming the dissolution of the hitherto existing world order, he argued (CCHPLI, CW3: 187), 'the proletariat merely raises to the rank of a principle of society what society has made the principle of the proletariat, what, without its own co-operation, is already incorporated in it as the negative result of society'.

Rather than compete with others for resources, we can produce more and better goods and services in collaboration. Furthermore, we gain satisfaction from such collaboration and it seems natural in the sense that it creates those conditions within which other aspects of the human can flourish. If Daniel Defoe's *Robinson Crusoe* had simply been the story of a person following a normal lifestyle it would not have been particularly interesting. It was because Crusoe was in an unnatural situation that made the story into a classic. Similarly, if St Simon Stylites' self-imposed ordeal of standing on top of a pillar in isolation (other than to receive food packages) for almost 40 years in the fifth century had been natural human behaviour then it is highly unlikely that his feat of endurance would have become legendary. As the socialist theorist Harold Laski (1925: 17) put it in *A Grammar of Politics* eight decades after the 1840s, before Laski came to consider himself a Marxist, 'Crusoe on his desert island, or St. Simon Stylites upon his pillar, may defy the normal impulses which make them men; but, for the vast majority, to live with others is the condition of a rational existence.' Humans, Laski argued, live with their fellows, this being a result of inherited instinct. Laski added that the fact that in the modern world humans live under the authority of governments and are obliged to obey governments arises from this communal nature. For Laski, what was important was that state sovereignty was a fiction, as states are influenced by powerful interests. The mask of sovereignty therefore needed to be removed and the obligation to obey governments was contingent upon their defence of both individual and social rights; the promotion of the social good; and upon the defence of equality and the equal freedom of people to enjoy fulfilling lives. Marx's view of human nature differed significantly from that of Laski. Marx identified two parts to human nature. First there was the changeable aspect which is conditioned by their environment. The environment itself changes as productive forces develop under the control of dominant classes in a series of temporal phases in which one class loses control and another gains it – for example, feudalism gave way to the system we now know of as capitalism. The other aspect was the permanent one which is always there but unrecognized by people in the condition of alienation. This permanent aspect is that of the cooperative, productive species-being. Like Laski's humanity, that of Marx's philosophy was characterized by community; but for Marx it was not enough for humans to hold their state to account. They needed, rather, to overthrow that state. The working class as the most exploited section of the community would need to lead the revolution. By means of revolution the state gives way to a new way of organizing society that people develop, and the changeable aspect of their nature comes into line with the permanent. The species-being is fully realized. This was not, however, realization as a *fixed* end point, as the human species-being continues to develop in its emancipated condition.

In *The German Ideology* Marx and Engels wrote that communist revolution would bring separate individuals 'into practical connection with the production (including intellectual production) of the whole world'. This would enable them to gain the capacity to enjoy the 'all-sided production of the whole earth (the creations of man)'. Until now the powers of mutual dependence of all human beings had been accumulated in a power alien to them. This was the power of the world market. 'All-round dependence, this primary natural form of the world historical cooperation of individuals,' would, Marx and Engels argued, 'be transformed by this communist revolution into the control and conscious mastery of these powers' (GI CW5: 51). The notion of transformation is hugely significant in the passage just quoted. Cooperation had hitherto been imposed, enforced on human beings. The cooperation needed for conscious mastery of their powers would require a transformation of the organization of production into free, voluntary cooperation.

This consciously guided revolutionary practice can be described, in a term often used in Marxist scholarship and activism, as *praxis* (Fraser and Wilde, 2011: 166). The need for a philosophical understanding of praxis on the part of the workers thus emerges as the outcome of Marx's broad analysis of the notion of production. As will be discussed in this study's chapter entitled Change, praxis is an important concept if one is to grasp how in his early political philosophy Marx built a theory of emancipation on the foundation of his understanding of human production. We have given a very brief characterization of this concept of production. Now, the task is to look at the roots of that concept within philosophy and subsequently to assemble a more detailed and complete picture of Marx's thought on the matter.

The history of the concept of production

To produce would seem to have several dimensions; let us lay these out as common sense might have it (by which we just mean: as everyday language uses the word 'production'). In the order of things, last of all comes the *product*, an object or perhaps activity that has come newly into existence. Prior to this, presumably, we find a *producer*, that being who exercises some agency and who 'does' the *production* or *producing activity*. First of all we find two original aspects, the *form* of the product (the idea or the plan according to which the product is produced) and the *matter* of the product (from what raw material the product is produced). So, for example, a cabinetmaker (a producer), through her various skills (the act of production), makes a cabinet (the product) from out of a design (the form) and some suitable wooden planks (the matter). We do not have to look very far to find this basic pattern all over the history of thought, albeit to be sure with some variations. For example, for a creationist, God is a producer who creates (produces) the world (product) according to a plan; the only thing missing here is the matter which one conventionally tends to believe is created at the same time as the world itself. Adam formed from clay and Eve from Adam's rib is more consistent with our model. Similarly, a fairly common model of education has the young person as material, who is formed into an autonomous, responsible and skilled adult through a process that looks very much like production, through the work and care of agents called teachers. The production of music presents a slight variation insofar as the act of music-making is itself the product (i.e. there is not something separable that can be taken away from the process); there are also therefore no raw materials that are used up in the process, except perhaps the energy and time of the performers.

Our references to the Judeo-Christian model of creation suggest that this broad characterization of production is very ancient indeed. It is found again in Plato (1974: 421–7) – for example, in the account of art as copy of copy in the *Republic*. Likewise, Aristotle, whose account of the four moments of causation is as clear a statement of this kind of thing as one could find. However, Aristotle introduces two new ideas that our model earlier did not include (Ackrill, 1978; Hocutt, 1974). First is the notion of *telos*, of production having not only a design and a product, but also spanning the act, from the one to the other, having a *purpose*. The cabinetmaker does not merely have a design and produce a cabinet, but the maker's purpose organizes all of the acts in between. Aristotle (1996: 146–7) called this the 'final cause'. In everyday language, we get close to this in saying that the cabinetmaker is 'busy' or 'being productive'.

Second, Aristotle argues that some processes, and most famously he has the living of living beings and especially human beings in mind, are *essentially productive*. Up to this point, nothing in our model suggested that the producer could not just stop his or her work and do something else, without ceasing to be the entity it always was; it seemed as though production was just *one* thing that those who were producers (again, thinking primarily of human agents) could do or be. It was, in other words, a *contingent or accidental* feature of human life. Aristotle suggests that it is of the essence of human beings to seek some end, that is, to seek to produce something. Other forms of life are more obvious examples: that everything about the flowering plant seems to be geared to the production of a seed, and thus the reproduction of itself and its species, and to do so in such a way as to ensure the species establishes the greatest and most secure possible grip on its ecological niche, has become something of a truism in the biological sciences. If the same holds of human beings, then what is the human end? Well, reproduction in the form of producing children to be sure, and Marx certainly stresses this as the basic form of all production (EPM, CW3: 276–7; GI, CW5: 41–3). However, both Aristotle and Marx add that this end is merely animal (indeed, plant-like too!), and is not an end that belongs to the human being as such. That is, it does not tell us how the human being is distinctive from the rat or the rhododendron. In our discussion earlier, a key phrase was 'establishes the greatest and most secure grip'. The flowering plant, both the individual and the individual as a representative of a species, does not just reproduce but 'seeks' (final cause) to *flourish*.

The question about the distinctive end of the human, for Aristotle, thus becomes the question of what does it mean for human beings to 'flourish', as opposed to rat or rhododendron types of flourishing. Very roughly, through the *Nicomachean Ethics*, he works out the answer as 'to live life according to reason'. The argument rests in part upon the observation that the most distinctive feature of human existence – what is different from plants and other animals – is the capacity for reasoning or thinking in all its various forms. It follows then that 'for human beings to flourish' as human beings must mean for them to attain their *distinctive* capacity to flourish, that is for their flourishing to consist in excellence in the use of reason (Aristotle, 1996: 1–30).

For our purposes, the key point here is that the model of production is still in operation. To be sure, the raw materials, the producer and the product are *all the same thing*: that is, human beings should (as producers) transform themselves (the matter) from relatively deficient to relatively proficient rational lives (the product, now refashioned in accord with the design, form or plan). Notice also that we are not talking *primarily* of individual human beings developing themselves, since it is a *species* characteristic that is at stake. The development of human beings is a species-wide project, which is why, for example, Aristotle's ethics leads naturally on to his politics, the study of the necessary role of communal organization in the species project of flourishing (Aristotle, 1962: 25–9). So, our model of production has been around – and we are speaking broadly here and do not wish to discount significant variations – since the beginnings of Western thought. Moreover, it is used to cover production in a quite ordinary sense (the cabinetmaker and the cabinet), in unusual senses such as music-making, and even self-production, something that in the history of thought is most common in understanding ethics.

In subsequent centuries, this Aristotelian idea of ethics as self-production waxes and wanes. Something akin to it, for example, is exceedingly prominent in the Roman period, with Stoic ethics. Christianity across its history sometimes took a broadly Aristotelian line, but then also often argued, for example, notably in the work of Saint Augustine, that the key agent in the production of human beings was the *grace* of God (still, note, based upon the model of production, but just not self-production by humans) (Haddock, 1992: 78–80). The issue typically hung upon whether the theology viewed human beings as innately sinful, and therefore abject and incapable of achieving salvation for themselves. In any case, over these centuries, the Aristotelian emphasis on human self-making being through and towards reason was also challenged. Perhaps reason is only a means for some other end. One could make a case that what was truly distinctive of human beings was the capacity for the production of art and beauty, for truly free acts or for faith. These could then be employed to understand flourishing. Another alternative is that the human should be defined not on the basis of what it produces, that is, any *specific telos*, but simply *that* it produces. The Latin phrase *homo faber* (man the maker) was used in the ancient world precisely to designate human beings (both collectively and individually) as having the unique capacity to alter and control their environment and lives. *Homo faber* became a common slogan among the humanists of the Renaissance and then again among political philosophers in the twentieth century (Ferrarin, 2000: 289–92). We mention this as it is an early anticipation of a key theme of the early Marx, which is a tendency to view any attempt to define the *telos* of human flourishing ahistorically as a limitation or alienation of the human.

Now, to be sure, one could write volumes on the ins and outs of the notion of production across the history of thought, but let this rough sketch serve. Again, we have identified two ideas: first, the basic model of production; second, the additional notion of self-production, perhaps self-production of the human as excellence in its rational life, or even production without any necessary and essential form or purpose, thus *homo faber* as a designation for the species. A crucial difference between Aristotle and Marx becomes significant at this point. While Aristotle saw the potential for human flourishing, for him this was on the basis of the actual essence of the human species – something that was innate and unchanging in human nature. Marx on the other hand saw both transhistorical and historical elements of human nature – in other words there was a constant aspect and also one that changed according to circumstances (Struhl, 2016). For Marx, the potential for flourishing is effected as the mutable aspect of human nature changes in accordance with conditioning as history passes through and into the different epochs, driven by the advancement of productive forces. Marx thus gave priority to potentiality rather than actuality (Jaffe, 2016), something as yet unrealized and certainly unconceived of (with the possible exception of Marx's fellow communists). There is a possible whole of human being, something which could only be realized and thought after other limited (and thus determinate) fragments of the human were achieved and then superseded. We must, Marx insists, avoid the all too common mistake of postulating some 'fictitious primordial condition' (EPM, CW3: 271) of the human. This, one can assume he would have agreed, applies as much to a past Eden as imagined by Rousseau, or a past (or future) Hell on earth such as Hobbes' state of nature. Likewise, this mistake would be found in any account of the human considered as having some ahistorical essence (so Marx accused a typical 'political economist' (EPM, CW3: 271) in his time). This is something to which we return in the chapters on change and emancipation later in the present study.

In the eighteenth century, insofar as we commonly identify it as the 'age of Enlightenment', the broadly Aristotelian notion had once again been prominent. This is in part because, although Enlightenment thought was by no means necessarily irreligious, it tended to emphasize the secular dimension of politics, ethics and other human affairs, thereby also emphasizing the efficacy of the productive acts of human agents. Also playing a key role, though, is the well-known Enlightenment stress upon *reason* as distinctive of humans and as a means of solving problems. No less important, finally, is the *optimism* with which many thinkers in the Enlightenment viewed social, political and ethical problems (not to mention the scientific and technological). This meant that, rather than stressing a concern with the preservation of existing social and political order, there was frequently an appetite for producing new – often radically new – forms of human order, in order to better achieve a flourishing of reason throughout human life. The French Revolution is the example usually raised at this point. Even among those who were politically or socially conservative, optimism in the ability of reason to achieve progress in other areas remained common; in other words, the belief in *progress*.

Production in Kant and Hegel

Working nearly contemporaneously with the revolutionary events in France, Immanuel Kant is one of the key figures in the history of the thinking about production and self-production, in the period leading up to that of the young Marx. Kant famously distinguishes between the theoretical and the practical dimensions of human experience, and thus also the theoretical and practical branches of philosophy. Governing each of these is reason, but reason in two distinct forms. The theoretical aspect of reason is concerned with our understanding of nature, where nature very much includes most aspects of human beings (our bodies, our senses, our psychology). Theoretical reason strives for ever more comprehensive or penetrating ways of understanding nature; above all, this means producing ever more comprehensive or penetrating *causal laws*, for nature is characterized by law-governed cause and effect. The practical, on the other hand, deals with our *actions* – and not just any actions, but only those accomplished from out of genuine *freedom*. In fact, Kant argues, most of my actions are a part of nature, because most actions are a part of the nexus of cause and effect. On Kant's analysis, there is no aspect of the cabinetmaker's productive work that, in and of itself, requires us to leave behind natural causation. It follows that most instances of production are also to be understood as part of theoretical philosophy. Free actions are the exception here because freedom, minimally defined, means freedom *with respect to* the nexus of cause and effect. When I act freely, Kant argues, I do not simply act randomly (which would presumably also be a way of not being part of the nexus of causes), but rather I act according to a law, but this is a law that I myself *set for myself*. I am 'autonomous' in the original Greek meaning of the word. Practical philosophy is the study of those laws that freedom freely imposes upon itself; it is ethics as distinct from any study of nature. If, for any reason, the domain of the theoretical (i.e. the domain of nature) imposes itself upon ethics, then we have a situation that Kant calls 'heteronomy' – a 'foreign' law is in play, and ethics ceases to be ethical (Williams, 1983: 64 and 226). So, for example, if I allow my self-interest (a part of my natural psychology) to influence my supposedly free choices, then I am not behaving ethically. Thus, Kant sees a need for moral education: my habits or desires must be trained so that either they agree with the moral law or they are not sufficiently powerful to sway my moral will. Some of this 'education' is my own duty as an adult to recognize and correct my prejudices, desires and so forth (Kant, 1993: 157–68).

As we mentioned in the Introductory chapter, Marx himself experienced a humanist education, both at home and at school, which encouraged the development of such Enlightenment ideals. In the letter he wrote to his father in 1837 he mentioned that his early idealism had been nourished by that of Kant before he 'arrived at the point of seeking the idea in reality itself' (LMFT, CW1: 18). The Kantian nourishment is clear to see in his

'Reflections of a Young Man in the Choice of a Profession' two years earlier,
where he declared a belief in the relation between individual and collective
aspects of morality. The chief guide to one's choice of a profession, he
suggested, was 'the welfare of mankind and our own perfection'. These two
interests were not, he went on, in conflict. One of them did not have to
destroy the other; 'on the contrary, man's nature is so constituted that he can
attain his own perfection only by working for the perfection, for the good,
of his fellow men' (RYM, CW1: 8). However much he might have been
uncomfortable with it, the Kantian influence never entirely disappeared
from Marx's thought.

In both the theoretical and practical domains, Kant was employing a
concept that he calls 'critique' – indeed, his series of three main philosophical
books all have 'critique' in the title. Critique means an investigation of
fundamental legitimacy and limits. A critique of theoretical reason (which
he provides in the *Critique of Pure Reason*) investigates how and why reason
has legitimacy with respect to the natural world – that is, how and why
reason can lead to the production of knowledge of nature – and on the basis
of this legitimacy, Kant thereby also determines what are the appropriate
limits of theoretical reason. Very crudely, Kant argues that knowledge arises
from an interaction of the human mind with nature as it is presented through
the senses. It follows that knowledge can be legitimate where founded upon
this interaction, but if either of the two sources (mind or sense) is omitted,
then reason will flounder. Since certain typical metaphysical avenues of
inquiry – such as 'Does the human being have a soul, and if so what is its
nature?', 'Does time have a beginning?' or 'Does God exist?' – all involve
leaving behind the sensual nature part of the equation, these questions are
meaningless, at least in the sense that no answer could ever be arrived at.
Were we to pursue our rational enquiry to the point of actually answering
such questions, or rather *seeming* to do so, then we would be positing false
or impossible objects (such as God's power, or the beginning of time). (A
similar conclusion is reached, by the way, concerning any pure empiricism,
which leaves out of play the transcendental concepts and activity of mind.)

In this way, Kant believed he had solved three enormously significant
philosophical problems. First, he had demonstrated that scepticism about
knowledge of nature is unfounded – knowledge can indeed be reliably
produced, within the appropriate limits of human reason. Second, he had
demonstrated that centuries of philosophical metaphysics were nigh on
useless and possibly harmful, producing false objects and false hopes. These
are 'false' in the sense that such objects, although products of untempered
pure reason, tempt us to take them as objects of knowledge. Third, he had,
despite the above, 'made room' for faith (Kant, 1996: 747–55) – for the
question concerning God's existence could not be answered *either way*, and
thus the relation between human knowledge and faith is settled as a draw.
For example, 'God's power' is not a false or impossible thing per se, but
certainly is so when considered as an object of human knowledge.

Practical reason too has its critique (see, not surprisingly, *The Critique of Practical Reason*). That a moral law is a self-imposed law of human freedom defines both its legitimacy and its limits. Kant conceives of the moral law as the 'form' of a law merely – that is to say, it is not so much a mechanism for determining what we ought to do than a procedure for reflecting upon our past or future actions. In order to assist with this reflection, Kant produces several versions of the moral law, which he claims are all equivalent. The two most well-known of these say (1) that we should act in such a way that the principle of our actions could be rendered universal, that is, apply to everyone; and (2) that we should in our actions treat other human beings as ends in themselves and not as means. The first of these ways of expressing the form of the moral laws means that, should I choose to act in a way that benefits me alone, or my group alone, then this is in principle unethical, for such an action cannot be 'universalised' – that is, it could not consistently be said to apply to everyone (Körner, 1955: 127–51).

The second will take a little more unpacking. By an 'end' is meant the purpose behind the action, or the end-point at which the action aims (in other words, it is a descendent of Aristotle's *telos*). By 'means' is meant a tool or resource that gets used in attaining some end. So, in our previous example, the cabinetmaker's supply of wood, and her tools and labour, are all means; the end is the finished cabinet (envisioned at the beginning and throughout, and achieved by the conclusion). Kant is clearly working within the ancient model of production that we outlined earlier. However, note two ambiguities: first, is it not contrary to the moral law as formulated earlier that the cabinetmaker's own labour should be understood as just another 'means' to the end? That is, is that not a case treating a human being as a mere means? And second, is the cabinet itself the end, or might perhaps the end be the subsequently satisfied customer, or even the uses to which the customer will put the cabinet? That is to say, where does the 'end' stop, among the series of events that ensue? These ambiguities will become very important later in talking about Marx's account of production.

In any case, in this formulation of the moral law, Kant is here effectively providing a definition (for ethical purposes) of the human being as an end in itself. This definition helps us with the ambiguities earlier. All other ends can *also* be means to a further end (e.g. the cabinet is an end, but also a means to the end of satisfying the customer, and that end in turn could be a means for something else, and so forth). Only a human being is an end in itself, meaning that (again for moral purposes) the series of ends finishes there. Thus also, the moral law would permit the cabinetmaker's labour to be a means to another's end (a cabinet for a customer) only if that labour is *also* directed to the maker's own end (the payment for the cabinet, and thus his or her livelihood as a cabinetmaker). A fair exchange, Kant implies, is no robbery. (Marx will of course object to this: by the time one gets to the stage where exchange is the basic form of interaction among human beings, the 'robbery' has already happened.)

From the second formulation of the moral law, it follows that when we consider the meaning or purpose of moral actions, that is when we consider what it is that is to be produced through moral action; there is only one possibility: every moral act must have a human being (one or more, or perhaps the species as a whole) as its ultimate end. What does it mean, though, to have a human being as the end of one's action: do we mean helping someone, enriching someone, educating someone, to say nothing of the innumerable other possibilities? Recall that in practical philosophy, the human being, the end in itself, is a free, rational being. That *capacity* to be free itself is thus the end; every other natural aspect of the human – for example, the need for food and shelter – is *ethically* significant only insofar as it is a condition of a human's capacity to be free. Moral action is defined as *nothing other than* acting so as to enhance or protect the rational freedom of human beings (both individually and collectively) (Williams, 1983: 34–6). *That* is a revolutionary idea. Freedom is the condition of any moral action, and any moral action produces freedom. Be gone with the interests of the King, parliament or state, or those of Pope or church; be gone with the wealth of nations or the power of estates – the purpose of freedom and the only possible moral action is freedom. This is what Kant says – or rather, what he *could have but did not say* – not only because he himself was a more modest personality, not inclined to politically revolutionary activity, but also because in the political climate of the day, he would have been censored, or worse. Nevertheless, it was what many other philosophers, in decades to come, *heard him say*.

Although this basic moral concept undergoes many transformations and additions over the next half-century, becoming nearly unrecognizable by the time of the 1840s, we will nevertheless rediscover freedom, as liberation or emancipation, as one of the pillars of the philosophy of the young Marx. In addition, it is worth adding here that the notion of critique itself – in a sense that traces its origin to Kant – is also a primary methodological preoccupation of Marx and many of his contemporaries (McCarthy, 1985). It is no accident, to point to only the most obvious example, that Marx uses the word 'critique' in several titles or chapter headings in his publications or notes, during this period. Likewise, in *The Holy Family* (HF, CW4: 55–211), he and Engels adopted 'critical critics' as a satirical label for their fellow, and still all too Hegelian thinkers, such as Bauer – by which they mean those who mistake critique, while assuredly an important stage of thought, with the whole meaning and purpose of thought. They resumed this attack on critical criticism in *The German Ideology* (GI, CW5: 109–16) and the short article 'A Reply to Bruno Bauer's Anti-Critique' (RBBA-C, CW5: 15–18). Thus, we will often have occasion to return to the broadly Kantian notion of critique – the study of principles as conditions and limits – in what follows; and in later chapters, we will show that Marx's critique demonstrates the limits even of *criticism itself*. In that critique Hegel was a key target.

As will have been clear from our Introduction, Hegel's thought was the dominant mode of philosophical enquiry in the German-speaking world for the whole first half of the nineteenth century. We will therefore be touching upon Hegelian ideas regularly and throughout the remainder of this book. Fortunately, this means that our account of Hegel here, under the heading of production, can be quite brief. We will pursue just two avenues: dialectic and freedom.

Hegel argues – or, perhaps more accurately, Marx and his contemporaries *take him to be arguing*, for Hegel is subject to subsequent battles of interpretation no less than other philosophers and probably more than most – that all things develop *dialectically*. By 'dialectic' is meant a specific type of production that occurs as the resolution of conflicts or insufficiencies that had emerged within some previous state. Another way of expressing this idea is that the dialectic is production that occurs through the reciprocal action of opposing elements within some existing state of affairs. Let us discuss two broad ways in which dialectic appears in Hegel. First, dialectic is an unavoidable philosophical method, one given to philosophy by the nature of thought itself. In his *Science of Logic*, Hegel begins with the mere concept of being. He then analyses this concept in order to show that it itself contains a contradiction such that, when being and its contradiction are worked through, they eventually yield another, new philosophical concept. Hegel holds that the complete and systematic set of concepts needed for philosophy can be arrived at by repeating this procedure. Moreover, being and thought are not originally at odds – that which *is* presents a rational order akin to and continuous with thought (Singer, 1983: 75–80). Thus, thinking cannot be understood to be essentially distinct from being, but at worst thinking taken on its own is an abstract moment of being. A complete system of philosophy is therefore also a true and adequate system, because it consists of nothing but the complete union (or reunion) of thought and being.

The second, and perhaps more familiar, way in which Hegel deals with dialectic is this: *over time* some form of thing (say, a form of social organization, some religious idea or one of the various types of human consciousness) comes to be insofar as it is the resolution of some inherent limitation in the previous form. In this respect he wrote about stages of history in his *Philosophy of History* (Avineri, 1972: 221–9). Hegel had thus begun where Kant left off, his thought evolving 'from the relatively static categories of Kant's intuition and understanding to a phenomenological reflection on the historical formation of consciousness itself' (McCarthy, 1985: 34–5). The new form will itself have limitations that eventually emerge, exhibiting an inherent 'contradiction', and in turn through what Hegel sometimes and famously calls 'sublation', yielding another, new form. The new form will possess all the positive features of the previous, but with the specific internal contradiction that plagued it overcome. This process of production continues until that form is arrived at which contains no contradiction. Dialectic is thus the mechanism, so to speak, within the historical development of natural forms, forms of mind and thought, as well as social and cultural forms. Although we should not classify this as 'historical' in any straightforward manner, the most famous example of such a dialectical analysis is found in Hegel's *Phenomenology of Spirit* of 1804. Namely, the so-called master–slave dialectic. Hegel is analysing a certain stage of self-consciousness that is in itself only 'abstract' (this is the same abstract self-consciousness that Marx discovers in Epicurus in his dissertation). It is abstract because it understands itself in isolation from concrete social relations. Both master and slave, as we shall see in greater detail in the next chapter, are *alienated*. A form of self-consciousness that realizes itself through awareness of social relations is the dialectical outcome.

In fact, of course, these two modes of dialectic (the 'logical' and the 'historical') are not in fact distinct for Hegel. We separated them only for purposes of explanation. The logic pursues the thinking of what is, while other writings pursue the history (or even natural history) of what is; however, since thought and being are to be seen as in an 'original unity', these are two sides of one coin. As Robert B. Pippin (1991: 534) notes, the traditional understanding of Hegel's position is as follows: 'Nature and finite spirit are supposedly compatible because both represent successively incomplete stages or modes of a developing, finally fully self-conscious entity, "World" or "Cosmic Spirit."' Pippin continues more modestly (1991: 535), suggesting that there is a key difference between Kant and Hegel: 'Hegel's account of the differing conceptual schemes necessary in understanding *Natur* and *Geist* [mind or Spirit] sees these schemes as continuous. Kant, famously, sees them as discontinuous.' (By the discontinuity in Kant, Pippin is referring to the two distinct dimensions of reason, theoretical and practical, which we discussed earlier.) We can thus see what is meant by an 'original unity' of nature/being with spirit/mind.

In either case, whether in logic or historical development, any stage prior to the attainment of that original unity will present internal contradictions. Important for understanding Marx is noting that these contradictions may manifest as *false objectivities*. We have seen, earlier, the role of critique in Kant – the uncovering of the legitimate employment of reason and the conditions of any knowledge or experience, and thus also the account of the limits of reason and of knowledge – leads to his discussion of the false objects posited by reason when it overreaches the limits of experience. In Hegel, in contrast, false objectivity refers to the various stages of the realization of the absolute, which *at the time* are taken to be universal or self-evident truths, and only subsequently discovered to contain contradictions leading to further stages. Because a limited or self-contradictory form of mind, life or thought only knows of itself, and has no tools to think beyond itself, it thus intrinsically posits itself as universal or unlimited. Christianity in the era of the early church, for example, posits just such a Christianity as the final state in the development of religious forms.

As George McCarthy (1985: 24) discussed, Hegel followed Kant, while having the very different concerns with false universality and false objectivity, so Marx followed Hegel with a very different, sociological, version of the concern with false objectivity of social reality. An excellent example of Marx's analysis would be his famous account of the Mosel wine-growers. Marx contrasts an objective analysis of the state of the wine-growing community with the official account given by the local and state authorities. The latter sees the 'distress' of the wine-growers as something 'natural', about which the state can do nothing, and indeed a distress brought upon these wine-growers by their own inferior products. 'The ruin of the poorer wine-growers is regarded as a kind of natural phenomenon, to which one must be resigned in advance' (JCFM, CW1, 342). This official account Marx sees as a kind of false objectivity, a 'truth' produced by the set of social, political and economic circumstances that encompass both the authorities and the wine-growers. He writes: 'one is all too easily tempted to overlook the *objective nature of the circumstances* and to explain everything by the *will* of the persons concerned. However, there are *circumstances* which determine the actions of private persons and individual authorities, and which are as independent of them as the method of breathing' (JCFM, CW1, 337). The constant process of evolution had brought humans into a period characterized by a mode of production that political economists tended to see as normal or natural. Marx instead believed 'that consciousness and the categories of political economy reflect the political-economic structures of capitalism' (McCarthy, 1985: 35). Humans needed to recognize that those structures could be replaced by ones that would foster human flourishing. We will return to these issues concerning a broad social structure and its effect upon individuals and groups, under the headings of 'alienation' and 'exploitation', in the next two chapters.

Hegel is sometimes interpreted (and certainly was by Marx; see e.g. CCHPL, CW3: 44) as holding that the form of the Prussian state circa 1830 – constitutional monarchy – albeit perhaps with a few tweaks here and there, was in the political sphere a final dialectical form. That is, the 'perfect' political state. A short statement that Hegel made in the preface to *Elements of the Philosophy of Right [Law]* was significant in provoking such interpretation: 'What is rational is actual; what is actual is rational' (Hegel, 1991: 20). Without actually quoting this statement Marx made the following comment in his *Contribution to the Critique of Hegel's Philosophy of Law*: 'Hegel is not to be blamed for depicting the nature of the modern state as it is, but for presenting that which is as the nature of the state' (CCHPL, CW3: 63). A broadly empirical 'depiction' of the state is a valuable thing to have done; a valorization of this state as simply natural or rational, rather than as something that either could be or should be changed, is not.

The issue of the ideal state leads us directly to the second avenue of discussion of Hegel, namely Hegel's reworking of Kant's issue of freedom.

While Hegel certainly had many issues with Kant's philosophical ethics, these in fact led him to bring out more clearly the self-production of freedom, which earlier we suggested could already be found in Kant. What, Hegel asks, are the *conditions* of freedom? That is to say, in what *situation* must a human being find himself or herself, in order that genuine freedom is possible – where 'situation' means everything from material conditions such as sustenance and shelter, to state of mind, to the social or political state? Let us stick to the latter for the moment. What is 'perfect' about the ideal state as Hegel describes it is that it is the full realization of an individual's freedom in harmony with that of others. The development of an advanced political state is thus the condition of human beings realizing their most complete freedom. This would be the case if the idea of the state, guided by spirit or rationality (God's rationality), had immediate actuality in a particular state (Hegel, 1991: 281–2). Of course, the key issue here is whether Hegel meant that the existing state *was* the ideal state. Now, Marx as a radical thinker in the 1840s would clearly not have accepted the view that the current Prussian state was this final state, and this despite the fact that he remains heavily influenced by Hegel.

However, Marx's argument was more complex than simply to reject the view that the Prussian state was close to a supposedly ideal state. He could, and in fact did, disagree with Hegel in two different ways. The first would be to show that the state as Hegel describes it is not final, but still contains contradictions that must eventually produce further political forms. Much of Marx's work in his notes on Hegel's *Philosophy of Law* (CCHPL, CW3) takes this kind of approach. The second would be to reject the very idea of the political as found in Hegel, insofar as it involves an original distinction between the political and private orders. This is Marx's approach in *On the Jewish Question* (OJQ, CW3). It is important to note that in this second approach, the development of new forms of social and political order is not necessarily to be considered *progress* towards ever more full realizations of human freedom (as Hegel would have held). Indeed, Marx now holds that new political forms can emerge that solve a previous contradiction by returning to an earlier and repressive form, and indeed he observed this happening when the Prussia of his time, since the death of Hegel, increasingly adopted Medieval forms (as we outlined in the Introduction). Also note that both of these lines of attack on Hegel are still very much compatible with a broadly Hegelian view of dialectic as production (we will discuss this more fully in the chapter on 'Change') and with a broadly Kantian–Hegelian view of the production of human freedom (to be discussed in the chapter on 'Emancipation').

As a dialectical thinker Marx considered Hegel's work to be an advancement – albeit a limited one – from that of Kant. The false objectivity that is a production of pure reason in Kant was therefore understood by both Hegel and Marx as part and parcel of a historical process. Thought must move forwards rather than backwards if it is to identify what really happens in the world. Marx, however, did not accept Hegel's view of abstract consciousness or his insistence that there was identity in absolute knowledge between the concept and reality. Nevertheless, as McCarthy (1985: 35) put it, Marx did not therefore simply revert 'to the Kantian distinction between phenomena and noumena, appearances and things-in-themselves'. Marx did not believe that an internal, dialectical dynamic emanated from the categories of political economy to explain or produce reality. Rather, consciousness and those categories *reflected the political and economic structures of the time*. Like Feuerbach, Marx considered that Hegel's speculative approach was a distorted one. For Feuerbach, by going from the abstract to the concrete, and from the ideal to the real, Hegel's was a procedure that could not reveal the true, objective *material* reality but in fact contradicted the latter. This is because the insistence that there is a God (or even an Idea or Spirit) independent of humankind relies on speculative and theological abstraction (Leopold, 2007: 200–3). Such criticism of Hegel's speculative thought was a fundamental feature of Marx's philosophy, beginning implicitly with the doctoral dissertation he submitted in 1841 (DD, CW1: 29–30) and also featuring, this time far more explicitly, in his *Contribution to the Critique of Hegel's Philosophy of Law* (CCHPL, CW3: 8–9) of 1843. Marx accordingly followed Ludwig Feuerbach in accepting Hegel's view that pretty much everything should be viewed as subject to historical, dialectical process. Like Feuerbach, he did so from a critical perspective, arguing that the liberation brought about by this process would require far more than the development of reason and mind. Liberation or emancipation would require a fundamental change in human activity and thus in human society. Marx's emphasis on the society, however, represented a break with even Feuerbachian Hegelianism (Kitching, 1988: 18–19).

Feuerbach and Marx on 'species-being'

Feuerbach had over a number of years developed a critique of Hegelian idealism and of religion more generally. For him, the essence of the human was that of a sensuous being. While he considered humans to be communal in their ways of living there was also a strong individualist element in his notion of a sensuous being (Breckman, 1999: 129–30). Marx was, like Feuerbach, a materialist, but nevertheless believed the latter thinker's philosophy to be static and unhistorical, for it did not appreciate either that human nature evolved as, in a constant process, humans created themselves and their communal nature (Parekh, 1975: 38) or that, as mentioned at the end of the previous section, future progress would require fundamental change in human society (Kitching, 1988: 19). Marx's materialism had been of a more dynamic character than that of Feuerbach as far back as his doctoral dissertation, in which he favoured Epicurus' theory of swerving atoms over Democritus' deterministic materialism (Schafer, 2006: 45–54).

Furthermore, Marx criticized the individualist aspect of Feuerbach's materialism (TF, CW5: 4). This aspect, Marx believed, was inconsistent with the notion of species-being – a notion which Feuerbach himself had introduced. Feuerbach had, in Marx's view, failed to grasp the collectivist implications of the notion (Breckman, 1999: 288).

In the Introduction, we provided an initial sketch of Feuerbach's account of religion as an alienation, wherein the human projects onto a being outside and above itself, properties that properly belong to the essence and perfection of the human itself. What we just called 'the human', in German just like in English could have also been rendered as 'man', in the sense that word is used in, for example, Thomas Paine's title 'The Rights of Man'. Clearly, the idea is that the human species as a whole has an identity or essence, separate from the summed-up identities of individual human beings (or rather, individuals have a form of being that, taken simply on its own, is something less than a part of the whole). This is what Feuerbach and, following him, Karl Marx call 'species-being'. In trying to understand this notion today, our most obvious first recourse is to biological science: in terms of biology, broadly speaking, there are clearly good reasons for asserting that human beings as such are a distinct entity – after all, statements can be made about the physiology of the human body, without reference to any particular individual, and indeed in terms that could not be expressed as properties of individuals (gender being the most obvious). (It is not difficult to imagine similar arguments being made on the basis of psychology, for example.) However, although the biological argument is not entirely alien to Feuerbach's way of thinking, it is also not its centrepiece. Likewise, there are apparently many precedents in earlier philosophy, such as ancient Greek attempts to define 'man' as a whole. Starting from ancient philosophy in this way is, again, not entirely misleading, but perhaps not the best place to begin. We need to try to reconstruct Feuerbach's analysis on his own terms, and that means starting with German Idealism, and Hegel in particular, as our horizon.

A rather old but nevertheless clear summary of German Idealism is as follows: 'The opposition between reality and the sphere of ideals is basic in their systems. Reality as the realm of objects, as the world of sense, as that world that the natural sciences explore and explain is not ultimate, it is not the All, or the Universe' (Kroner, 1948: 6). Hence, according to the Idealists, for the thinking mind 'duties and ideals cannot be derived from facts and events' but, rather, form a class of their own, a sphere that lies beyond the horizon and the reach of the natural sciences and of their merely theoretical knowledge (Kroner, 1948: 6). Feuerbach insists that in Hegel one encounters not just a difference between two spheres, but an *order of precedence* of the ideal, prior to, above and indeed productive of, natural sensuous reality. Feuerbach argues that this should be reversed, putting the original emphasis solely on sensuous being. It is this Feuerbachian materialist turning upside down of Hegel that Marx finds so stimulating in the early years of the 1840s.

In so doing, Feuerbach asks what is the relation between the ego (the thinking, reasoning, 'I') and its objects (such as ordinary physical things)? The ego is that which is able to say 'that is a cup' or 'that is a cloud'; it posits things as existing, and existing as this or that kind of thing. The object is that which is posited by an ego. Expressed formally: I, qua subject, posit objects. The 'I' is active; the object is passive. If we try to step outside of this formal relationship, however, we observe a *material* relationship, that of a human body on the one hand, which is in a physical, sensual relationship to something (a cup or a cloud). Light reflects off the cup, into the eye, which then stimulates the nervous system, and so forth. Such a materialist view of human perception and thought is hardly unique to Feuerbach, but what is unusual is to introduce it into the framework of an idealist view of the ego. Now, the material relationship of subject to object is clearly reversible: there is no reason to think that some kinds of objects could not also be subjects, and that the ego, the 'I' as subject, would then be an object *for it*. If I was positing *another human being*, most obviously, that other is in a position to be able to posit me. Light reflects off of me, into the eyes of another, stimulating the nervous system, and so forth. There is nothing necessary, then, about the ego always being on the side of the subject, always being the one that actively posits. We can now see that this analysis is a specifically materialist reworking of Hegel's master–slave dialectic – introduced earlier – where what is at stake is not the recognition of the subject by another subject, but the recognition of the subject, by way of *another* subject, of its own sensuous object-hood. By thinking materialistically, and thus by not simply discounting from the beginning human sensuous perception, Feuerbach believes he has made a significant discovery about the essential nature of the human: every subject is also an object.

For Feuerbach, this conclusion entails two others. First, that in order to understand the ego fully in its essence, we need to understand also the ways in which an ego can be *passive* and immediately related to particularities (i.e. object-like). This first result Feuerbach discusses under the heading of 'sensuousness'. Second, that even if we start with a lone ego – the ego understood in isolation – it is clear that intrinsic to the essence of that ego is the possibility of its being an object for another. To believe that the ego as subject is sufficient in and of itself is a form of alienation from our 'species-being' which, here as in Hegel, is essentially social. By 'alienation' he means a misunderstanding that is not only about but affects us in our species-being. Feuerbach's materialist account of alienation builds on Hegelian roots and is in turn taken up and radicalized enthusiastically by Marx, as we shall see in detail in the next chapter.

In Marx's appropriation of Feuerbach's philosophy, he emphasizes that species-being is not an abstraction, that is, a general concept of man. It is not that the human has a species-being, the way that some natural object has an essence (e.g. the hardness of a mineral, the life cycle of a butterfly). As Marx suggests in the brief notes that are now known as *Theses on Feuerbach*, such a claim would first of all reduce the human to an abstraction, rather than a totality of real social relations (TF, CW5: 3–5); moreover, second, this would render it very difficult to understand how species-being could be variably manifested or subject to historical contingency. Rather, human beings exist ('the ensemble of social relations' as Marx puts it) *as* their real essence. The way that human individuals live, produce and relate to one another constitutes the essence of the human, which is thus not a separate and abstract idea. However, what we will later be calling the immutable aspect of human essence is always more or less fulfilled in the current state. To the extent that the way human beings exist is alienated, then its essence, at that historical junction, will be some stunted fraction of that species-being that would, in reality, belong to it under more favourable conditions. That species-being is not something other than my human essence (again, not a separate idea), but rather is the full flourishing of that human essence. Consciousness of this alienation is thus the first glimpse of the other possibility of human life. (In fact, Feuerbach comes very close to arguing just these points, although he does not carry the *historical dimension*, and certainly not the more radically social implications, of this argument through to Marx's satisfaction.) We will return to these difficult ideas, including the important notion of 'abstraction' here, in the chapters that follow.

In *The German Ideology* one finds a marginal note by Engels (GI, CW5: 78) that clarifies the issue raised by the lack of historicality specifically. The note is made to recap a point he and Marx had made a few pages earlier, which was that for Feuerbach the actual being of a human was its essence. This, Marx and Engels (GI, CW5: 58–9) went on, meant the mode of life and activity of an individual were those in which that individual's essence felt satisfied. Hence, if exceptions emerged, even if these were to number millions of proletarians who had begun to feel that their essence was unsatisfied, then theirs was an unavoidable misfortune. For Marx and Engels, Feuerbach's acceptance of existing reality in this way was simultaneously a misunderstanding of that reality. This was because Feuerbach was overlooking the reasons and mechanisms for possible social, revolutionary change. Change would happen because advances in industry would create the conditions for an improvement in human lives. The supposedly unfortunate proletarians would be able to bring their being into harmony with their essence. What Marx and Engels were thus arguing was that the human essence is the totality of all acts and relations and is identical with the historically contingent formation of these acts and relations. That there could be *other* ways for human beings to exist, and therefore other essences less stunted with respect to full species-being, and that these other might remove the contradictions, limitations and failures of the current formation (might allow human beings maximum freedom, maximum consciousness in Feuerbach's 'strict sense') is one of Marx's key discoveries.

Notice, however, that species-being is not only mutable historically, but also its highest or most authentic form has no *content*, in the sense of prescribing any *determinate* features of human life. Is the human truly flourishing, fulfilling its species-being with its existence, when it lives in a village or in a city? When it speaks German or perhaps English? Has a large family or a small one? Fulfilled species-being would be possible in all these ways. This follows from the notion of production as we discussed in Kant (freedom lies in the production of universal freedom, and not necessarily in the promotion of any determinate ethical law) and in Hegel (mutual recognition as subject per se, and not as any particular this or that, is a key moment in the full constitution of the self). In other words, in our discussion of self-production, we have been moving increasingly towards the *homo faber* account: the human is that being that produces and indeed produces itself, but without any further specification concerning *as what* it must produce itself. These 'definitions' of the human are *formal*, not in the sense of that word that is opposed to the material (which is how 'form' gets used generally in discussions of production), but rather in opposition to any determination of content, and especially any content set in advance and for all time concerning what it means for human beings to 'flourish'. (Analogously, we might say that the basic notion of a 'duty' is formal, lacking any determination concerning *who* has a duty to do *what*, under *which* circumstances.) To be sure, the full, free and authentic form that species-being can take when emancipated is indeed a producing being, is a being that is conscious of itself as a species, is characterized by freedom and is a communal being. However, Marx insists, and he is again following both Kant and Hegel here, these features too are to be understood as formal in the above sense. Communism is predominately a non-alienating productive structure, not a 'way of life'. As Marx stated in a note added to the margins in the manuscript of *The German Ideology*: 'Communism is for us not a state of affairs which is to be established, an ideal to which reality [will] have to adjust itself.' Communism was, rather, 'the real movement which abolishes the present state of things. The conditions of this movement result from the now existing premise' (GI, CW5: 49). That is, there are indeed historically determined ways in which the human being can be limited, misunderstood or enslaved, but there is no 'right' way to be free, but only the 'right' conditions for it. So there may be many tokens of such freedom, but the right conditions allow for this free type of existence. (We will return to and elaborate upon this notion of formality later in the book, both in discussions of whether and in what way Marx is a determinist and also when we discuss the type/token distinction at greater length.)

The way in which Marx thus fits into the German critical tradition has huge implications for production. Marx had taken the German philosophical tradition of critique, which originated in the work of Kant, to the point where social production for the good of humanity could be seen as immanent in the present, capitalist system of production which was exploitative and unnatural – that is, it had become possible to anticipate a new, un-alienated form of social and political organization. Hegel believed that humans can achieve universality and thereby freedom by means of mutually recognizing their universality in their community, under the guidance of the state. For Marx, this neglected a crucial aspect of human nature. According to him human beings produce cooperatively. This meant that freedom and universality could only be achieved in a communist society, in which mutual production would no longer be mediated by private property (Chitty, 2011: 486). Marx could not have arrived at these positions unless Kant, Hegel and Feuerbach had paved the way. On this basis Marx's was a distinctive view of human nature that was not only historically materialist but also transhistorical. For him, an essential – or trans – part of human nature was to produce collectively but also freely and creatively (unlike creatures such as bees which produce through necessity), whatever social and economic arrangements they may be in at a particular time (Byron, 2014: 245–6). As we stressed earlier, however, the 'permanent' part of human nature is formal with respect to various forms of life that could fulfil it.

Having compared and contrasted Marx and Feuerbach on the issue of production, we need, in order to present the argument that a coherent political philosophy can be found in Marx's early work, to consider a question prominent in the literature. The question is whether this notion of production and self-production is a constant in Marx's work, from the earliest texts, to those of the mid-1840s, and indeed the work later still. In order to identify such consistency the first step is to seek for evidence that there is in Marx's early work a constant understanding of human nature itself, notwithstanding for the moment the question whether this is also a view in which production is significant. Norman Geras' (1983) influential book *Marxism and Human Nature: Refutation of a Legend* serves this purpose very well. He in fact argued that there is a consistent theory of human nature throughout all of Marx's philosophy, from the early to the later writings. What is hugely significant for the present study is Geras' argument that the theory of human nature in Marx's writings of the early 1840s was not abandoned in the *Theses on Feuerbach* in 1845, as is sometimes suggested.

Geras began by acknowledging that Marx's sixth thesis of Feuerbach is not entirely unambiguous regarding the issue whether the thesis was in effect abandoning the idea that there was such a thing as human nature. Geras (1983: 29) quoted the entire sixth thesis. While this was essential for his purpose of painstaking scrutiny to demonstrate not only the ambiguity but also the likelihood that Marx did still hold a theory of human nature, it will suffice here to quote only the first three sentences. 'Feuerbach,' Marx argued, 'resolves the essence of religion into the essence of *man*. But the essence of man is no abstraction inherent in each single individual. In its reality it is the ensemble of the social relations' (TF, CW5: 4). To begin with, notice again Marx's emphasis on the essence of man not being an abstraction, an 'idea'. More significantly here, the very last sentence could be understood in several ways. The wording of the sixth thesis may indeed, Geras conceded (1983: 29–58), conceivably be a statement that the nature of humans is dependent on, or dissolved into, the changing ensemble of social relations. Instead, Geras argued that a close analysis of the words in the sixth thesis indicates strongly that in presenting this theory of the 'essence of man' as the ensemble of social relations Marx was not abandoning his earlier views that humans have a nature – that by nature humans are social and communal, and that by producing the human community as a social entity they each manifest their own nature. He was not satisfied to leave the matter having offered textual analysis of the thesis. Instead, he sought and found passages from a range of Marx's writings including *The German Ideology* of 1846 that do in fact make quite clear that Marx was retaining a consistent theory of human nature (Geras, 1983: 61–81). However, rather than summarizing Geras directly here, it will be more useful for us to make our own journey through a number of his works including his 'Comments on James Mill', the *Economic and Philosophical Manuscripts* and *The German Ideology*.

Production in Marx's writings of 1844

To understand Marx's views on production as a feature of human nature one should focus on what has become perhaps the most well-known work of the mid-1840s – the *Paris Manuscripts* of 1844. To be sure, production in various ways had been a theme since the beginning. As we mentioned in the Introduction, he was quite clear in the *Manuscripts* that this was part of a larger project which drew on earlier works and would include later ones. But the *Manuscripts* are where things really start to come together. Now, some commentators argue, as Marcello Musto (2009: 392) puts it: 'Not homogeneous or even closely interconnected between their parts, the manuscripts are an evident expression of a position in movement.' That is, we should not expect to find a single, internally consistent political philosophy therein. As he wrote the notebooks that accompanied the Manuscripts Marx was, Musto goes on, 'assimilating and using the reading material that fueled them'. Corresponding excerpts were 'spaced out through the period, from the articles for the *Deutsch-Französische Jahrbücher* to *The Holy Family*' (Musto, 2009: 391–2). Now, there is no doubt that Marx's ideas developed as he was writing this lengthy document, but we see these works as surprisingly coherent in the overall philosophical narrative given. Moreover, we also see them as the bridge that allows us to grasp the underlying, broader coherence between Marx's works in the early 1840s and texts like *The German Ideology*.

Among Marx's notes of 1844 are his 'Comments on James Mill, *Elémens d'économie politique*', in which he criticized liberal, bourgeois political economy for its anti-historical reading of human nature in terms of the relations of an immutable capitalist system. In such terms: 'Political economy – like the real process – starts out from the *relation of man to man* as that of *property owner to property owner*' (CJM, CW3: 217). He summarized as follows the way in which the relation of production to human nature was misrepresented by economists such as Mill: 'The community of men, or the manifestation of the nature of men, their mutual complementing the result of which is species-life, truly human life – this community is conceived by political economy in the form of exchange and trade' (CJM, CW3: 217). This is the view of human species-being, however:

> the real, conscious and true mode of existence of which is social activity and social enjoyment. Since human nature is the true community of men, by manifesting their nature men create, produce, the human community, the social entity, which is no abstract universal power opposed to the single individual, but is the essential nature of each individual, his own activity, his own life, his own spirit, his own wealth. Hence this true community does not come into being through reflection, it appears owing to the need and egoism of individuals, i.e., it is produced directly by their life activity itself. (CJM, CW3: 216–17)

Marx continued: 'The existence or non-existence of this community does not depend upon man; but as long as man does not recognise himself as man, and hence give the world a human organisation, this *community* appears in the guise [*Form*] of estrangement. [...] Men, not as abstractions, but as real, living particular individuals *are* this community' (CJM, CW3: 217). According to the view of species-activity presented by the economists, the interaction between humans is mediated by the process of exchange. As Christopher Berry (1989: 126) suggests, by stating that exchange is the equivalent of species-activity, he was saying that exchange was considered to amount to 'the direct mediation of human to human'. As, however, the logic of private property was the driving force, this was an unnatural situation as it ran counter to human need. Marx's use of the term 'need' can be understood more clearly if one turns to his distinction between practical, animalistic need and human need in the *Paris Manuscripts*. As Berry (1989: 127) suggests, in the latter work Marx 'was more forthcoming about his notion of human need' than in 'Comments on James Mill ...', suggesting that people produce for human need only when they have transcended the egoistic perspective and are focusing on the needs of other people, thus becoming communal beings. Nevertheless, the 'Comments on James Mill ...' are useful for the way in which they show how Marx devised his clearer argument in the *Manuscripts* while he bore in mind the liberal economists' misrepresentation of human activity and need.

Given this clarification, let us paraphrase the whole passage in which Marx mentioned need in the 'Comments on James Mill': The real and conscious form of species-existence for the human is community; human beings are essentially social beings. Nevertheless, no community is just given some natural object (an ahistorical essence, like the properties of a mineral), but rather is produced by the concrete life activities of individual humans. Further, the community is not determined by the choice of men (e.g. by social contract or democratic consensus), nor by their reflection upon their nature or condition (e.g. through political philosophy per se), but it is the social form directly corresponding to their life activity. There is, then, no mediation, between the material conditions of human activity and the social form, by *abstract* will or by thought. This direct correspondence is true whether the community produced is an authentic one or some caricature of his real community (CJM, CW3: 217). Now, where that life activity involves human estrangement, as in conditions characterized by *exchange*, the corresponding social form will be estranged likewise. Economics (Marx means Smith, Mill and so forth) takes the current state of human life activity, in which estrangement is the rule, as essential, that is, it takes a historically contingent form of human activity as universal and necessary; therefore, it also understands the consequent 'caricature' of a community as essential, and projects that back onto the conception of human nature itself. Marx concludes by writing: 'It is seen that political economy defines the estranged form of social intercourse as the essential and original form corresponding to man's nature' (CJM, CW3: 217). The form of human activity and consequently of social organization that *is*, in fact, appropriate to the vocation of man, and which permits human beings to have full consciousness of themselves as a communal species-being, rather than understanding themselves in some limited and estranged fashion, is of course communism.

Turning to the *Paris Manuscripts*, one finds Marx's main discussion of production in the section on estranged labour, upon which the next chapter of the present study will focus in discussing Marx's theory of alienation. The life activity of labouring to produce, he argued, appears to humans as simply the means of satisfying their need to maintain their own physical existence. Productive life, however, was in Marx's view something more than this. 'The whole character of a species' was 'contained in the character of its life activity; and free, conscious activity is man's species-character' (EPM, CW3: 276). This meant that the human species was unique among others. He elaborated as follows:

> In creating a *world of objects* by his practical activity, in his *work upon* inorganic nature, man proves himself a conscious species-being, i.e., as a being that treats the species as its own essential being ... . Admittedly animals also produce. They build themselves nests, dwellings, like the bees, beavers, ants, etc. But an animal only produces what it immediately needs for itself or its young. It produces one-sidedly, whilst man produces universally. It produces only under the dominion of immediate physical

need, whilst man produces even when he is free from physical need and only truly produces in freedom therefrom. (EPM, CW3: 276)

Let us elaborate on this passage. The mention of consciousness refers us back to Feuerbach's analysis that introduced the notion of species-being. For production to be entirely related to a creature's own sustenance (food, shelter and reproduction) is animal-like; everything is immediately related to its own need. For the animal, its sustenance is not even an object for consciousness, that is, something in any way understood to be distinct from itself and its activities. Only in freedom from need is there true human production, which is 'universal' – what I produce is understood from the beginning to be something that is or could be an 'object', for the use of others, and which joins a world of objects of such use. I am not building a nest, but a house, that *people like me* can live in, and that others will recognize as a house, even if in fact it is for my use in the first instance. Moreover, in so doing I am perhaps using a tool that others could understand as a tool and also use. Such production is from the ground up related to species-being and communal life and can be of value to all. Historically, this means that only when the technologies of production developed to the point where food and so on could be plentiful enough so as to no longer present an immediate need for anyone could human beings free themselves in this way. It also means, though, that in any economic or political system where some human beings are kept in a situation of immediate needs (regardless of the plenty that is, in fact, available or possible), true human free production is not possible. Under conditions that are not free of such need, man produces like an animal (given the aforementioned this is a tautology) and, more importantly, under such conditions human beings do not produce themselves as a 'conscious species-being', that is, a possibility of consciousness of authentic human being is denied. They remain human beings, of course, but the social forms generated and the capacity for self-understanding are both in some way stunted. Such situations Marx calls 'estranged' or 'alienated'.

Marx had by 1844 also already begun to think in terms of the necessity of the capitalist mode of production in the historical process that would bring about the conditions for a fulfilling life for all. Collectively, the society would produce the genuinely wealthy human beings, rather than a few wealthy ones in terms of the capitalist conception of wealth. As he put it in the *Paris Manuscripts*:

Just as through the movement of private property, of its wealth as well as its poverty – of its material and spiritual wealth and poverty – the budding society finds at hand all the material for this development, so established society produces man in this entire richness of his being – produces the rich man profoundly endowed with all the senses – as its enduring reality. (EPM, CW3: 302)

The way in which Marx is writing about the 'senses' here is founded upon a Feuerbachian account of the sensuous; the appropriate place to discuss it though is in the next chapter on 'Alienation'. So, for the moment, something of the meaning of this sentence must elude us. Nevertheless, the play on 'wealth' and 'richness' should be clear. What is clear is that the 'wealth' possible through capitalism (the kinds of things that we called 'animal sustenance') is possible only on the basis of 'poverty' (some humans remaining in a condition of immediate need, and thus also alienated in a variety of ways); nevertheless, this wealth in turn creates the conditions under which it becomes possible to release all human beings from immediate need, so that the human can produce, in genuine freedom, a more profound sense of 'richness'. In brief, capitalism produces the conditions for its own overthrow.

While the *Paris Manuscripts* thus present Marx's views on human production clearly and concisely, they do so only briefly. For a fuller treatment of the concept and process of production one needs to turn to Marx and Engels' *The German Ideology*.

Production in *The German Ideology*

The German Ideology was a rather different work than Marx and Engels' earlier efforts, being the first in which what would later be known as the material conception of history was presented. Rather than a text in which the authors abandoned Marx's earlier political philosophy, however, it was one in which the notion of production of the human community, mentioned in 'Comments on James Mill …' two years earlier, was explored more extensively. While there was thus a very significant development of Marx's political thought, his work of 1845 and 1846 should be seen as building on earlier ideas which he did not abandon. As was mentioned in the Introduction to the present study, he noted in 1844 that he was in the process of assembling the broader political and philosophical work. To be sure, the language these writings use changes in some ways – Marx and Engels more or less drop the expression 'species-being', for example – but the concepts and the analyses behind those concepts remain in play. As C. J. Arthur (1974: 21) put it in his introduction to a popular abridged edition of *The German Ideology*, the most fundamental idea in it had already been introduced in the *Paris Manuscripts*. This idea was 'that man produces himself though labour'. Human nature was neither unchanging and biologically determined on the one hand nor developed in accordance with some form of spiritual essence on the other, as German idealist philosophy had suggested. This, however, did not mean that people and their social lives were simply produced by their circumstances. They also actually produced those circumstances, including unnatural situations such as that imposed by the capitalist mode of production. Hence, they were capable of so doing again and differently. This, of course, had revolutionary implications and at this point Marx's famous eleventh thesis of Feuerbach, mentioned in the introduction of the present study, becomes significant. The point was to change the world (TF, CW5: 5) to enable humans to regain control of and to change their circumstances. Already in his 'Dissertation', Marx (DD, CW1: 84–5) was thinking along these lines, for there he accused conservative interpreters of Hegel (who were at the time the dominant voice) of abandoning the integration of theory and practice found in Hegel and merely 'reflecting' in their system the existing state of the world. Marx was here implicitly defending the Young Hegelians, such as Feuerbach, although later he accuses them of exactly the same mistake.

As Arthur (1974: 22–23) suggests in *The German Ideology* Marx and Engels were making the case that to understand the place of production in human nature one needs to 'examine the basis of their own activity'. As they produce by means of their labour humans are involved in a dialectical process. In this process their mutable labour activity is transformed as they both alter their circumstances and in turn are altered by them. Humans needed to grasp what was happening to them in their existing circumstances and change the latter. It is in this context that we should read the opening few sentences of the preface to *The German Ideology*:

> Hitherto men have always formed wrong ideas about themselves, about what they are and what they ought to be. They have arranged their relations according to their ideas of God, of normal man, etc. The products of their brains have got out of their hands. They, the creators, have bowed down before their creations. (GI, CW5: 23)

Marx and Engels built their theory on a materialist basis, being concerned primarily with actual people rather than ideas. 'The first premise of all human history is,' they insisted, 'the existence of living human individuals. Thus, the first fact to be established is the physical organisation of these individuals and their consequent relation to the rest of nature' (GI, CW5: 31).

There were, Marx and Engels observed, many ways in which human beings could be distinguished from other animals, such as the nature of their consciousness or their ability to have religion – and philosophers have variously used these distinctions. None though was original. There was also a fundamental way in which they made themselves distinctive. This happened 'as soon as they begin to *produce* their means of subsistence, a step which is conditioned by their physical organisation'. 'By producing their means of subsistence', they were 'indirectly producing their material life' (GI, CW5: 31). The point being made in *The German Ideology*, rather too quickly, is not essentially different from the analysis Marx gave in the *Manuscripts*. Humans differed from other animals in that at any one time and place they produced their material life in a particular mode of production which did not simply reproduce their physical existence:

Rather it is a definite form of activity of these individuals, a definite form of expressing their life, a definite *mode of life* on their part. As individuals express their life, so they are. What they are, therefore, coincides with their production, both with *what* they produce and with *how* they produce. Hence what individuals are depends on the material conditions of their production. (GI, CW5: 31–2)

Let us elaborate upon this passage. Marx and Engels are assuming that animals reproduce their material existence as follows: a particular species of bird hunts certain kinds of worms; a particular species of rodent lives in certain kinds of tunnels. They thus assume that there is no adaptation to environment within a single species, which is probably untrue but that does not necessarily invalidate the argument. Humans, however, produce *food* and *shelter* not of one kind, but of whatever kind the environment permits. Unlike animals whose 'mode of life' is fully determined by their physical organization, and thus can in turn only inhabit certain narrowly defined habitats, humans can fulfil their needs in a number of possible ways. Humans even understand that this is the case: I might not like the food eaten by another way of life, but I recognize it *as* food. Humans in this way express their life in a mode of life – what in anthropology might be called a 'culture' – and thus, as Marx puts it in the *Manuscripts*, they produce 'universally'. This is certainly not to say that human beings *freely choose* how to express their life, not at least in any previous historical era. The choice is made *for* individuals, so to speak, by the conditions in which they find themselves (e.g. climate, raw materials, proximity to water etc.). Similarly, we must not think that, apart from the 'physical organisation' of the body itself, there is some transhistorical essence to the human being, such that this essence is held distinct from some definite way of expressing life. 'As individuals express their life, so they are.' Human beings, in producing, produce themselves. For Marx, productively active individuals find themselves in social and political relations. The social structure and state evolved continuously out of the life-process of those definite individuals, 'not as they may appear in their own or other people's imagination, but as they really are; i.e. as they operate, humans evolve materially, and hence as they work under definite material limits, presuppositions and conditions independent of their will' (GI, CW5: 35–6).

The phrase 'productive forces' is used to describe the whole set of material, social productive activities that are found at a particular time. To grasp what the terminology of productive forces is all about, it is useful to bear in mind the historical context of Marx's work in the 1840s. He and Engels would have been aware of the developments in what we now know as the industrial revolution. The feudal era was fading (unevenly among countries) as productive forces became so advanced that the feudal social structure was becoming outdated. Those productive forces included inventions and developments in industry, tooling, science and technology. Those forces also, very importantly, included humans themselves. Humans have, as they have done so throughout history, developed new skills and ways of working. The developments happened as humans experimented or as they reflected on previous experiments that had led to developments (sometimes these were not even consciously perceived as experiments). Ideas thus did not just appear in the minds of humans; they reflected real human activity. Relations of production – relations between humans individually and in their classes – were consequently changing from feudal to capitalist as the developments in productive forces paved the way. Marx and Engels (GI, CW5: 36) expressed this as follows:

> The production of ideas, of conceptions, of consciousness, is at first directly interwoven with the material activity and the material intercourse of men – the language of real life. Conceiving, thinking, the mental intercourse of men at this stage still appear as the direct efflux of their material behaviour. The same applies to mental production as expressed in the language of the politics, laws, morality, religion, metaphysics, etc., of a people. Men are the producers of their conceptions, ideas, etc., that is, real, active men, as they are conditioned by a definite development of their productive forces and of the intercourse corresponding to these, up to its furthest forms.

Marx and Engels (GI, CW5: 36) insisted that a mistake of German philosophy had been to begin with what people thought, conceived or imagined 'in order to arrive at men in the flesh'. The correct method was, rather, that of 'setting out from real, active men, and on the basis of their real life-process demonstrating the development of the ideological reflexes and echoes of this life-process'.

For humans to make history by means of developments in productive forces and the subsequent changes in relations of production, the first premise of all human existence was crucial. This premise was, according to Marx and Engels, that they must be in a position to actually live. This, of course, meant basic activities such as drinking, housing, clothing needed to be fulfilled. The first historical act was 'thus the production of the means to satisfy these needs, the production of material life itself' (GI, CW5: 41–2). Only then would they be in a position to 'make History' (GI, CW5: 41). Human recognition of the relative significance of universal and social material activity on the one hand, and thought and consciousness on the other, also of course developed as the productive forces became more advanced, and especially as productive forces became sufficiently advanced that immediate need did not absorb all human energy. Revolutionary social change would be required because the existing relations of production were and are based on exploitation. Insofar as exploitation, and the alienation underlying it, must also be founded in the material conditions of human life, it was possible to become conscious of them as such. This new consciousness was what enabled people to think outside the box (to use a much more recent phrase) of the intellectual structure of their day, see the errors of these ways of thinking and glimpse possibilities of thought yet to come. Revolution will bring about emancipation. We will examine all these ideas in detail in the remaining chapters of this book.

For Marx and Engels making history was, moreover, something that was accomplished not by human beings individually but, rather, collectively. Humans produced not only themselves but also their collective communities. Marx and Engels expressed this view as follows:

> The production of life, both of one's own in labour and of fresh life in procreation, now appears as a twofold relation: on the one hand as a natural, on the other as a social relation – social in the sense that it denotes the co-operation of several individuals, no matter under what conditions, in what manner and to what end. It follows from this that a certain mode of production, or industrial stage, is always combined with a certain mode of co-operation, or social stage, and this mode of co-operation is itself a 'productive force'. Further, that the aggregate of productive forces accessible to men determines the condition of society, hence, the 'history of humanity' must always be studied and treated in relation to the history of industry and exchange. (GI, CW5: 43)

The underlying conditions of production are always already no less social than natural. Therefore, they determine a form of social life, a set of social, political and economic institutions, such as the family, property and the state. (There are greater or lesser degrees of determination, however; we'll look at this issue at the end of the chapter.) These latter forms, though, are also one of the conditions of production; that is, there is what we might call a 'feedback loop' between the activities of individuals and their social form. This feedback loop provides a mechanism both of continuity and of change and thus drives the 'history of humanity'. In a later chapter of the present study Marx and Engels' understanding of the nature and necessity of social change between modes of production will be examined. For now, let us look briefly at their vision of the nature of production in communist society.

In a well-known and widely discussed passage, Marx and Engels described production in the communist society which they believed would follow dialectically from the capitalist. In the present capitalist society the mode of production, or in other words 'industrial stage' (see the passage just quoted), involved a division of labour. As soon as such a division comes into being, they argued, 'each man has a particular, exclusive sphere of activity, which is forced upon him and from which he cannot escape'. Each of these individuals in the present and previous modes of production was, 'a hunter, a fisherman, a shepherd, or a critical critic, and must remain so if he does not want to lose his means of livelihood'. In communist society, by way of contrast,

> nobody has one exclusive sphere of activity but each can become accomplished in any branch he wishes, society regulates the general production and thus makes it possible for me to do one thing today and another tomorrow, to hunt in the morning, fish in the afternoon, rear cattle in the evening, criticise after dinner, just as I have a mind [*wie ich gerade Lust habe*], without ever becoming hunter, fisherman, shepherd or critic. (GI, CW5: 47)

The passage just quoted, which has attracted the scorn of their critics and confusion among sympathetic scholars, may seem to suggest that Marx and Engels were looking forward to an idyllic, pre-industrial society. This, however, would be entirely inconsistent with the view that they would always hold that communism would take advantage of advanced productive forces to provide an abundance of goods and services to provide all with a life of human fulfilment. One explanation for this puzzling passage is that Marx and Engels were not really offering a serious analysis. The reference to criticism is directed at the continuing parody of the Young Hegelians, and the phrase '*wie ich gerade Lust habe*' – which might be better translated as 'just as I fancy' – trivializes the issue. As William James Booth (1989: 2007) put it: 'That this passage contains a tongue-in-cheek, polemical barb directed at Marx's erstwhile philosophical allies is certain.' However, in recent years a more complex explanation has been offered.

Following the research of Waturu Hiromatsu, who produced a Japanese-language edition of *The German Ideology*, based on scrutiny of the original manuscripts, Carver (1998: 104–6) suggests that the passage, which includes crossing outs and notes in the margins, is actually a concoction of comments by each of Marx and Engels. Engels was basically having fun presenting the kind of jobs that might be found in utopian schemes. Engels crossed out some of the more ridiculous ones. Marx, by way of contrast, was scribbling brief notes in the margin about criticizing after dinner to indicate that this is something that the critical critics or German idealists might propose, and in so doing also reminding Engels to take the issue more seriously. After all, in the preface to *The Holy Family*, written in the second half of 1844 and published the following year, Marx and Engels had stressed that Critical Criticism and the broader tradition of speculative philosophy could now be ignored, after the polemical work they were prefacing had pilloried Bruno Bauer and other writers at the latter end of that tradition. As Marx and Engels put it in that preface:

> Critical Criticism is in all respects *below* the level already attained by German theoretical development. The nature of our subject therefore justifies our refraining *here* from further *discussion* of that development

itself .... We therefore give this polemic as a preliminary to the independent works in which we ... shall present our positive view and thereby our positive attitude to the more recent philosophical and social doctrines. (HF, CW4: 7–8)

While *The German Ideology* carries on the polemic to a great extent, it would also have been the first 'independent' work putting forward a positive case. The concocted passage about fishing, hunting, critical criticism and so on in *The German Ideology* actually obscures a very serious and relevant point about production in the next paragraph that may easily be missed, especially if the reader's mind remains focused on the controversial passage. In the next paragraph they make the following point:

> The social power, i.e., the multiplied productive force, which arises through the co-operation of different individuals as it is caused by the division of labour, appears to these individuals, since their co-operation is not voluntary but has come about naturally, not as their own united power, but as an alien force existing outside them, of the origin and goal of which they are ignorant, which they thus are no longer able to control ... whereas with the abolition of the basis, private property, with the communistic regulation of production (and, implicit in this, the abolition of the alien attitude of men to their own product), the power of the relation of supply and demand is dissolved into nothing, and men once more gain control of exchange, production and the way they behave to one another. (GI, CW5: 48)

As mentioned earlier in the present chapter, the issue whether cooperation is voluntary or not is significant. Marx and Engels were suggesting that a feature of the future society will be a community in which cooperation is voluntary and not enforced. Booth (1989: 217–18) suggests that Marx and Engels' mention of the activities of fishing and so on in the communist society indicates that people will be able to do them without pressure of time or necessity freely with the associates they mutually choose. However, what this overlooks is that the words in the passage after 'production', which combine Engels' playful comments and Marx's addition which aimed to highlight the absurdity of those comments, form a misrepresentation of communist society. Without this misrepresentation their treatment of production in *The German Ideology* is consistent with that of Marx in the *Paris Manuscripts* of 1844.

We therefore are justified in interpreting the infamous passage in the following manner: human beings have 'a mind', where this is understood to mean the *capacity* to have free activity and choice, and to be aware of their choices as free, but certainly *not* understood to mean some mind or soul, separable from the materiality of their bodies and environment. Moreover, this possibility of the human belongs to the human quite independently of whether one is a hunter or fisherman, that is, independently of the current configuration of their productive acts. No human being is *essentially* this or that type of labourer, either in his or her own eyes, or in the eyes of others. As humans produce, so they are – but the very assertion confirms the idea that the human being could be otherwise. However, the current configuration of productive acts may be such as to alienate human beings from themselves, from each other (i.e. from an authentic form of community) and from the products of their labour, making it impossible for them to arrive at a consciousness of their genuinely free 'mind'. They find themselves subject to an alien power such that the labourer in fact does identify his or her humanity with the form of labour, or at least with being a labourer, rendering him or her little more than how Marx and Engels both had described the condition of animals.

Significantly, it does not necessarily follow from Marx and Engels' reasoning here that in communism productive tasks will not be specialized, only that this specialization will not interfere with human beings attaining their full potential as free, communal beings. Only under conditions where labour is not *essentially* 'divided' by an external, 'alien' force as it is in capitalism are humans consciously able to grasp their species-being, and thus (as mentioned in the passage just quoted) 'gain control of exchange, production and the way they behave to one another'. Again, the point is not that under communism the worker is able to choose capriciously *as an egoistic individual* what work to do and when, but that the relative wealth of advanced industrial society, and above all his or her consciousness of communal benefit (of 'species-being'), means that the alienation caused by the division of labour under capitalism is removed. The list of different forms of labour (hunter, fisher, etc.) is indeed intended jokingly, insofar as it seems to allude to some pre-industrial idyll, but is definitely not a joke in its chief point: that human beings are essentially freely productive but *not* essentially specialized and alienated individual labourers. This argument regarding the status of individualism, however, raises the question whether Marx should be considered a philosopher of holism.

The question of holism and the individual

According to Marx in the *Paris Manuscripts*, 'just as society itself produces man as man, so is society produced by him' (EPM, CW3: 298). Marx was identifying a dialectical process. As people produced their society they brought into being something more than the sum of the individuals who constituted its parts. This institution of society in turn affected the actions and thought of those individuals and those that would be born later. Indeed, their activities, including those that brought them enjoyment, were necessarily social as they could not have arisen from and to isolated individuals.

Some of Marx's critics, including notably Joseph Femia (1993: 157–70), have argued that Marx's work in the *Paris Manuscripts* was holistic to the degree that it had despotic implications. Such criticism does not, however, capture the reciprocal relationship that Marx saw between humans as individuals and the society which they collectively constituted. Marx's thought can, instead, be grasped with reference to the distinction drawn by Erik Olin Wright, Andrew Levine and Elliott Sober (2003) between radical holism and anti-reductionism. Radical holism holds that, having no independent explanatory force, particular relations among individuals simply reflect the operation of the whole, from which they are generated. The whole is considered the sole genuine cause, with only macro-social categories providing explanations of social phenomena. Anti-reductionism, while accepting that properties of aggregate social entities and relations among them are irreducibly explanatory, does not deny that relations among individuals *also* have explanatory force. Unlike methodological individualism, however, anti-reductionism does not accept that all social explanations can be reduced to micro-levels of analysis, or in other words to relations between individuals. Methodological individualism is thus the mirror image of radical holism (and perhaps should be termed 'radical individualism' for that reason). Wright, Levine and Sober introduce the distinction between types and tokens, which we mentioned earlier in the present chapter, in order to understand how Marx fits neither of these extremes. There are types of situation but in many cases more than one particular case, or token, of human behaviour that can be identified as belonging to the type. Simply discussing the token does not capture significant points that can be understood in terms of the social explanation (the type); describing the type does not fully determine the tokens.

It is in the *German Ideology* that such concerns about radical holism are most clearly found. The materialist account of history *seems* to leave no room for individual decisions, relations, thoughts or freedoms. Marx and Engels' thesis here is a very unforgiving one, suited to their ongoing war with the philosophers of mere criticism, of 'ideology'. However, even if we accept the strong version of the materialist thesis, the implications are still not 'despotic'. The *material basis* of human reality comprises concrete individuals and their productive activities. This basis in turn determines a *form* of social relations. This means that individual relations are (of course) influenced by but not strictly determined by the underlying material basis. That is, they are determined in their type but not in their token. The closest Marx and Engels get to a radical holism is in their analysis of conditions of private property: the labourer understands himself or herself as a labourer, abject to a 'foreign power', and has no intrinsic opportunities for a different mode of consciousness. Capitalism is indeed 'despotic' in this sense, for it is not just a form of relations but also tends to hold its actors rigorously in place. This part of the analysis in *German Ideology* is a clear continuation of the account of the alienation of production in *Paris Manuscripts*. Even then, however, because changes happen slowly in one or the other level (i.e. the underlying collection of relations of production among individuals and the social, political or economic form that emerges out of these relations), one level can get 'ahead' of the other, revealing a 'contradiction' in human reality (GI, CW5: 45). It is this contradiction that yields change, but it also yields conflicting ideas or analysis of the human condition. In this way, for example, the labouring class can become aware of its alienation. Historical materialism may pose the problem of holism, but also provides an account of change (see corresponding chapter in this book). Thus, 'criticism' is possible and important, provided that it does not understand itself as the basis for change, rather than a means by which historical change occurs.

With Wright, Levine and Sober's consideration of method in terms of types and tokens in mind one can clearly see Marx's point in the *Paris Manuscripts*. There, he elaborated as follows:

> The human aspect of nature exists only for social man; for only then does nature exist for him as a bond with man – as his existence for the other and the other's existence for him – and as the life-element of human reality. Only then does nature exist as the foundation of his own human existence. Only here has what is to him his natural existence become his human existence, and nature become man for him. Thus society is the complete unity of man with nature – the true resurrection of nature – the accomplished naturalism of man and the accomplished humanism of nature. (EPM, CW3: 298)

Nothing in the passage just quoted suggests that the type can be reduced to only one natural, human token of behaviour. Now in the new society, in which private property will have been transcended, the conception and perception of human achievement will no longer be restricted to 'immediate, one-sided enjoyment, merely in the sense of possessing, of having' (EPM, CW3: 299). Collectively humans will achieve *as individuals* such fulfilment as could never have been gained by individuals per se. As Marx put it:

> Man appropriates his comprehensive essence in a comprehensive manner, that is to say, as a whole man. Each of his human relations to the world – seeing, hearing, smelling, tasting, feeling, thinking, observing, experiencing, wanting, acting, loving – in short, all the organs of his individual being, like those organs which are directly social in their form, are in their objective orientation, or in their orientation to the object, the appropriation of the object, the appropriation of human reality. (EPM, CW3: 299–300)

We will endeavour to explain these ideas in greater detail from out of their opposites, or their more limited forms. So, in the next chapter we will talk about the 'mere' sense of 'possessing' (an idea borrowed from Hess, as we shall see) and also about the fragmentary man and reality conceived not as human reality but as a power over the human. All these topics fall under the heading of 'alienation'. Similarly, we shall see why the individual of liberal political economy (or, for that matter, the radical individual of Max Stirner's *The Ego and his Own*), while appearing to have the greatest range of freedoms in civil society, is in fact grossly limited in its being, and cut off from its fulfilment as species-being.

As will have been noticed at several places in this chapter, the issue of alienation was a key concern for Marx in the *Paris Manuscripts* and also came into the picture in several of his other works of the early to mid-1840s. Before moving on to examine alienation in his thought in the next chapter, it will be useful to consider very briefly what David Brudney (2001; 2002) sees as a problem for Marx's theory that production will be fundamentally transformed by means of revolution, so much so that humans will produce a new, communist society which will in turn produce a new outlook in the minds of those humans. Brudney raises the interesting question of how, if thought is essentially a product of material forces, the idea can emerge of a form of social organization different from the current one. It should be clear by now that Brudney's analysis involves an error. Ruth Abbey (2002) suggests that Brudney fails to see that in Marx's view humans have unrealized potential to become cooperative producers of goods, of their society and ultimately of themselves. The possibilities of human being are not an abstract idea, but lie in our material existence. We *are* our essence, and only because of this could the practical activities of production ever alienate us from it. Abbey's response does not, however, deal with the problem of how people, in their alienated condition under capitalism, recognize and thus realize such potential. The point is that while Marx did believe that in such a condition people are not fully aware of what is really happening to them, and thus could not envisage the better type of society that they could subsequently try to achieve, this does not mean a transition to communism is impossible. This is because it can happen gradually *through dialectic*. The underlying productive forces are already in dialectical opposition to the relations of production – that is to say, recognition can happen as consciousness of and critique of alienation emerge in the minds of people who begin to suspect that, as they gain nothing from the developing capability of their society to provide a better life, there is something not quite right. We will discuss such issues in more detail in the chapter on Change. Revolutions result from sparks, however small and weak those sparks may be.

CHAPTER THREE

Alienation

To recap on the main point of the previous chapter, Marx considered production to be an intrinsic feature of humanity. According to Mészáros, as we saw, Marx thus perceived productive activity as an absolute ontological factor, in that the human mode of existence is inconceivable without it. Humans by nature produced not only material things, but also their economic, social and political environment, and even themselves. If they failed to produce they would be losing an essential feature of their species-being (or indeed, cease to be entirely). If they did indeed produce, then they were enabling themselves to continue to be properly human. As for whether or not they could do so, this was dependent upon the conditions of their society; this is Marx's materialism. It was those conditions which might facilitate or obstruct this process. In the present chapter we turn to alienation, examining Marx's view in the 1844 *Paris Manuscripts* of the four forms it takes and the broader condition that they compose. Alienation can be quickly and roughly defined as a condition of human self-production that is deficient, not fully human. This chapter also discusses the development and appearance of the concept of alienation in some of his other early writings and indicates how the concept fits into the broader political philosophy that he built in that period. 'Alienation' is the most common translation of *Entfremdung*. However, the standard *Collected Works* uses 'estrangement'. Marx frequently uses the term *Entäusserung*, 'externalisation' in a closely related way, and the Collected Works translate this as 'alienation'. This creates a confusing picture for the reader, which is alleviated only by the fact that Marx does not make any consistent distinction between these terms, and so we can treat them as equivalent for our purposes.

The notion of alienation has its origins in a Roman legal term, for the voluntary relinquishing of title to property. Marx, by way of Hegel and Feuerbach, uses the notion in a much-altered and broadened meaning, although as we shall see, it retains some analogies. It is no exaggeration to say that alienation is, in fact, a key feature of the early political philosophy of Marx. The word 'key' was used carefully rather than casually in the previous sentence. It was used not simply to mean 'important'. Alienation is, rather, key in the more specific sense that Marx's discussions in the early to mid-1840s of the various other aspects of human life in capitalist society constitute a theory of the main problem of the human condition in a system of relations dominated by the institution of private property. For him, this was a problem that would need to be overcome if people were to escape from the exploitation that was presently a part of their lives. If they were to do so they would thereby experience emancipation, leading to the communist society in which they could produce collectively and cooperatively.

Alienation, which Marx considered to be the most debilitating factor of the condition that humans would continue to endure in the absence of emancipation, can be perceived as a pathological rather than natural trait. This is because people who experience it as a feature of their lives endure it as an artificially produced societal arrangement. As Bertell Ollman (1976: 132) put it: 'Both the individual and his way of life can be spoken of as "alienated", and in the latter case the tag "realm of estrangement" is applied to the most infected areas.' Alienation, therefore, is not an inevitable feature of human life, but rather 'a mistake, a defect' (EPM, CW3: 346). It is, indeed, a consequence of an arrangement that they can conceivably escape. As will be discussed in the chapters on Change and Emancipation in the present volume, for this reason the issues of transcendence and emancipation can only be fully understood in relation to alienation.

As was mentioned in the previous chapter, Mészáros (2005: 79) argued that Marx saw alienation as a second-order mediation of humanity with nature, in that it can only arise on the basis of the first-order productive activity. For Marx, alienation was one of the most damaging problems of the existing capitalist society, in terms of its effect on the lives of human beings. It was also a problem that could not be overcome by means of mere reform of such a society. This was because, in his view, although production as the first-order mediation was constant in human existence, alienation was not an intrinsic feature of production – and thus a necessary feature of human existence – but arises because of various forms of social organization. The capitalist form, though alienated through and through, is not unique.

Marx considered alienation to be damaging in that, as Ian Fraser and Lawrence Wilde (2011: 23) suggest, he perceived it as a representation of the 'process through which human beings suffer a loss of control over their interactions with nature and their fellow human beings'. (In fact, 'control' is not a broad enough term here, as we shall see, but it will serve for the moment.) This process happens when the human being in question produces something that comes to be owned by another or others and, moreover, thereby reproduces the human condition which is, artificially, dominated by the institution of private property. When products become private property, people have to exchange some of those things for other things as each person needs or desires some items that others produce. Usually, exchange occurs through the additional mediation of money. Self-reliance is not a viable, universal solution. The products of a person appear as alien to her, in that, under necessity she merely produces objects that are exchanged for the means to continue living, and sees work as simply a means to an end rather than as part of being herself. The very act of production in these circumstances therefore amounts to alienation. As Marx (EPM, CW3: 274) put it in terms of a question in the *Paris Manuscripts*: 'How could the worker come to face the product of his activity as a stranger, were it not that in the very act of production he was estranging himself from himself?' This is an important quote. It indicates something that will become evident towards the end of the present chapter: that, for Marx, people must begin to suffer alienation *before* the institution of private property can become entrenched in society.

As mentioned earlier, alienation from the product was in fact one of four forms of the broader condition that Marx identified in the *Paris Manuscripts*. Because, however, productive activity is the first-order mediation of humanity and nature, alienation from the product needs to be understood before the other three forms can begin to make proper sense to us. Whether or not this is the reason why he mentioned alienation from the product first, this ordering serves us well in both our endeavour to understand Marx's theory of alienation and our thesis that this was an element of a broader political and social philosophy that he was building in the early to mid-1840s. We will return to alienation from the product and the other forms later, but first we need to inquire into the history of the concept, in order to make Marx's conception of it as clear as possible.

Hegel and Marx

As was the case in the previous chapter on production, one can get a better picture of Marx's view of alienation by first comparing and contrasting it with that of Hegel. After all, had Hegel never written his philosophical works Marx simply would not have had the particular ideas that he did. Each saw the social world as having been alienated from the humans who comprised society; but they differed in their views of both what alienation actually was and how it might be overcome.

Marx argued that alienation was a product of human activity, in that humans alienated themselves because, in a society guided by the institution of private property, their labour produced objectifications of their creativity that were beyond their own control. For Hegel, objectification and alienation were conditions of the as-yet-unrealized idea, which would be overcome by means of the development of mind (Kitching, 1988: 19). Alienation in a broad, analogical sense, is part of the condition of any state of development, right up until the final stage. Within the political sphere, Hegel considered that the French Revolution of 1789 had brought about significant, progressive change in this respect. Obstacles to the political transformation in accordance with the absolute will could be overcome if the post-Napoleonic European states, in which the positive aspects of the revolution had made their mark, were to be duly reformed (Mah, 1990). Humans would thereby be reconciled with their society. For Hegel this meant that alienation, which was an aberration from the proper operation of the existing form of society, could be overcome by means of reform (Sayers, 2011: 26–7). Marx took a very different view of the legacy of 1789. He believed that the significant revolution would be one which replaced capitalism with communism and that such a revolution was, of course, one that was yet to take place. In fact, for Marx, the system of capitalism had intensified the problem of alienation that transpires in any society of which the institution of private property is a feature. Marx believed that reconciliation would require real, radical action to bring about the necessary fundamental social, concrete change, whereas Hegel considered that the necessary reconciliation would be philosophical.

For Hegel, the required philosophical explanation would enable people to see that their society was a sort of home, within which freedom was possible, despite the appearances that made them think otherwise (Hardimon, 1992: 169–72). The reconciliation that Hegel had in mind would be of a positive nature, rather than involving submission to something they might rather resist, as the English translation from the original German *versöhnung* might imply. It would be positive in that humans would be reconciled with God (or with the Idea), as they would see that the social world and the state, which God created, is ultimately good. It was ultimately their real community and thus their home, in that there was no single, objective way in which they are split from it. Once they recognized that this was so and identified with its social roles and institutions, their condition of alienation would end (Hardimon, 1992: 173–85).

One well-known discussion in Hegel's work is the master–slave dialectic. We very briefly mentioned this passage earlier in the book. (In fact, this passage occurs in *The Phenomenology of Spirit* in 1804 and is thus more of a propaedeutic to Hegel's later account of human societies and politics than a contribution to it. Nevertheless, the master–slave is often *taken to be* a key element of Hegel's political philosophy, and for that reason it is important that we discuss it here.) To grasp Hegel's point the terms master and slave ('bondsmen' or 'servants' according to some translations) can best be understood as analogies of two possible alienated states of consciousness. These states are explored by way of a thought experiment to examine why a person who dominates another who does the necessary work for them will remain in a condition of alienation while that dominated person eventually can overcome alienation. There are two premises to the argument. The first is that human beings, through their work, transform nature according to their desires. By 'desire' here we could substitute the more neutral Kantian idea of an 'end', that which initiates, coordinates and ultimately is the end point of any act of production. So, for Hegel, the transformation of nature according to ends permits human beings to become aware of themselves as producing beings. The second is that awareness of my own productivity is still a deficient, abstract stage of self-consciousness.

Abstraction is an important concept in this discussion. It carries two chief meanings, which are related. The first, which is normally the primary meaning in Hegel, is what results when something is taken from out of, or considered in isolation from, its real context. 'Abstract' in this meaning is the opposite of 'concrete'. The second meaning is of a concept or idea, a mental representation (for lack of a better phrase) that refers to the shared features of many different particulars. 'Abstract' here is the opposite of a sensible particular. We can use the term 'general' to refer to what is abstract in this second sense. Although in many philosophers these two definitions are essentially the same, they are not for Hegel. In Hegel, through dialectic the idea can become *realized*, which is to say, it can be both concept and concrete, in unity. (Indeed, Hegel normally uses the term 'idea' to mean just such an absolute realization.) Much of the critique of Hegel in Feuerbach, other Young Hegelians and Marx centres on abstraction. The issue is not so much that Hegel's notion of realization might be false, as that it needs to be understood to happen in the opposite direction (this is one of the reasons why both Feuerbach and Marx talk about turning Hegel 'on his head').

Consciousness within the master/slave situation is abstract because its idea involves the removal of the individual self-consciousness from out of any concrete social relations. On Hegel's analysis, neither the slave nor master are complete subjects: the slave is not because his producing belongs immediately to another, the master is not because the master does not produce at all. Each is alienated. A higher stage is reached when my desires enter into interaction with the desires of another, the other comes to *recognize* me in my humanity (i.e. not as a natural object, nor a product, but as myself a desiring and producing being), and this recognition by the other is part of the constitution of my self-consciousness.

Although it might seem common sense that the master will be the one capable of full human realization, while the slave is necessarily held back, Hegel's argument runs that in fact *both* are alienated by the relationship. Moreover, and importantly, the slave will be better placed to overcome alienation, and to carry the dialectic forward to the next, higher stage of self-consciousness. The master neither gains the recognition of his authority (i.e. of his possessing of ends) freely from the slave he dominates – for the slave being a slave hardly gives this recognition freely – nor experiences the seriousness or necessity of any work of his own – that is, does not himself transform nature according to his desires. In both these ways, he is thus prevented from achieving full self-consciousness. He is *alienated* from any recognition of his full humanity. Now, the slave, to be sure, is compelled to produce according to another's desire, and so is also alienated. However, he may thereby become aware of the essential nature of the human as productive; he may also become aware of the dependence of the master upon him (in effect, aware that the master himself is alienated). In this way, the slaves are better equipped to achieve that full, human self-consciousness; or, more properly expressed, it is through modifications in the self-awareness on the side of the slave that the human dialectic can progress towards a fully realized self-consciousness (Beiser, 2005: 189–90; Chitty, 2011: 482; Speight, 2008: 42–6).

It is a moot point whether Marx was to any degree influenced by Hegel's master–slave analysis (Sayers, 2011: 14–15), first of all because the problems of human production, recognition and alienation are clearly present in his work, and because more generally Hegel is the philosophical atmosphere that most intellectuals breathed in German-speaking Europe. As we saw in the last chapter, the Hegelian notions that the essence of the human includes production, that production is the basic model of the development of both history and thought, and that human beings must come to realize their essentially social nature are all important in Marx. Nevertheless, the master–slave passage in particular is significant because it points us to a fundamental difference between these two thinkers. Hegel considered (or at least the Young Hegelians tended to interpret him in this way) that the slave's experience illustrates the situation of a person gaining the *knowledge* that would enable them to end their alienation, if only the social arrangements could be reformed such that the interaction of the human production of things towards individual ends did not result in domination and universal alienation. In other words, the required reform (i) occurred primarily at a philosophical level, rather than a material one; and (ii) would not necessarily eliminate – but in fact enshrined all the more – the idea of one *owning* the transformed products of nature, and establishing a market for exchanging them. On Hegel's analysis, that is, the essential sociability of human beings was compatible with capitalism, broadly speaking. Marx believed those social conditions that generate alienation could not be altered while capitalism was still in place. Capitalism, moreover, could only be abolished when the exploited people would begin to campaign together to overcome it through action rather than thought. Only then would they develop the consciousness of themselves as the species-being, as they recognized that working cooperatively was making them into such a being.

Marx perceived humans as object creators; but as he saw it the process of creation was taken out of their control. His theory of alienation is concerned with the specifically material process by which human beings come to be dominated by things they create from nature and by the institution of private property. In this respect he agreed with Hegel's critic Feuerbach that the sole foundation of human consciousness was the material world. Marx would rapidly come to hold, however, the inadequacy of Feuerbach's argument that the way to overcome alienation would be to recognize and confess that what had been portrayed in terms of a god was actually no more than the human essence. For Marx it was not sufficient to recognize that, so long as we failed to recognize that our own creations had no supernatural causes, those creations would oppress us. What was needed in addition was to recognize that the existing social conditions, guided by the principle of private property, took the creations, including goods, social relations and even human lives, out of the control of workers. In order to dispel myths that oppressed them, people would need to recognize this problem and, most importantly, subject their social conditions and relations to fundamental change (Allen, 2011: 36–9).

For Marx, workers who were unable to master their material conditions were dehumanized, and thus left with only biological, animal-life functions. Motivated by greed, the exploiters were driven by an urge that was beneath the standards of humanity. When this happened, the human creative origins of those things were neglected, ignored or denied. As people lost control of their creations this entire process became institutionalized by social and economic arrangements. Creations thus came to be perceived by their creators and others in society as having lost the value associated with their own production as they came to represent only the money they could fetch in the market. Human labour itself was considered to be nothing but a commodity, to be exchanged on the market at its lowest price. The more fruitful the worker's production was, the poorer that worker became as the division between her and the things she produced grew proportionally greater. Meanwhile, the relationship between workers and their products became increasingly that of persons and alien objects, and the poorer those workers became, the greater was their alienation and exploitation. While, as will be seen later in this chapter, the 1844 *Paris Manuscripts* is where Marx expressed these views on alienation most coherently and fully, the development of this way of thinking can be detected in some of his writings of previous years.

Feuerbach and Hess on alienation

As we saw in the Introduction, one of the most important influences on the young Marx was Feuerbach, especially the latter's writings between 1839 and 1843. Feuerbach in fact is no less significant than Hegel to Marx's account of alienation. There are two broad and interconnected aspects of Feuerbach that we need to consider here. The first is Feuerbach's criticism of philosophy (especially but not exclusively Hegel) on the grounds of its abandonment of the real and the sensible (i.e. its being merely 'abstract'). The second is Feuerbach's critique of religion per se, especially as found in his famous book *The Essence of Christianity* from 1841. As we shall see, both hinge on issues of alienation.

In 1839, in a journal edited by Ruge – one of several publications that Ruge set up, trying to stay ahead of censorship, including a few years later a collaboration with Marx in Paris – Feuerbach published an extended essay entitled 'Towards a Critique of Hegel's Philosophy'. (It is not incidental that Feuerbach in fact established among his younger contemporaries something of a rush of papers with 'critique' in their title, including Marx's own *Contribution to the Critique of Hegel's Philosophy of Law*.) With the exception of a few passages where Feuerbach gives careful consideration to the exact wording of some bit of Hegel, the essay is for the most part an attempt to demolish the very conception of Hegel's whole philosophical project (and that of Schelling, just to add to the implausible audacity of it). Although Feuerbach could not be more gushing in his praise for Hegel as the greatest of philosophers and his works as 'unsurpassed models' (Feuerbach, 2012: 68), nevertheless his choice of language in describing the illegitimate presuppositions in Hegel's philosophy is most damning: he jokingly refers to that philosophy as a grotesque insect (53–4), speaks of the 'imprisoning of the intellect' by Hegel's writing (68) and the 'violence' of Hegel's suppression of the sensory (75).

The analysis hinges on the accusation that there is an illegitimate *abstraction* (in the sense of generality) in Hegel's work, something that Hegel is never entirely able to overcome. Hegel, Feuerbach argues, *assumes* an original distinction and moreover an original *priority* between concept and thing, between generality and sensuous life. So, for example, he claims that Hegel's monumental *Logic* appears to begin with an analysis of Being but, in fact, begins with an analysis of *the idea of* Being. So, instead of a presuppositionless point of beginning, as Hegel would like, the *Logic* in fact makes the same presuppositions that nearly every philosophy since Plato has: namely, that ideas or concepts exist alongside real, material being, that thought is something separable from such being and indeed (in Hegel's case at least) the presupposition that ideas are the *more fundamental* form of existence.

Feuerbach turns to Hegel's *Phenomenology of Spirit*, and discovers the same illegitimate move. The *Phenomenology* begins with an account of immediate sense certainty, a state of primitive consciousness in which there is no distinction made between the sensation and what is sensed. Now, this sounds at first very much like what Feuerbach is calling for – for it seems that no distinction between particular and general, or between thing and concept, is being assumed here. However, on Feuerbach's reading, in the course of the analysis it becomes clear that Hegel is not taking that initial point sufficiently seriously. Consciousness, Hegel argues, quickly comes to notice a distinction between a 'here', and the changing content of the here. I see a tree here, then a house here; the 'here' remains the same while the sensory content changes. So, Hegel notes, the *general* emerges as a 'here' that is indifferent to the particularity of what is here; likewise, a 'now' that is indifferent to what is in the now. Immediate sense certainty (for which there was no distinction between generality and specificity) is refuted, and a new stage of consciousness – one that deals with concepts – emerges. Feuerbach argues, though, that this refutation is an arbitrary decision on

Hegel's part: for, there is no reason to think that, rather than immediate sense certainty being refuted by this analysis, instead it should be the general that is considered refuted. Why should I not side with the philosophical position of nominalism, and insist that particulars are the real, and generality a superfluous artefact? In other words, that 'here' or 'now', as formal features of something general called space and time, respectively, are in fact illegitimate and misleading phantoms? 'My brother is called John … but there are innumerable other people besides him who are called by the same name. Does it follow from this that my brother John is not real? Or that John-ness [the generality] is the truth?' (Feuerbach, 2012: 77). Feuerbach accuses Hegel of having already decided on the primary reality of the concept, and thus the stage of immediate sense certainty is just a straw man argument for him. Being as sensuous, material reality never was the real starting point of the *Phenomenology*, and it follows that Hegel is by no means without his presuppositions. These observations about the *Logic* and *Phenomenology* are reiterated four years later in Feuerbach's 'Principles of the Philosophy of the Future' (Feuerbach, 2012: 214–16). Feuerbach thus sees his account of Hegel as a reductio ad absurdum of Hegelian thought: the distinction between thought and being, and the elevation of the former, amounts to an a priori rejection of materialism, and this is in direct contradiction to its own claims of presuppositionless thought.

All this adds up to an account of *alienation*. According to Feuerbach, philosophical thought (where Hegel is the chief because the most advanced and influential example), although it purports to be an overcoming of alienation, is in fact founded upon the primary alienation of human thought from human sensuous life (and ultimately from materialism). Philosophy, it appears, begins by a dismissal or rejection of the legitimacy of the sensual or the material. Whether we call it a soul, a mind or a spirit, such ideas arise out of a kind of abhorrence of the body. Philosophy, Feuerbach insists, must be thoroughly reformed lest it continues to be in a state of alienation. Not surprisingly, the word 'reform' occurs regularly in the titles of Feuerbach's publications over the next few years.

However, it is not just philosophy in its thinking that is alienating; philosophy in its public practice is in fact also deeply alienating. If the distinction between concept and sensual real particulars is not original and thus not a true foundation for philosophy, then the *form* that philosophy happens to take is not a necessary one, but only a means of communication. By 'form', Feuerbach means the arguments, logical structures, definitions and the order of presentation. The form is the conceptual articulation of some insight; the insight should be indifferent to it, in the sense that it should be possible to express or think about that insight *in a different form*. If, however, the concept is taken to be a primary reality, then the result is that a specific form *is* necessary to the philosophical insight (as Hegel insists). Philosophical logic is not just a tool for this or that analysis, but produces from out of itself all the 'content' of analysis. This particular way of writing about the master–slave dialectic (for example) is therefore word for word and line by line necessary, if the writing is to be philosophical. Such a philosophy is no longer communicating in an ordinary sense, meaning to 'awaken' a philosophical insight in another person, Feuerbach then insists. Instead it is *forcing* others to agree (Feuerbach, 2012: 66), that is, it is 'communicating' in the secondary sense that a quantum of momentum is communicated from one billiard ball to another. There is no hesitation, doubt or partial acquiescence permitted, no criticism; Hegel's writings function like a sacred text – they are not just words describing something, but the holy words of God. Thus Feuerbach (2012: 58) half-jokingly talks about the philosophical 'incarnation' earlier in his essay. Again, then, a form of alienation: the philosophical audience is alienated from their own human capacity to think (because they are 'imprisoned' by Hegel's thinking); this means, Feuerbach explains, they are treated not as a subject who can think and judge for themselves, but as an object; and Hegel's readership is also alienated from their own human capacity to judge the validity of something (because the concept is always already more true than the sensuous reality against which one might want to judge it). Feuerbach accuses Hegel's philosophy of being *nothing but theology*, both in that it places power in an absolute (the 'idea') that lies beyond the embodied, sensuous human as such, but also because in its act it *performs* this very subjection of the human.

Feuerbach's criticism of Hegel's philosophy in terms of theology is of particular interest because of the affinities to it borne by Marx's view of ideology as idealism and apologism. In this period, Marx's conception of ideology differs from the most common usage in contemporary political discourse, namely ideology as descriptive of any organized body of beliefs and its related political activities. Marx's view also differs from another usage today, this being essentially a term of abuse to belittle opposing political beliefs as inflexible and dogmatic (thus the word 'ideologue'). Marx's view was, however, consistent with a conception of ideology in circulation during the early nineteenth century. Ideology, in this conception, was seen as a particularly uncritical way of studying ideas. What distinguished Marx's view was its critical aspect. He used the term ideology in *The German Ideology* to represent an illegitimate way of portraying ideas, where the ideas were seen by idealists such as Hegel and the Young Hegelians – including Feuerbach (GI, CW: 38–41) – as detached from the concrete reality of actual human activity and interaction in social context. He was thus using the term *ideology* to signify what in the early 1840s, in *Contribution to the Critique of Hegel's Philosophy of Law*, he had portrayed as *idealism*. Marx criticized the Hegelians for thus universalizing the ideas and institutions of their own time, giving them a legitimacy that has no basis in a critical understanding of what they represent in today's world (Parekh, 1982: 1–14). Marx was thus using the term 'ideology' to portray what the critical theorist Herbert Marcuse would 120 years later perceive as false, repressive tolerance and false consciousness. As Marcuse (1969: 81) saw it, 'what is proclaimed and practiced as tolerance today, is in many of its most effective manifestations serving the cause of oppression'. The 'marketplace of ideas' had, Marcuse (1969: 110) argued, come to be 'organized and delimited by those who determine the national and the individual interest'. 'In this society,' he went on, 'for which the ideologists have proclaimed the "end of ideology," the false consciousness has become the general consciousness.' Organization and delimitation seem to have served to produce the legitimacy that Marx had mentioned. Marx's inclusion of Feuerbach among the thinkers to which he applied the term 'ideology' was, however, rather unfair in that there were distinct affinities between the views of Feuerbach and Marx in this respect.

There is another meaning to 'ideology' at work in Marx and Engels' writing that is worth bringing out at this point, because it is central to how alienation is understood. 'Ideas' do not mean just any concept or general notion – that is, Marx does not mean thinking in all its forms, but rather 'ideas' in a Kantian and especially a Hegelian sense. As we have seen, for Kant an Idea is a special type of concept such that it has no relation to the sensible conditions of possible experience. An Idea might have use in a regulative sense, but could not itself be referred to any possible object. Had Kant used the term 'ideology', he would have meant by it empty metaphysics. The situation is different for Hegel, insofar as the Idea is capable of realization through dialectical progression. Nevertheless, Feuerbach and Marx both interpret Hegel as if he had ignored the lessons of Kant, and specifically had ignored the vital role of the sensible. So, for example, we have seen Feuerbach argue that Hegel begins with the presupposition that reality (sensible reality) is subordinated to thought. Again, then, 'ideology' does not mean any kind of thinking whatsoever, but rather a specific kind of thinking that continues this Hegelian mistake: ideology holds that all of reality (or at least human reality) is ultimately a *product of thought*, or should be reformed in accordance with concepts of pure reason, and that therefore *critical thinking* (Marx and Engels are thinking specifically of the Young Hegelians when they use the word 'critique') will form the foundation of a change in human reality, for the better. This faith in the idea, and in the independent power of thought, is what Marx and Engels dismiss as merely the German Ideology. Importantly, this rejection of critical thought as *foundational* is not the same as a rejection of its instrumentality, as if thought is simply powerless and that all change rests with 'revolution'. So, in the *Theses on Feuerbach*, Marx says that Feuerbach's account of religious alienation rests on a secular basis – that is, the ideas about God that determined how human relations were to be organized were in fact founded upon the material conditions and activities of human beings; he adds, importantly, that the secular basis of religious projection needs to be overcome *both* in theory and through practice (i.e. revolution). Thus, the point is that thought is efficacious – both in a positive sense, as in Marx and Engels' own studies of political economy, and in a negative sense, as in the theological projections studied by Feuerbach. It is, however, only efficacious and indeed exists at all, to the extent that it is already a by-product of the underlying sensible reality of human affairs, and especially of contradictions within that reality. Critical thought or philosophy is a product and hence a tool in the hands of historical forces, rather than some kind of independent or founding force in and of itself. The name Marx gives to a revolutionary practice that can employ critique not as an independent power but as a tool is *praxis*, which usually translated as practice but with the connotation of revolutionary, practical-critical activity. We will discuss this further in our chapter on 'Change'.

Now, what we have just presented is the core of Feuerbach's criticisms of Hegel (and, again, by extension, all philosophy in the Western tradition). What matters is not so much whether the criticisms are well-founded, and whether Hegelian thought is genuinely vulnerable in these ways, but that Marx certainly viewed these criticisms as valid and important. For example, Feuerbach's suggestion that Hegel's writings performed like holy texts in their demands on their readers surely influenced Marx and Engels' satirical title *Holy Family* in its accounts of several key Young Hegelians. As yet, though, it must be difficult to see why these two types of specifically philosophical alienation matter – that is, why such alienation is a social, ethical or political issue, and thus why the young Marx would find these ideas so important. Feuerbach is not, to be sure, as directly concerned with political issues of the day, or with radical politics, as Marx – but there is a definite and significant political message in his work. In order to see this, we need to move to the second strand of Feuerbach's analysis, the critique of religion. Hegel's speculative philosophy is viewed by Feuerbach as essentially religion in a rarefied form, so the account of religion will in the end also be a further elaboration of the basic points in the critique of Hegel.

There is a long philosophical tradition, often but by no means always on the 'left', offering a critique of established religious institutions or practices on the grounds either that they degrade human beings or that they are part and parcel of some form of political injustice. Thus also there have been various calls either for religious tolerance or for a clear demarcation of the powers of the state from any religious doctrines, ideas found in various forms in, for example, Locke or Rousseau (Lessnoff, 1986: 59–67 and 74–82). Rather unusually, Pierre Bayle argued that atheism was fully compatible with moral order (Martin, 1962: 46–54); it is significant that Feuerbach wrote a book on Bayle in the 1830s. Kant insisted that moral principles were derived primarily from reason (Lessnoff, 1986: 90–4), and not from either revelation or religious orthodoxy, which carries the implication that a morality derived from either of these two sources will by that very fact not be fully moral. The thinkers of the French Revolution were thorough-going in the attempt at the dismantling of Christian institutions on political grounds (Martin, 1962: 1–3 and 277–81).

Feuerbach's immediate predecessor in these matters was David Strauss, whose *The Life of Jesus* (published in 1835) is also a Young Hegelian critique of religion (Breckman, 1999: 135–9). For Marx, Feuerbach's is the more important account, both because Feuerbach is less orthodox in his Hegelianism than Strauss – indeed, Feuerbach's is written in the context of his thorough-going critique of Hegel that we outlined earlier – and also because Feuerbach's is the more radical in terms of its implications for the understanding of human beings, and for its political dimension. The basic thesis of Feuerbach's account of religion can be stated quite quickly: a religion involves the positing of an entity above the human. This occurs because the human projects outside of itself its own unlimited essence, onto some imaginary entity beyond the human. Then, with respect to this beyond, the human is viewed as mere object, as limited and determined. This is self-alienation. Becoming conscious of this alienation, both in practice (the content of religion) and in theory (theology and philosophy), must mean the liberation of the human from its self-imposed subjection. Religion as an institution or as a way of human living their lives is one of the key models of alienation for Marx. Separate from the particular topic of this alienation, that is, religion, the formal model has several features that become important for Marx well beyond the sphere of religion itself. First, we have two states of the human: the unlimited or the 'whole', as distinguished from the limited, determined or fragmentary. Moreover, this whole human is not an idea for the future, but is immanent: real human perfections when properly understood (not alienated). Second, we have an invention of an entity in which the essence proper to the human is made manifest, apparently originally. Third, this entity that is beyond the human is in a state of dominance over the human.

The second and third of these features concern objectification. Marx argued in the *Paris Manuscripts* that the product of labour is a material object in which labour is embodied, and which confronts that labour 'as something alien, as a power independent of the producer'. As under the conditions of private property the realization of labour is thus objectification, 'this realisation of labour appears as loss of realisation for the workers; objectification as loss of the object and bondage to it; appropriation as estrangement, as alienation [*Entfremdung* and *Entäusserung*, respectively]' (EPM, CW3: 272). This objectification becomes entrenched in the creation of money as a mediating alien power. This result will be discussed in more detail later in the present chapter. In the case of the first feature, this concerns the division of labour and labour specialization. This concern is illustrated very clearly in Marx's *Paris Manuscripts*. The industrial division of labour portrayed as the norm in modern political economy was actually, Marx suggested, limited by the market. In this condition human labour was 'simple mechanical motion: the main work is done by the material properties of the objects'. 'The fewest possible operations,' he went on, 'must be apportioned to any one individual' (EPM, CW3: 322). The consequences of this situation were as follows: 'The savage and the animal have at least the need to hunt, to roam, etc. – the need of companionship. The simplification of the machine, of labour is used to make a worker out of the human being still in the making, the completely immature human being, the child' (EPM, CW3: 308). Historically, that is, human beings were alienated long before they had realized themselves as full flourishing beings possible for humans (i.e. in Marx's metaphor: adulthood). Marx thus takes the model as developed by Feuerbach, agrees with it broadly, but also claims that *more fundamental* than religious alienation *is alienation in production*. That is, alienation in production is seen as the bigger picture, of which religious alienation is only a subclass or a derivative effect.

The second result directly also concerns species-being. In the 'Introduction' to his *The Essence of Christianity*, Feuerbach begins not with religion per se, but with 'The Being of Man in General'. Animals have no religion, and this is because (he asserts) they have no consciousness in a 'strict sense'. Now, in a broader sense – the ability to distinguish between objects and to perceive or judge – animals certainly do have consciousness. However, there is one object of which animals can never be conscious, namely, of their 'own being', of their species-being. The animal experiences itself as an individual, but not as a species, and thus is not aware of itself vis-à-vis the species. The human ego can understand itself as a possible object for other egos; that is, it can see itself as others see it, and can thus *see itself as of the same kind as these other egos*. The individual ego, then, has 'built in' to it, so to speak, an awareness of itself as a *member of a species*. This, Feuerbach calls consciousness in the 'strict' sense, or 'self-consciousness'. So, an ego might factually be alone (I might happen to be the only human being in existence, or I might happen to be stranded on a desert island), but even so it also includes this reference to other egos. Human self-consciousness is consciousness of its own being, that is, its species-being. The human ego is understood fully only if it recognizes the possibility of being an other's object, only in community is the truth of human essence revealed. Thus, seeking to understand the individual *without* this absolutely intrinsic reference to others and to the species is not only a philosophical mistake, but a form of alienation. Thus, Feuerbach can accuse a whole line of philosophers of illegitimately espousing solipsism, egoism or individualism. (The little-known J. F. Reiff is just a convenient, contemporary target for Feuerbach in his review of 'The Beginning of Philosophy' (Feuerbach, 2012: 135–144).) There is also a political implication, although it is mostly drawn by Feuerbach in separate publications: so, for example, in 'The Necessity of a Reform of Philosophy', he argues that any monarchical system is basically the alienated power structure of religion translated into a political system. It follows that only by means of a thorough republicanism could 'the powers of man differentiate and unfold themselves in order … to constitute an infinite being […] The true state is the unlimited, infinite, true, perfect, and divine man' (Feuerbach, 2012: 150). As a primarily sensuous being, the perfection proper to me is a sensuous one. So, if perfection of the human is to be understood by way of abstract concepts (ultimately theological concepts, Feuerbach insists) then my sensuous nature must be denigrated, seen as a problem or a burden. I am thereby alienated from my essence. As unalienated, my (i.e. the human) ideal, my perfection, the fulfilment of my essence and my image of the divine, all must be understood in terms of sensuous particulars, not mere concepts.

With that, we are back to Feuerbach's critique of Hegelian thought as having a surreptitious dependence upon abstraction. By sensuousness, Feuerbach means that the sensing of things, of being in a broadly passive relation of smelling or tasting, is the key part of the essence of the ego. That we are sensory beings is not, for instance, just a result of a pure mind or soul being dropped against its will into a body. The passivity does not emerge from the ego on its own, considered as activity, but arises because of the activity of objects, objects that, for example, reflect light, make noises and so forth. There is no 'pure' mind or soul, other than as a fictional abstraction created by philosophers. Rather, the ego is originally corporeal, embodied (cf 'On "The Beginning of Philosophy"', Feuerbach, 2012: 142). This does not mean, incidentally, that the age-old 'mind–body' problem that has been preoccupying philosophy for centuries is finally solved. On the contrary, Feuerbach insists that 'The conflict between the spirit and the body is alone the highest metaphysical principle' (Feuerbach, 2012: 144). What Feuerbach's analysis does show, however, is that certain ways of posing (and of solving) the mind–body problem arise because of an illegitimate abstraction of mind from body: the problem of the interaction of mind and body is the problem of interaction between things presumed to be, respectively, intellectual and material. The mystery that needs exploring is embodiment itself, and not the connection of two vastly different things. Only recognizing that human beings are essentially sensual beings could frame the basis for its solution: 'Only sensuous beings act upon one another' (Feuerbach, 2012: 224). Importantly, as long as sensuousness is denigrated with respect to the pure mind, then it is also misunderstood. Freeing our capacity to sense from various misconceptions is not simply a move within philosophy, but must change the way humans sense; we can sense fully and properly for the first time.

Feuerbach's approach was far too simplistically materialist for Marx. For Marx, the human being is, as Sidney Hook (1994: 274) put it, 'active in knowing'. Sensuous nature implies that humans simply react to experience. Hence, Feuerbach's thought takes him into the same predicament of earlier materialists who had not been able to resolve the antithesis between material nature and human consciousness. As was discussed in the previous chapter, human beings produce themselves and their surroundings. They develop in their communities as they find ways of providing for their needs. As Marx put it in his first thesis on Feuerbach:

> The chief defect of all previous materialism (that of Feuerbach included) is that things [*Gegenstand*], reality, sensuousness are conceived only in the form of the object, or of contemplation, but not as sensuous human

activity, practice, not subjectively .... Feuerbach wants sensuous objects, really distinct from conceptual objects, but he does not conceive human activity itself as objective activity .... Hence he does not grasp the significance of 'revolutionary', of 'practical-critical', activity. (TF, CW5: 3)

Feuerbach developed the notion of species-being as community in a very different way than Marx; human activity as 'objective activity' takes us to Marx's notion of *self*-production, the products of activity being part of the communal production.

Let us continue, though, with Feuerbach's account. In accordance with the earlier notions, he discusses the concept of 'love', clearly appropriating the concept back from Christianity. In the *New Testament,* God's love for man or the world is the basis for the redemptive sacrifice of Christ, and John goes so far as to claim that 'God is love' (John 1, 4:8 and 16). The Greek word used there is 'agape', which is to be distinguished both from dutiful or filial love shown, for example, to one's family, and sexual love; agape is thus seen as unconditional and universal. In his 'Principles of the Philosophy of the Future', Feuerbach argues as follows: to think of myself as *sensed* is for me to be another for someone else, I am passive with respect to another's activity, I am an object for them. To *love* though is to affirm this other's sensing of me; to love is thus to value or pledge oneself to this communal human essence (Feuerbach, 2012: 224–6). Marx takes up this idea explicitly in the 'Excerpt-Notes' from his reading of James Mill, in 1844. There he writes, concerning any genuinely free human production, that 'I would have been for you the mediator between you and the species, and therefore would become recognised and felt by you yourself as a completion of your own essential nature and as a necessary part of yourself, and consequently would know myself to be confirmed both in your thought and your love' (CJM, CW3: 228). Reference to this notion of love appears again in the *Paris Manuscripts,* at the end of the discussion of money (EPM, CW3: 326).

For Feuerbach, it also follows that only a being whose own being is an object of thought can then have the essential nature of other beings as an object of thought – in other words, species-being is the condition of possibility of *science*. This arises because specifically human consciousness is able to see not only itself but also its world as others see it, indeed as the species taken as a totality would see it, thus forming an *objective* view of that world not confined to an individual and its contingent perspective. My individual perspective stands to be corrected or confirmed by that of others; that this objectivity is the cornerstone of science. Notice, importantly, that this 'total' view of objects that forms the basis of the objectivity of science is built from out, not of the identity of human beings with each other, but precisely their *differences*; if everyone had the *same* view of an object, then we would be back with an individual and contingent perspective, albeit one multiplied many times over. Accordingly, Feuerbach writes 'The *true* dialectic is *not a monologue of the solitary thinker with himself*; it is a *dialogue between "I" and "You"* ' (Feuerbach, 2012: 244).

Feuerbach's materialism not only entails that sensuousness is part of the essence of the ego, but also that truly existent things are always determinate and particular. In Hegel, Feuerbach asserts, the particularity of things was only a moment or stage within a notion of Being conceived of abstractly (Feuerbach, 2012: 217). It also follows that on the Hegelian model only God could be perfect, because He qua existence beyond sensuousness includes all possible attributes of being, while all other things are imperfect because they are determined; again, only God could be unlimited or infinite for the same reasons, while all subordinated beings are limited and finite. But this Hegelian way of thinking about particularity is only possible when sensuousness is also denigrated below the level of human essence. 'Being,' Feuerbach writes, 'is not a general concept that can be separated from things. It is one with that which is' (Feuerbach, 2012: 214–15). This means that the existence of something and its properties are one and the same. Moreover, Feuerbach insists that this line of analysis entails that the perfection of something is for it to *be* its essence. Human beings find their true essence in species-being, in consciously communal life; but this essence is not merely how a human being is to be defined – it is not an abstract definition at all – but also *forms the real perfection of human existence*. Human beings exist fully and in perfect accord with their essence, only in existing as the totality that is the human species. This notion of human essence as immanent is clearly important for Marx, as we have seen.

In religion, this perfection was projected onto a transcendent deity, and the possibility of its own perfection denied to the human; in fact, what was formerly called the perfect and infinite deity is nothing other than human being itself, projected surreptitiously onto a 'transcendent' being. Under conditions of religion, whether explicitly recognized as such (as in Christianity), or in political scenarios that replicate the alienation structure of religion (such as monarchy), or in philosophies that covertly introduce and justify religion (such as Hegel's), the human species is incapable of realizing its perfection. They are *alienated*. The conditions under which human beings can fulfil their essence and thus their perfection thus become a matter of urgent political, social and moral reform.

As noted earlier, one key reason that Marx was interested in, and adapted for his own use, Feuerbach's account of religion was the way that Feuerbach framed the distinction between a full or whole account of the human and a partial, fragmented or alienated one. This distinction between a full and a partial account of the human is shown in three topics that we have just been discussing. First, in the distinction we are now able to draw between a view of the ego as embodied necessarily and embodied contingently (i.e. where body is an imposition upon some spiritual 'purity'). Feuerbach sees this as the human alienating itself from its full essence as embodied. Second, as the distinction between the ego as in its essence not only sometimes passive but also intrinsically positing the existence of other human egos, indeed of the species per se, as opposed to the illegitimate view of the ego as essentially self-sufficient in its activity. Feuerbach sees this as the human alienating itself from its essence as a social or species-being. Third, in the notion that the realization of the perfection of species-being is not impossible, and is held back by the misunderstanding of perfection as being something other than humanity's own immanent social essence, which misunderstanding occurs under conditions of religious alienation.

Marx adapts Feuerbach's analysis in the *Paris Manuscripts*, where we find a lengthy discussion of the alienation and emancipation of the senses. He writes 'In the place of *all* physical and mental senses there has therefore come the sheer estrangement of *all* these senses, the sense of *having*.' (On the notion of 'having', please see immediately below where we introduce the analysis of Hess.) The passage continues: 'The abolition of private property is therefore the complete *emancipation* of all human senses and qualities' (EPM, CW3, 300). Here we point to these passages as evidence of the importance of Feuerbach (and Hess) for Marx's account of alienation – although of course Marx clearly rethinks the notion in terms of alienation with respect to private property, rather than (as in Feuerbach) in terms of alienation from an abstract conception of the ego. What emancipated sensibility means, and the role it plays in Marx's notion of emancipation, we will discuss further in the chapter 'Emancipation'.

As we have seen, Marx and Engels wrote two polemics against the young Hegelians, *The Holy Family* and *The German Ideology*. In both, Feuerbach comes in for criticism, of course, but also a recognition of his importance and influence. In the latter book, they wrote, and this is clearly an echo of the last of the *Theses on Feuerbach*: '[L]ike the other theorists, he merely wants to produce a correct consciousness about an *existing* fact; whereas for the real Communist it is a question of overthrowing the existing state of things.' However, the book then continues, 'We fully appreciate, however, that Feuerbach, in endeavouring to produce consciousness of just *this* fact, is going as far as a theorist possibly can, without ceasing to be a theorist and philosopher' (GI, CW5, 58).

A thinker of the period by whom Marx and Engels were far less impressed was Max Stirner. In the early 1840s, Stirner was a Young Hegelian in terms of the circles he moved in, but much less so in terms of the ideas he propagated, having a fairly tangential relation to Hegelianism. Today he is remembered more as part of the history of anarchism, or for his striking anticipations of existentialism, than for his contributions to anything resembling Hegelian thought. His book *The Ego and its Own*, published late in 1844, was an important event in the developing Marx's intellectual trajectory, however. Stirner argued for a radical egoism; the ego is the 'unique' (unavailable to concepts or 'names'), not an object (a pure creator) and thus entirely transcendent to both the sensible and the spiritual. Anything that exerted a sovereign influence over the ego, whether as a material force outside of me or as an idea within, that ego could (and should) reject. The main forces that Stirner identified were religion (the Deity and the idea of the sacred were essences that positioned themselves *above* me), the humanism of Feuerbach (where the idea of the human was elevated above the individual ego's real and authentic interests) and any form of state (thus the link to anarchism). Anything external to me is material and sensuous, and beneath me in value – and, indeed, to the extent that I can control it, it is my *possession* (thus the 'its own' in the title of Stirner's book). There are and could be no external ideas or 'essences', and this broadly materialist claim already shows, Stirner argues, the absurdity of such external forces as the sacred, the species-being of the human or justice. Anything internal to me is thought and, because I myself am nothing but pure creation, the moment I think a thought, it becomes 'alien' and again beneath me, to be accepted or rejected as I choose. Thus even what I hold to be truth does not obligate me to consider it so, or act accordingly. Stirner thus accused the revolutionary communists of plotting the downfall of the power of the state over the individual, in itself something he approved of, but only to bring back that power in the still more disturbing form of the power of the collective (Thomas, 2011).

Engels was briefly impressed by Stirner's book, and recommended it urgently to Marx. He argued that communism had to progress by convincing individuals that communism was indeed in their interest (LM 19/11/1844, CW38: 11–12). Their joint critique of Stirner (satirically renamed 'Saint Max') takes up more than half of the manuscript pages of *The German Ideology*, showing the significance they attached to it. From a distance of 170 years, though, it is difficult to understand why, for Stirner is clearly something of an intellectual lightweight. Certainly, it seems possible that the influence of Stirner accelerated Marx's break with Feuerbach after 1844, and the till then key terminology of the sensuous and of species-being. However, this was happening anyway, and more importantly, the reasons why it was happening had little to do with Stirner. Stirner might also have made more urgent Marx and Engels' clarification of the ontological status of the individual within their thought; but again, this was happening anyway in the *Paris Manuscripts*, written months before Stirner's book appeared. In *The German Ideology*, Stirner is dumped in with the rest of the ideologues, shown to be fruitlessly advocating the power of ideas and abstractions. For that is what Stirner's unique individual is, an abstraction – where that word is understood in its proper Hegelian usage of something stripped of its real context. Stirner's materialism is a sham. Who I am, Marx and Engels insist, is not a pure creator, transcending even my own thoughts, but rather a flesh and blood person, sharing a material world with others. That my thoughts and sensations are 'mine' is just a tautology, of no ontological significance. The polemic against 'Saint Max' is extensive because Stirner's work was such an immediate and widespread intellectual vogue, but in substance the critique is not different from Marx and Engels' treatment of all the other Young Hegelians.

While Feuerbach's notion of species-being might look like an abstraction (now using 'abstraction' in the more familiar meaning of a mere idea, without a foothold in the materially real), as Stirner claims, this was certainly not Feuerbach's intent. After all, the rescue of the sensuously real from its devaluing with respect to the idea is Feuerbach's whole campaign. To be sure, Marx and Engels abandon the word 'species-being' (and in the same gesture accuse Feuerbach of abstraction), replacing it with the less ambiguous 'life'. By 'life' they mean the actual totality of material states, actions and relations of people. For example, in *The German Ideology* they say 'the being of men is their actual life-process' (GI CW5: 36). Only when there is a universal union, which in turn must follow a proletarian revolution in which the power of the previous mode of production, intercourse and social organization is overthrown, they suggested later in that volume, 'does self-activity coincide with material life, which corresponds to the development of individuals into complete individuals and the casting-off of all natural limitations' (GI, CW5: 88). Until then, self-activity is constrained, because individuals are subject to the division of labour, alienated and stunted with respect to the always immanent possibility of their completeness. At the very end of the section on Feuerbach in the manuscript of *The German Ideology*, one finds a note stating, 'Individuals always proceeded, and always proceed, from themselves. Their relations are the relations of their real life-process.' 'How does it happen,' the note continues, posing a question concerned with the problem Marx had in earlier work referred to as alienation, 'that their relations assume an independent existence over against them? and that the forces of their own life become superior to them?' 'In short' the answer to this rhetorical question is: 'division of labour, the level of which depends on the development of the productive power at any particular time' (GI, CW5: 93). Nevertheless, notwithstanding the change in terminology, we argue that all these analyses retain the link back to Feuerbach and to the sensuous essence of the human as species-being. The proper bone of contention with Feuerbach is not primarily his humanism, then, but rather (as the *Theses on Feuerbach* also made clear) that his definition of the human ignores the concept of objective self-production, and thus he (like all the Young Hegelians and materialists) misses the notion of revolutionary praxis.

Another important source for Marx's emerging account of alienation is Hess, usually classed as one of the Young Hegelian communists, but one rather more sympathetic to Marx's brand of materialism. Hess becomes the proximate source for the young Marx's account of possessing or having, although the core of the idea comes ultimately from Feuerbach. Hess was a close colleague and friend of both Marx and Engels in Paris, and certainly a fellow admirer of Feuerbach. However, by the late 1840s they had distanced themselves from him. Among other things, this distancing occurred because Hess held what Marx called an 'utopian' (or anarchist) socialist view that no form of state would be required after the abolition of private property. Reciprocally, Hess found he could not agree with the predominately *economic* analysis of history that Marx and Engels were producing, instead reserving a vital role for both racial and theological differences, and he became one of the key founders of socialist Zionism. From 1843 to 1845, though, Hess published several papers that clearly show influence on and affinities with Marx's thinking in this period. Indeed, Marx in the Preface to the *Paris Manuscripts* ranks him with Wilhelm Weitling and Engels as the only real German contributors to socialism, and also puts a brief forward a reference to his work in the section of that work on private property. Here, we want to sketch two of Hess's analyses from this period, because they are of particular significance for our reconstruction of Marx: namely, the concept of 'having' or 'possession' from 'The Philosophy of the Act' (originally published anonymously in *Twenty One Sheets from Switzerland* in 1843) and the corresponding analysis of money (found in 'The Essence of Money', published in the *Rheinische Jahrbücher* in 1845).

Explicitly following both Spinoza and Fichte, Hess argues that the key characteristic of the 'I' is activity and continual change. Descartes' 'I think' does not lead to the abstract being of some 'I', but rather to the act of thinking itself; the ego exists only to the extent that it is actively becoming something else. As Hess writes, 'This constant altering of the "I" is necessary, because there is an "I" [...] only so long as it defines itself, limits itself, and perceives, in this act of the self becoming another, or limiting itself, its likeness to itself, or free self-determination' (Hess, 1964: 251). The identity of the self arises not through the constancy of a substance, but through the merely formal constancy of the law of activity; likewise, its freedom consists in its self-limiting (which we can recognize as a broadly Kantian conception of freedom, i.e. autonomy).

Reflection, however, turns things 'upside down' (another instance, notice, of the motif of inversion, common in the Young Hegelians): in reflecting upon the difference between thinking and the thought-about, and between the act and the acted-upon, it mis-identifies the latter two as the domain of constant change, and the 'I' as constant. In other words, any act of reflection is intrinsically vulnerable to producing an alienating illusion, which is that the self is a constant and permanent substance, within an ever-changing world. (Hess takes this as not only a philosophical mis-step, but also and perhaps more importantly, the original *theological* mis-step. Here, we will not discuss these theological implications.) In this alienating illusion, that in the objective world which appears to be a constant that is correlated to my constant self is called 'my property'. The objectification of my own activity is taken as something that I can 'have' or 'possess'. Thus, for example, in Locke ownership of land is equivalent to having invested into it one's labour. In the objective world, which is also a public world, this amounts to an illegitimate barrier or mediation between me and others, and among others. Collective production is obscured by the mediation of property. Thus, Hess concludes, 'This is the curse that has weighed upon mankind throughout history until now: that men do not set up activity as an end in itself, but constantly conceive of its gratification as something separate from it' (Hess, 1964: 265).

Hess elaborates further on this idea two years later in his analysis of money. To the earlier account of material property, Hess expands upon the intrinsic social dimension. *The Essence of Money* begins (after an extended quote from Shelly's *Queen Mab*): 'Life is exchange of creative life-activity,' and this is as true at the level of the social as at a simply material level of the body. Although as bodies we act *as if* we were separable individuals, actual separation would mean literal asphyxiation; likewise, men act in the social sphere *as if* separable individuals, but again actual separation would be deadly. It follows, he states in Section 2, that 'any real practical as well as theoretical activity is a species-act, a collaboration of individuals', and these collaborations are the 'real essence of each individual'. In Section 5, Hess continues, again using the image of inversion, 'The individual who wants to live not through himself for the species, but through the species for himself alone, must create practically an inverted world.' (To live 'through himself for the species' would mean to recognize that the end of individual action must be the 'species-act' or 'collaboration'.) That 'inverted world' he names as 'our world of shopkeepers', concluding 'here, there is money'. The specific alienation under discussion is not just material property, but the 'general means of exchange' as the economists would have it, such that, as he put it in Section 7: 'What cannot be exchanged, what cannot be sold, has no value' (Hess, 1845, online).

At this point, Hess again makes the link to theology, and this time we must follow him. Christianity placed the value of the world in the next or higher world. Thus, it had (i) to distinguish between spirit and body, where the next world is the proper home of the former; and (ii) had to treat the body, resident in this world, as intrinsically evil or polluted. That which pertains to or is linked to the body is likewise polluted. Material property, something that I own because of my activity, must carry this theological pollution. Money, however, precisely because abstract, can be considered holy. Thus, if a man is the material property of another, as in literal slavery, then both owner and slave are touched by this corruption; however, if I exchange my activity for money, then I am considered to have done so freely and this 'exchange' is not polluted. Money represents an appropriately spiritual way of valuing human beings. The wage-earner is in fact no more free than the slave, but by way of this theological sleight-of-hand, liberal economics can deem him to be. Obviously, the phenomenon of money predates Christianity, so Hess argues that his is the theological genesis not of money per se but of the significance ascribed to money within modern economic theory. In the world of shopkeepers, 'The actual atmosphere of man, which in Heaven is God, the superhuman good, is' he stated in Section 11, 'in Earth the extra-human or unhuman ... money' (Hess, 1845, online). Money, we might say, is immaculate acquisition.

Marx of course has much less interest in religion or in theology, and certainly not as a foundation of key concepts; Hess in this analysis is still close to Feuerbach's critique of religion. However, without question, much of Hess's analysis of abstract 'possessing' and of money was important to Marx's development. Part of Hess's analysis was published before Marx set to work on the philosophy of political economy in 1844, and part after – so exactly who influenced whom is difficult to pin down. At the very least, Hess is a useful mirror with which to view, and understand, Marx. At the end of the 'Excerpt Notes' of 1844, Marx is contrasting alienated production from fully human production. The ideal relationship to objects which one had produced was mutual need, but the alienated condition is described in Hess's terms: '[T]he real, true relationship, which actually occurs and takes effect, is only the mutually exclusive possession of our respective products. What gives your need of my article its value, worth and effect for me is solely your object, the equivalent of my object' (CJM, CW3: 226). Fully human production, on the other hand, is described in terms of species-being and love, as we saw earlier. We will of course return to the latter analysis in our chapter on 'Emancipation'.

The significance of *On the Jewish Question*

The significance of alienation in Marx's earlier thought is evident in his views on civil and human rights, of which he was particularly critical in *On the Jewish Question*. In that article of 1843 he derided the notions of such rights. Ostensibly rights of man, they were in fact based on a misunderstanding of humans as selfish, egoistic creatures. Furthermore, the social division between private and public in modern capitalist society meant that people saw themselves as both private individuals and citizens pursuing the common good. This dualism that characterized modern bourgeois society prevented individuals from associating in communities. Human beings were thus separated from their essential social nature, becoming atomistic individuals, rather than species-beings (OJQ, CW3: 146–68).

Although Marx wrote *On the Jewish Question* before the 1844 *Paris Manuscripts*, the synergies are clear. In the earlier of these two works, he criticized the attempt to achieve revolutionary political change in the absence of fundamental social reform. 'The establishment of the political state and the dissolution of civil society into independent individuals,' he argued 'is accomplished by one and the same act' (OJQ, CW3: 167). In this situation the natural human being appeared to be the unpolitical person who was a member of civil society. As conscious activity was focused on political activity, egoistic activity in civil society appeared passive and natural. This view of humanity, he elaborated,

> regards civil society, the world of needs, labour, private interests, civil law, as the basis of its existence, as a precondition not requiring further substantiation and therefore as its natural basis. Finally, man as a member

of civil society is held to be man in the proper sense, homme as distinct from the citoyen, because he is man in his sensuous, individual, immediate existence, whereas political man is only abstract, artificial man, man as an allegorical, juridical person. The real man is recognised only in the shape of the egoistic individual, the true man is recognised only in the shape of the abstract citoyen. (OJQ, CW3: 167)

Notice again the Feuerbachian way of describing the supposed difference between sensuous individuality and the abstract. As we will discuss further in a later chapter, Marx thus distinguished between political emancipation and human emancipation.

Marx went on to offer what may seem to be rather a peculiar quote from Jean-Jacques Rousseau's *On the Social Contract*. Marx announced that Rousseau was correct to describe as follows the abstract idea of political man:

Whoever dares undertake to establish a people's institutions must feel himself capable of changing, as it were, human nature, of transforming each individual, who by himself is a complete and solitary whole, into a part of a larger whole, from which, in a sense, the individual receives his life and his being, of substituting a limited and mental existence for the physical and independent existence. He has to take from man his own powers, and give him in exchange alien powers which he cannot employ without the help of other men. (OJQ, CW3: 167–8)

Now, this is a strange passage in Rousseau's work in any case, referring to a figure he calls the 'law-maker', who is virtually God-like in the establishment of broad frameworks; the broad framework then makes possible men having sufficient moral qualities to be able to form the general will. Marx's use of this quote may appear more odd to readers who have an awareness of Rousseau's argument in the book, which was that citizens should forgo their natural liberty in exchange for the civil and moral liberty that can be achieved by participating in the community and accepting that one must abide by the general will. The general will would be what anyone who knew what was in their best interests would will, and the collective sovereign, comprising the people, would decide what this would be (by majority decision if unanimity could not be achieved) (Rousseau, 1993: 214).

Lucio Colletti (1974: 188) argued that Marx was misinterpreting Rousseau. This, however, seems unlikely given that the previous year, in a leading article in the *Kölnische Zeitung* newspaper he had discussed Rousseau briefly in words that capture the latter thinker's intentions very well (LA179, CW1: 201–2). Marx was actually using the tactic of the reductio ad absurdum which one finds time and again in his writings, perhaps most prominently in the case of the spectre haunting Europe in the *Communist Manifesto* (Lamb, 2015: 26–8). Marx was criticizing Rousseau indirectly in *On the Jewish Question* for advocating political emancipation. Rousseau was trying to achieve two things, neither of which was possible in conjunction with the other. That Rousseau even admits that the law maker seems impossible or a 'miracle' is precisely Marx's point. As Marx put it: 'Political emancipation is the reduction of man, on the one hand, to a member of civil society, to an *egoistic, independent* individual, and, on the other hand, to a *citizen,* a juridical person.' Rousseau's argument was thus absurd given that both of these were merely abstractions, fictions invented so as to prevent any real change, and his tortured language shows it.

The acceptance of alien powers that Rousseau had urged, because of this fictional division into civil and political, was exactly what Marx wanted people to overcome. Marx stressed that the abstract citizen of the political realm needed to be absorbed into each person's nature as 'a *species-being* in his everyday life, in his particular work, and in his particular situation'. Human emancipation could only be accomplished, he went on, 'when man has recognised and organised his "*forces propres*" as *social* forces, and consequently no longer separates social power from himself in the shape of *political* power' (OJQ, CW3: 168). The power that was thus being recognized was not alien; it was, rather, a part of the natural human being – albeit a part that was not presently recognized as such. The human species is one that can have power over nature and thus creativity. Through power and creativity we can recognize and affirm ourselves as humans. This involves the overcoming of alienation (Sayers, 2011: 31).

Galvano della Volpe (1979: 21–48) noted that Rousseau's argument about the general will overlooks the problems of class that were central to Marx's later work. The general will would not be recognized, and still less achieved, in a society dominated by the class which gained so disproportionately as was the case in capitalist society. Andrew Levine (1987: 11–13) suggests that in this respect Marx's work helps illustrate the limitations of Rousseau's political philosophy but also to provide a remedy for those limitations. What seems clear is that, even before he began to focus specifically on class struggle, Marx was aware in the early 1840s that Rousseau had overestimated the utility of simply political revolution in the absence of social change of a more fundamental nature. Marx's ideas at this time did in fact contribute to his views on class struggle. He became convinced that criticism and philosophy alone could not overcome human alienation. In his article *Contribution to a Critique of Hegel's Philosophy of Law [Right]: Introduction,* which he wrote in late 1843–early 1844, Marx referred to the proletariat as the class with radical chains (CCHPLI, CW3: 186). If those chains were broken, humanity would be emancipated. The proletariat, by liberating itself, could emancipate all other spheres of society. At this time Marx saw the proletariat in terms of specifically German emancipation but thought this would develop into the wider human emancipation. The proletariat's universal suffering and role as the object of injustice in general meant that its recovery would require the complete redemption of humanity. This would happen in part through the

unmasking and overcoming the social and economic source of alienation/
estrangement (CCHPLI, CW3: 176).

By means of this example of absurdity in Rousseau's philosophy Marx
was exposing the myth of the naturally egoistic individual. He did so as
follows a few pages before his quotation of Rousseau in *On the Jewish
Question*, with reference of the French revolutionaries' Declaration of the
Rights of Man:

> It is puzzling enough that a people which is just beginning to liberate
> itself, to tear down all the barriers between its various sections, and to
> establish a political community, that such a people solemnly proclaims
> (Declaration of 1791) the rights of egoistic man separated from his fellow
> men and from the community. (OJQ, CW3: 164)

Why tear down barriers just in order to erect one no less fundamental? To
grasp why Marx was so critical of the French revolutionary declaration
of the rights of man it is useful to focus for a moment on the distinction
between the civil and the political in this text. We have seen Marx's way
of describing the distinction, but something like this distinction had been
mainstream in political thought for decades. Indeed, it was key to what
was portrayed in liberal thought as a great emancipatory development.
Protection from a domineering state – the sphere of politics – was considered
necessary, and the best way to achieve this was to establish civil society as
a benign sphere of individual freedom. This ostensibly benign sphere would
be guarded against the political, and indeed even the democratic, decision
making of the state. Marx believed that the acceptance of this separation
of civil society from political decision making meant that civil society had
become the dominant partner in its relationship with the political sphere of
the state. The autonomy of civil society in turn meant that those with the
resources of property were free to exploit the labour of the disadvantaged
(Pierson, 1996: 67–8). Marx found the French declaration of rights

> still more puzzling when we see that the political emancipators go so far
> as to reduce citizenship, and the political community, to a mere means
> for maintaining these so-called rights of man, that therefore the citoyen
> is declared to be the servant of egoistic homme, that the sphere in which
> man acts as a communal being is degraded to a level below the sphere in
> which he acts as a partial being, and that, finally, it is not man as citoyen,
> but man as bourgeois who is considered to be the essential and true man.
> (OJQ, CW3: 164)

It was not enough to build a supposedly perfect political state, while
leaving the existing civil society in place. As he put it: 'All the preconditions
of this egoistic life continue to exist in *civil society outside* the sphere of the
state, but as qualities of civil society' (OJQ, CW3: 153–4). Even if a political

state were fully developed, he went on: 'a human being] leads a twofold life, a heavenly and an earthly life: life in the *political community*, in which he considers himself a *communal being*, and life in *civil society*, in which he acts as a *private individual*, regards other men as a means, degrades himself into a means, and becomes the plaything of alien powers' (OJQ, CW3, 153–4).

'Heavenly' and 'earthly' echo Feuerbach's account of the projections and abstractions of religious thought. Marx notes that in the North American states where there was no longer a state religion, a still greater religiosity was fostered. People thought they were free, because they were free to worship as they pleased, but they were actually influenced by the ideology associated with private property (OJQ, CW3: 150–3). Religious freedom obscures this exploitation. Marx's view on the separation of civil society from the political sphere is related to his view of religion and ideology. As Denys Turner (1991: 323–4) has suggested, Marx considered that religion had an ideological function and a recursive nature. Religion was ideological in that it misconstrued the particular world by presenting that world through the prism of a belief in a false world. This is recursive in that feedback occurs as individuals as social agents act in their relationships on the basis of the misconstrual. This fostered false consciousness and indeed alienation.

The relevance of this discussion in *On the Jewish Question* for Marx's theory of alienation can be seen if one turns to the pages of the *Paris Manuscripts* where Marx criticized mainstream political economy for starting with the fact of private property and for expressing the material process though which it passed in 'general, abstract formulas' (EPM, CW3: 270). Political economy accepts these formulas as laws without comprehending them and thus without demonstrating that they reflected the institution of private property. Political economy could, therefore, not account for the division between labour and capital. It took as necessary what was historically contingent. On the other hand, it took for granted as accidental circumstances (both things like economic crises or imbalances, and industrial or social innovations), what was actually the 'expression of the necessary course of development' (EPM, CW3: 271) of the society based on private property. It was, therefore, necessary now 'to grasp the whole estrangement connected with the *money* system' (EPM, CW3: 271). In this process the more wealth the workers produced the poorer, proportionately, they became as they in turn became in effect ever cheaper commodities themselves. The object which labour produces, he went on,

> confronts it as *something alien*, as a *power independent* of the producer. The product of labour is labour which has been embodied in an object, which has become material: it is the *objectification* of labour. Labour's realisation is its objectification. Under these economic conditions this realisation of labour appears as *loss of realisation* for the workers; objectification as *loss of the object and bondage to it*; appropriation as *estrangement, as alienation*. (EPM, CW3: 272)

To better appreciate what Marx was saying about the connection of estrangement/alienation with the money system one needs to recognize that, for him, the basic cause of alienation in modernity is money. For this purpose, it is useful to turn to the comments Marx made in the same year (1844) on James Mill's book *Elements of Political Economy*. 'Mill', he argued, had, like many other modern political economists, committed the mistake 'of stating the abstract law without the change or continual supersession of this law through which alone it comes into being' (CJM, CW3: 211). In brief, Mill is not a historical or dialectical thinker. To discuss the money system in the abstract terms of scientific law was to overlook the dynamic human activity which created that system and thereafter maintained it. 'The essence of money is not,' Marx insisted, 'in the first place, that property is alienated in it, but that the mediating activity or movement, the human, social act by which man's products mutually complement one another, is estranged from man and becomes the attribute of money, a material thing outside man' (CJM, CW3: 212). Money was the fictional entity projected from out of human social production. It is clear that Marx is analysing the situation in a manner parallel to how we discussed Hess, earlier. As it was human beings themselves who had produced the alienated, mediating activity served by money, they had dehumanized themselves, and continued to do so, thus maintaining the system which enslaved them. Humans, moreover, did not recognize what they were doing themselves, instead perceiving their activity and the relations between them as a power independent of them. The alien mediator, as Marx described the money system, 'now becomes a real God, for the mediator is the real power over what it mediates to me'. In Marx's thought money had come to take the place of the God which Feuerbach saw as the most important creation of the alienation process – a creation which mediated and maintained that process.

Important, but unstated here is the human trait of emotion. We cannot understand human beings and their society if we continue to view their thought solely in terms of rationality, thus ignoring emotion. If we do so, then we miss something important in human nature. Moreover, this was fully understood by Marx. Without emotion the feeling of shame that would enable us to escape the egoism that is unnatural to the species-being could never arise. We could never escape alienation (Weyher, 2012). We could never feel exploited, never want change and never engage in the struggle for emancipation. Hence, as will become clearer in the chapter of this book on Emancipation, emotion is a key, implicit feature of the theory of the first Marx.

Alienation in the writings of 1844

In 1843, one year before Marx wrote the *Paris Manuscripts*, Engels had written his paper *Outlines of a Critique of Political Economy*, which was published in 1844 in the final issue of Marx's journal the *Deutsch–Französische Jahrbücher*. Marx was impressed with Engels' work and the 'Outline' is often considered to be the inspiration for Marx's critique of the economics and politics of the capitalist system (Seed, 2010: 24–5). Marx himself acknowledged its influence in his preface to the *Paris Manuscripts* (EPM. CW3: 232) and, reflecting on his own intellectual development in 1859, its brilliance (CPE, CW29: 264). Certainly, starting in 1844, Marx's account of alienation and human emancipation became increasingly economic in its focus. Engels' 'Outline' also had a more specific impact on Marx's view of alienation. The following words by Engels are interesting in this respect:

> Just as capital has already been separated from labour, so labour is now in turn split for a second time: the product of labour confronts labour as wages, is separated from it, and is in its turn as usual determined by competition – there being, as we have seen, no firm standard determining labour's share in production. If we do away with private property, this unnatural separation also disappears. Labour becomes its own reward, and the true significance of the wages of labour, hitherto alienated, comes to light – namely, the significance of labour for the determination of the production costs of a thing. (OCPE, CW3: 431)

The connection of alienation to labour in the domain of private property had obviously struck him as important. In the brief notes he made in summary of the 'Outline', Marx did not mention Engels' comment that the true significance of the wages of labour is alienated when human relations are dominated by the institution of private property. However, the passage in which Engels made this point had clearly struck a chord with Marx, as he made the following notes:

> The separation of capital from labour. The separation of capital and profit. The division of profit into profit and interest ... Profit, the weight that capital puts in the scales when the costs of production are determined, remains inherent in capital, and the latter reverts to labour. The separation of labour and wages. The significance of wages. The significance of labour in determining the production costs. The split between land and the human being. Human labour divided into labour and capital. (SFEA, CW3: 375–6)

In the 'Comments on James Mill' that he wrote early in 1844, Marx discusses alienation as a consequence of private property in terms not dissimilar to those of Engels.

> Let us suppose that we had carried out production as human beings ... .
> In the individual expression of my life I would have directly created your

expression of your life, and therefore in my individual activity I would have directly confirmed and realised my true nature, my human nature, my communal nature .... My work would be a free manifestation of life, hence an enjoyment of life. Presupposing private property, my work is an *alienation of life,* for I work *in order to live,* in order to obtain for myself the *means* of life. My work *is not* my life. (CJM, CW3: 227–8)

(The full significance of what Marx means by 'My work *is not* my life' will become clear in the 'Emancipation' chapter of the present study.) The focus on political economy that Marx began to adopt, influenced by Engels, was thus being interlinked with Marx's earlier philosophy in a way that developed a distinctive view of alienation. As Mészáros (2005: 69) suggests, in *Critique of the Hegelian Philosophy of Right [Law]* Marx had already begun to express considerable concern about division in society, the external determination of the individual and the divorce of man from his objective being in the existing civilization. Mészáros (2005: 73–4) also notes that in the separate article *Critique of the Hegelian Philosophy of Right: Introduction* Marx had (as mentioned in the previous section of the present chapter) begun to insist that human self-alienation in its secular form needed to be unmasked, and that the primary task for philosophy was to do so. Thus, the earlier work remained crucial to the development of his views in 1844; Marx became a *philosopher* of political economy. The convergence of these ideas can be seen in a passage from his 'Comments' on James Mill's writings on political economy. 'To say that *man* is estranged from himself', Marx insisted,

is the same thing as saying that the *society* of this estranged man is a caricature of his *real community,* of his true species-life, that his activity therefore appears to him as a torment, his own creation as an alien power, his wealth as poverty, the *essential bond* linking him with other men as an unessential bond, and separation from his fellow men, on the other hand, as his true mode of existence, his life as a sacrifice of his life, the realisation of his nature as making his life unreal, his production as the production of his nullity, his power over an object as the power of the object over him, and he himself, the lord of his creation, as the servant of this creation. (CJM, CW3: 217)

Turning to the *Paris Manuscripts* of 1844 one finds, in the section entitled 'Estranged Labour', four aspects of alienation which take place as ownership and control of the work process is taken over by the capitalist employers, and the capitalist division of labour subsequently prevents people from accomplishing creative work. These aspects are alienation from (1) the product; (2) the activity of labour as mentioned at the beginning of this chapter; (3) the species-being, humanity being a particular creative species characterized by their work and production of things from nature; and

(4) other workers who are seen as rivals, this being the practical expression of alienation from the species (EPM, CW3: 272–7). This elaboration may have been inspired by Engels, but Marx's analysis is much more nuanced and philosophically penetrating, and takes its lead from his own account of human being as essentially productive.

The object which labour produces, Marx argued, 'confronts it as *something alien,* as a *power independent* of the producer' (EPM, CW3: 272). The 'more powerful labour becomes', he stressed, 'the more powerless becomes the worker' (EPM, CW3: 273). Marx presented the first two aspects of the estrangement or alienation of labour, as practical human activity, as follows:

> (1) The relation of the worker to the *product of labour* as an alien object exercising power over him. This relation is at the same time the relation to the sensuous external world, to the objects of nature, as an alien world inimically opposed to him. (2) The relation of labour to the *act of production* within the *labour* process. This relation is the relation of the worker to his own activity as an alien activity not belonging to him; it is activity as suffering, strength as weakness, begetting as emasculating, the worker's *own* physical and mental energy, his personal life – for what is life but activity? – as an activity which is turned against him, independent of him and not belonging to him. Here we have *self-estrangement,* as previously we had the estrangement of the *thing.* (EPM, CW3: 275)

Notice, in the first of these, the reference to Feuerbach's notion of the 'sensuous'. My being as a sensuous being is alienated insofar as my senses can only apprehend things in terms framed by the alienation, by private property. The senses become conceived as subjective and 'neutrally' receptive to what philosophers later would call 'sense data' – something that we, as individuals, just 'have' (EPM, CW3: 300). (That is the same passage where Marx makes appreciative reference to Hess.) Such objects bear no relation to me or my activity. Thus, within the domain of private property, then, I am alienated both from the product of my labour and, for the same reasons, from all sensuous existence. Sensuous objects should however be originally social in their nature, objects of human need and activity, sensed as part of a produced human world. In other words, the genuine meaning of an 'object' is to be within a world that human beings have produced, and to which human beings belong, as the realization of their fulfilled species-being. 'Through this production, nature appears as *his* work and his reality. The object of labour is, therefore, the *objectification of man's species-life:* for he duplicates himself not only, as in consciousness, intellectually, but also actively, in reality, and therefore he sees himself in a world that he has created' (EPM, CW3, 277). Importantly, when Marx writes 'sees himself' in that last sentence, he means both 'conceives' and 'is consciousness' of himself, but he also means quite literally, the *sense* of seeing. 'The abolition of private property is therefore the complete *emancipation* of all human senses and qualities' (EPM, CW3: 300).

The second form of alienation is self-alienation. Human being or life is productive, that is to say, *active* through and through. For there to be a part of my activity that is conceived of as *not mine* is grotesque, an 'emasculation' of the worker's life. Thus, the worker 'feels at home when he is not working' and is most free when he pursues primarily animal functions (eating, sleeping, procreating), and least free, least human, when producing (EPM, CW3: 274–5).

The third and fourth aspects Marx argued could be deduced from the first two. Human beings each treated themselves as universal in that they saw themselves in terms of the actual, living human species. Each human must maintain a continual interchange with nature. Nature is thus each person's 'inorganic body' not just because it provides the material means of life (air, food, etc.), but because nature becomes, as a produced object, an integral part of the fulfilment of humans as productive beings (what Marx here calls the 'spiritual' nature of the human). This idea follows from Marx's treatment of the genuine meaning of an object, which we looked at earlier. Alienation from the active functions of life changes his view of life activity into merely a separable means of satisfying individual needs. The species character of human life is thus neglected, along with its human realization *within* nature (EPM, CW3: 277). This means that the human being is thereby estranged not only from his/her own body, but also from the very *human* aspect of life.

The first three forms of alienation thus bring about the fourth, for when each person confronts herself, s/he also confronts other human beings. 'What applies to a man's relation to his work, to the product of his labour and to himself,' Marx argued, 'also holds of a man's relation to the other man, and to the other man's labour and object of labour.' This, he went on, meant that 'the proposition that man's species-nature is estranged from him means that one man is estranged from the other, as each of them is from man's essential nature' (EPM, CW3: 277). Consciousness of ourselves as belonging to a species or, equivalently, consciousness of others as constitutive for our own being is a key part of what differentiates us from animals. Human species-being is cooperative production. Labour within private property individualizes human beings, making the liberal characterization of the 'real' human being as the egoistic being in civil society (which Marx analyses in *On the Jewish Question*) seem plausible or natural. Consciousness of sociability is ruled out, the possibility of cooperation seems fanciful (workers are put in competition with one another) and so workers are alienated from the species-being.

Marx went on to make a crucial point that had important implications in linking the different parts of his philosophy together. He argued that although alienation appeared to be the result of private property, in fact private property was originally the product of alienated labour. After this initial causation the relationship between private property and alienation becomes reciprocal (EPM, CW3: 279–80). What Marx meant was that as what they produced became alien to them, in the course of their exploitation, the notion of property as something that could be private came to be institutionalized, and was conceived as the 'natural' and 'just' way for human beings to be. Through alienated labour, initially failing to understand their cooperative species-being, human beings produce themselves and their world as one characterized by alienation at every turn in the form of private property. The money system becomes crucial once again in this respect. 'The distorting and confounding of all human and natural qualities' which, for Marx, was in effect 'the divine power of money', lay in 'its character as men's estranged, alienating and self-disposing species-nature. Money is the alienated ability of mankind' (EPM, CW3: 325). As was discussed earlier, in his comments on Mill's *Elements of Political Economy* Marx identified the mediating function of money. 'In effecting this mediation', Marx stressed in the *Paris Manuscripts*, money was 'the truly creative power' (EPM, CW3: 325).

Marx had complained in his comments on Mill that humans had themselves created money as this alien mediator and, moreover, produced the world in such a way as to maintain it so. Now if the mediator had been created and maintained, one can assume that it could be abolished. This is a hugely significant step in that it indicates that Marx did see a way out of the condition of alienation. In the case of human beings this involved the production not only of goods, but also their society and indeed themselves. Because the condition of alienation, and the system of private property, had been historically produced by human beings, it could be produced otherwise. If they could become aware of their own alienation, people would see private property for what it was: an institution which was contrary to the fulfilment of human nature. They could, to return to the eleventh thesis on Feuerbach which he penned the year after the *Paris Manuscripts*, thus change their own world, themselves included. Marx believed that humans would eventually overcome alienation by regaining control over their creations – the material and other things they produced – in a communist society. This would not be a crude form of communism involving simply the communalizing of property, but true communism where private property would no longer be even desired. Individual egoism, and egoism 'fulfilled' as the having of things, is a historical product of an alienated, inhuman world. As Ollman (1976: 132) put it, 'for Marx, unalienation is the life man leads in communism'.

Alienation continued to feature in Marx's writing in *The German Ideology*, written in 1945 and 1846, although importantly the terminology changes (we discussed this in the previous chapter). He and Engels argued that the abolition of alienation could only be achieved when the condition had become intolerable, with the majority of the populace becoming propertyless at a time when a great increase of productive power had contradicted the existing wealth and culture (GI, CW5: 48). People would gain control of the mode of their mutual relations. Marx and Engels developed the materialist conception of history (which they had earlier discussed less systematically in *The Holy Family*) arguing that the socio-economic process forms the basis of human society, from which politics, the law, religion and so on all derive.

In his later works, Marx would refer to these derivative elements as the superstructure and sometimes uses the word 'estrangement'. There has, however, been considerable debate in recent decades whether the later Marx actually considered estrangement/alienation to be an issue worthy of debate, and whether he held a different view of human nature – or perhaps did not hold one at all (Cowling, 1989; Hammen, 1980). Nevertheless, we are concerned in this book only with the first Marx, and the aspects of a political philosophy that he was building before he and Engels left the manuscript of *The German Ideology* for the mice.

Alienation means that cooperative production, the essence of the human, somehow loses its original meaning. Marx believed that alienation was a process that provided the conditions for *exploitation*. Hence, the discussion in the next chapter of his views on exploitation builds on that of the aspects of his thought – production and alienation – which the present and previous chapters have offered.

CHAPTER FOUR

Exploitation

Having examined the place of production and alienation in Marx's early political philosophy, this chapter turns to the related but rather less prominent theme of exploitation. It is not uncommon to find discussion of exploitation as a theme in Marx's later work, such as *Capital* (see, e.g. Holmstron, 1977; Cohen, 1988: 209–38; Laycock, 1999; Fine and Saad-Filho, 2010: 27–43). What is less widely acknowledged is that exploitation and a number of related issues represent a theme which is intertwined with those of production and alienation in his work of the early to late 1840s – even though this is less pronounced than in the later works.

In the 1840s Marx used the German term *Ausbeutung* when he referred to what is in English, which in turn follows the French, termed 'exploitation'. Before Marx's time, 'exploitation' had mainly been used to refer to the industrial use of land or materials (Williams, 1981: 130) – just as today we might talk about the 'exploitation of natural resources' without necessarily implying anything negative about such activity. Indeed, Marx (EPM, CW3: 264–5 and 270) himself sometimes used the word in this way in 1844. This raises the question, which we will discuss later, concerning how to understand exploitation in its newer, normative meaning. The concept is in play, though, much more often than the word *Ausbeutung*. So, like with 'production', we shall have to use the context in order to ascertain its presence.

Our broad, initial definition of exploitation is that exploitation occurs when one individual or group uses another for the former's ends. Such a formulation obviously evokes one key version of the Kantian moral law, about treating others as ends in themselves and never as means. In that sense, exploitation designates a very broad moral category indeed, and as we shall see, this is where the very early Marx begins. However, such exploitation is easy to identify; exploitation becomes a problem requiring some other, more subtle form of analysis only when it is the condition of alienation that lies behind it, permitting some act to serve the interests of one group at the expense of another. Indeed, for Marx, as the mutable element of human nature undergoes change, the contradictions driving this change, and generating alienation, as well as the experiencing of these contradictions will vary. In this way, the condition of alienation appears and feels normal, and human beings individually and collectively thus become ripe for exploitation. Some people in the powerful classes, moreover, take advantage of opportunities to exploit not only other individuals but also the system that enables them to help their own situation by in some way harming others. Of course, this exploitation need not be conscious or malicious – it too will have been naturalized, and may even bear the banner of, say, liberalism.

Now, one would look in vain for a lengthy analysis of exploitation focusing specifically on this problem in one of the early books, chapters or papers of Marx. It is, rather, found in a variety of other discussions in Marx and Engels' work of the period. Later this chapter will consider the usefulness of Wolff's work to the analysis of Marx's view of exploitation. Wolff's discussion is mainly, but not entirely, concerned with Marx's writings in political economy, but nevertheless has broader significance. First, however, it is worthwhile to note another very relevant article. Written by Allen Buchanan, it identifies various examples of the several types of exploitation one finds in Marx's work, including some from the period of the early to mid-1840s with which we are concerned.

The meanings of exploitation: reflecting on Buchanan's three-way distinction

To a significant extent, Buchanan's article helps clarify what might seem to be a rather confusing array of examples of the term 'exploitation' in the works of the early Marx. For Buchanan (1977: 122):

> Marx's work includes three distinct but related conceptions of exploitation: (a) a conception of exploitation in the labor process in capitalism, (b) a transhistorical conception of exploitation which applies not only to the labor process in capitalism but to the labor processes of all class-divided societies, and (c) a general conception of exploitation which is not limited to phenomena within the labor process itself.

To start with the last of Buchanan's trio, the *general* conception of exploitation refers to the very broad definition with which we started: exploitation as immoral use of others as means rather than ends. Now, within its scope Buchanan's threefold categorization makes good sense given the complexity of Marx's views of not only exploitation but also human nature – his thought on each of these two concepts identifying both transhistorical and historical elements. The transhistorical element of human nature was, as we have said, immanent to human beings; Marx's thought on this transhistorical element was characterized by the analysis of social production as a core feature of humanity (Struhl, 2016: 86–7). The transhistorical aspect – or in other words the aspect which remains constant despite changes in the social, economic and political environment, and indeed changes in humans themselves – can potentially lead to change in the temporary, historical element as people realize that their experience in the present epoch does not allow them to achieve human flourishing. They can thus overcome their condition of alienation and subsequently engineer their own emancipation. This will mean that people need to recognize, address and surmount the exploitation which, being a condition of capitalist society, may have hitherto appeared to be something that simply has to be endured.

Another way of distinguishing between the types of exploitation in what Buchanan refers to as conceptions (a) and (b) can be found in Gill Hands' introductory book on Marx. As she puts it: 'Marx believed that there had always been exploitation but it was only under the capitalist system that exploiting others became the normal way of working' (Hands, 2010: 101). Hands certainly packs a lot into this simple sentence, which is for that reason illuminating as a way into Marx's thought on the topic. Perhaps the key word here is 'normal', which includes both the naturalizing typical of alienation and the systematic character of the exploitation that we will be emphasizing here. We take it that Hands, although very briefly, indicates the systemic aspect which Buchanan neglects.

Buchanan's three conceptions do help draw attention to the richness in Marx's thought on exploitation – richness which is neglected if one takes a reductionist approach such as that of the analytical Marxist philosopher Jon Elster. From his methodological individualist analysis of Marx's work Elster (1986: 79) suggests that 'Marx's notion of exploitation has a very specific content.' 'A person is exploited, in Marx's sense,' Elster (1986: 79–80) goes on, 'if he performs more labor than is necessary to produce the goods that he consumes.' While Elster's interpretation is indeed useful to account very concisely for Buchanan's first and second types, it neglects the third, general type which, as will be discussed in the present chapter, is crucial to the understanding of Marx's thought on exploitation in the early to mid-1840s.

Within its own terms Buchanan's analysis helps one grasp some key points and purposes that arise from Marx's rather casual uses of terms – usage that can be mistaken for situations which T. D. Weldon (1953: 52 and 121–4) once identified as 'question-begging'. That is, in using the word the user assumes what s/he is trying to conclude. Specifically, Weldon (1953: 52) suggested that 'Marx employed ... words like "exploitation" which have no place in the kind of positivist account of political phenomena which he professes to offer us.' Whether or not Weldon was including Marx's work of the early to mid-1840s in the positivist account, it is significant that the philosophical aspect of this early work was indeed normative rather than positivist (we use the term 'philosophical aspect' here because, as we have seen, Marx (TF, CW5: 5) claimed to go beyond philosophy as previously understood, and seek to change the world). We are not concerned in this study to question whether Weldon was right in his suggestion that Marx sought in his later work to be positivist. It is certainly the case that in *The German Ideology* which is clearly a transitional text, Marx and Engels claim to employ a positivist method. 'The premises from which we begin,' they insist, 'are not arbitrary ones, not dogmas but real premises ... They are the real individuals, their activity and the material conditions of their life' (GI, CW5: 31). But even here, they have a hard time disguising their repugnance at the condition of such real individuals, which would seem to lend weight to Weldon's argument that Marx tried (perhaps unwittingly) to combine positivist and normative aspects coherently.

Obviously enough, normative words are permissible provided there is no attempt to surreptitiously smuggle them in, under the pretence of being dispassionate observations. Normative terms are perfectly permissible in explicitly normative writing. A standard definition of normative philosophy, which is a tradition of stretching back at least as far as Plato, is that it seeks not only (1) to clarify concepts but also (2) to engage in the critical evaluation of beliefs (Raphael, 1990: 5–20).

Weldon's objection, however, might be understood as the claim that Marx and Engels could not, in principle, be normative in this sense. A positivist cannot offer value judgements; facts do not lead to values. According to such a way of thinking, within dialectical materialism the end of capitalism in a communist revolution was a historical necessity, and not some kind of moral or political 'ideal' to be pursued. But this is a profound misunderstanding of Marx (and Engels), at least during this early period. The positivist approach adopted in *The German Ideology* does not require them to put their normative evaluations to one side. This is because behind the scenes, so to speak, is a conception of the full possibilities of a liberated human essence. This latter *also* is arrived at, later in the same book, in a positivist manner, but is understood to contain immanently a normative sense of justice or morality. We indicated this in the previous chapters by using the Aristotelian notion of flourishing. The full conception of the human is a normative one, however, without our therefore having to doubt (on that basis) Marx and Engels' broadly positivist method. Similarly, we would have no cause to dispute a cancer researcher's scientific objectivity just because she desires to help people. Weldon's objection assumes a fact-value distinction that it was precisely Marx's project to dismantle (and here again following Feuerbach). Morality is not an idea distinct from and above the human condition, but rather nothing but this condition properly understood. Or, to express the same point differently, positivism as distinguished from some normative evaluation is just another version of philosophy seeking to understand the world, rather than to change it. While Weldon was correct in his own terms in asserting that such terms have no place in positivist philosophy Marx may well, if he had lived until the 1950s, have offered the following answer: 'So what? The point is to change the world not just philosophise about it.' To recognize what Marx was doing we need to understand that he and Engels were key thinkers of their time who were introducing a new interpretation of exploitation in order not only to try to make sense of social problems but also, crucially, to find a way to resolve those problems.

Alternatively, the 'question-begging' accusation of Weldon might refer to the use of evaluating terms prior to or independently of the justification of their content. In other words, Weldon might have accepted our analysis of Marx's project, or at least been willing to accept that a positivist form of analysis might eventually yield a result that had normative implications; specifically, it might demonstrate that certain people live in conditions of exploitation. However, his point is that Marx and Engels do not, so to speak, wait until the evidence is in, but rather use the normative terminology in order to manipulate the evidence. Their 'professed' positivism is therefore not genuine. This is indeed a serious claim (in our analogy earlier, the cancer researcher would be falsifying data). However, this cannot simply be a case of 'at what point' in a text a term is used; an author should be able to anticipate the future course of her or his argument with impunity. What is important for our purpose is that question-begging terms such as 'exploitation' – terms that clearly offer an evaluation rather than just a description – do have a place in normative philosophy to emphasize a point as long as the meaning is elaborated and justified elsewhere in the argument. So, what we need to do is to show that Marx and Engels do have such a justification, and do not simply either make assumptions or allow their values to twist the evidence. This we have been doing since the beginning, reconstructing Marx's overall analysis in a way that does not simply leave any concept unexplained.

Turning again to Buchanan (1977: 124–5), he elaborates on his suggestion that one can find a general conception of exploitation in Marx's thought by focusing on a passage in *The German Ideology* in which Marx and Engels criticize the Enlightenment philosopher Holbach for being an early bourgeois, utilitarian thinker. Utilitarianism is basically a doctrine that the well-being of individuals should be maximized. The actions that are deemed right by utilitarians are those that maximize well-being, whether it is aggregate or average utility that is to be maximized (Knowles, 2001: 23–37). Whichever form utilitarianism takes, it is based on an analysis of the utility of individual human beings. There are indeed grounds for portraying Holbach as such a thinker (Arblaster, 1984: 182–91). Nevertheless, even if there is any doubt about this, it is insignificant for our purpose. What is significant is the relevance of Marx and Engels' criticism of Holbach to the general conception of exploitation. Holbach, according to Marx and Engels, depicted 'the entire activity of individuals in their mutual intercourse … as a relation of utility and utilisation' (GI, CW5: 409). In this case, Marx and Engels suggested, the utility relation means 'that I derive benefit for myself by doing harm to someone else (*exploitation de l'homme par l'homme*)'. This is important because, once we recognize that Marx thus conceived of exploitation in a general way *as well as* in the way specific to the labour process in capitalism, we can begin to see how exploitation was a concern even *before* his work came to be influenced by Engels (as was discussed in the previous chapter), leading Marx to turn his attention in 1844 to political economy.

By focusing their attention on harm in relation to exploitation, Marx and Engels were engaging with an issue on which, in the early- to mid-nineteenth century, influential British and German intellectual traditions overlapped one another. One of the concerns shared by the traditions was in the sorts of encroachments upon individual actions that were deemed justifiable and the extent to which such encroachments should be allowed. John Stuart Mill (1991: 2, 64, 114–15) acknowledged in his essay *On Liberty* of 1859 that he was drawing on the German thinker Alexander von Humboldt's philosophy. In his *Autobiography* of 1873, moreover, Mill (1924: 216–17) said that his own political philosophy in *On Liberty* reflected ideas that had been circulating around Europe in previous generations. The work of German intellectuals such as Humboldt and Johann Wolfgang von Goethe was, he suggested, particularly important in this respect. Mill had as early as 1832 been considering the implications of what he would later call the harm principle for governmental policy, which should ensure that society does not inflict evil on any of its members for the sake of good for others (Ten, 1980: 76). Marx and Engels cited Goethe's work throughout *The German Ideology* to support their arguments. As will be discussed later in the present chapter, where in that book Marx and Engels were concerned with exploitation this was because of the consequences in terms of *harm*, to both particular people and the system of which they were parts, in the pursuit of self-interested, individualist benefit. Whereas with his harm principle in the 1850s Mill sought to devise a better form of self-interested individualism, Marx was concerned in the previous decade to criticize such individualism and replace it with a collectivist alternative. While Mill considered that he was contributing to the overlapping British and German intellectual traditions, Marx in the 1840s was arriving at views that would later be considered to have founded a parallel, socialist tradition to the liberal one into which Mill placed himself. That Mill (1976: 335–58) later became aware that this was so can be seen in his 'Chapters on Socialism' of 1879 in which, without mentioning Marx by name, he criticized the continental, revolutionary form of socialism because of its attack on individual, private property.

A problem with individual private property, in Marx's view, was that it lay at the heart of exploitation in modern times. In *The German Ideology*, Marx and Engels criticized utilitarianism for not grasping that attempts to make systems of private property less exploitative of some people by others would, even if they could be implemented, merely result in mutual exploitation. Utilitarianism is concerned with usefulness, and therefore to arrange a society on utilitarian principles would be to consider human beings simply in terms of how useful they are to one another. Such principles had been influential in recent centuries and by the eighteenth century liberation was considered, from the standpoint of the bourgeoisie, as free competition. The sort of consciousness corresponding to this bourgeois practice was 'the consciousness of mutual exploitation as the universal mutual relation of all individuals' (GI, CW5: 410). Marx's most memorable comment on mutual exploitation appears at the point where he teases Stirner for advocating that society become a voluntary union of egoists. Stirner (or Sancho as Marx nicknames him), Marx and Engels (GI, CW5: 416) assert playfully,

> therefore, expresses the pious wish that in his union, based on mutual exploitation, all the members will be equally powerful, cunning, etc., etc., so that each can exploit the others to exactly the same extent as they exploit him, and so that no one will be 'cheated' in regard to his 'most natural and obvious interests' or be able to 'satisfy his needs at the expense of others'.

Mutual exploitation here can be considered as a variant of Buchanan's third category: general exploitation.

Marx and Engels' criticism of utilitarianism and the ideas of Stirner are also relevant to the issue of the division of labour we have discussed in previous chapters. The link between exploitation and division of labour is indeed important. Having ridiculed Stirner's idea of the voluntary union of egoists, Marx and Engels outlined its implications. Stirner's union must, they insisted, mean one of two things. First, the equal power of all that Stirner envisaged would consist 'in that everyone should become "omnipotent", i.e., all should become impotent in relation to one another' (GI, CW5: 416). Alternatively, Stirner presupposed 'a society in which each can satisfy his needs unhampered, without doing so "at the expense of others", and in that case the theory of exploitation again becomes a meaningless paraphrase for the actual relations of individuals to one another' (GI, CW5: 417).

For Marx and Engels, neither of these possible implications reflected the reality of societies based on the accumulation of private property by means of exploitation of others. Such societies necessarily involved division of labour. Marx and Engels noted the following feature of utility theory: 'With division of labour, the private activity of the individual becomes generally useful' (GI, CW5: 413). Now sometimes one may simply mean a division of work involved in a project which does not involve exploitation, such as the joint authorship of the present book for example; but the social aspect of labour's division is a feature of Marx and Engels' use of the term. As Sean Sayers (2011: 133–4) has discussed very clearly, they were concerned with societies in which labour is socially organized, involving the confinement of individuals to limited and specific activities in their work. Moreover, this was a vertical division of labour that involved social hierarchy in which those above had authority and those below endured subordination. This division of labour was thus a division between rulers and ruled. Division of labour, as Marx and Engels saw it, involves people of different social positions. Even if mutual exploitation is a feature of people of similar social positions, the exploitation involving a division of labour is actually the exploitation by people of one such social position of those of another such position. Marx and Engels expressed this division as follows in their assessment of modern society in *The German Ideology*: 'By taking into account the economic relations of rent, profit and wages, the definite relations of exploitation of the various classes were introduced, since the manner of exploitation depends on the social position of the exploiter' (GI, CW5: 413). Here, they were discussing bourgeois society. Hence, this is Buchanan's first category of exploitation: exploitation in the labour process that is a feature of capitalism.

The meanings of exploitation: looking beyond Buchanan's categorization

Although useful in the ways just discussed, the scope of Buchanan's threefold categorization is nevertheless rather too thin; nor does it help us to see exploitation in its link to the Feuerbachian account of alienation. We will be proposing a *five-way* distinction. The fourth, to be added to Buchanan's taxonomy, is that alienation in the sphere of religion, or even abstract philosophy such as Hegel's, makes possible a form of exploitation in those fields. Feuerbach (2012: 248), in the angry second edition Preface (dated 1843) to his *The Essence of Christianity*, writes of the effect the book has had: 'I have brought upon myself the displeasure of politicians … [including] those who use religion as a political weapon to suppress and repress people'. This is one example of a number of ways that alienation involved in Christianity can be manipulated to treat some individual or group as a means to an end.

In his introduction to a recent selection of Feuerbach's writings, Zawar Hanfi quotes a sentence he attributes to Marx from an article which praises Feuerbach's account of miracles over Strauss's. The latter does not realize that the 'wish to be free' is the 'first act of liberty'. The sentence quoted by Hanfi insists that 'there is no other road for you to *truth* and *freedom* except that leading through the Fiery-Brook [a pun on Feuerbach]' (Hanfi, 2013: 42). The sentence is in a short article of 1842 titled 'Luther as Arbiter Between Strauss and Feuerbach', which is included (in a slightly different translation to Hanfi's) in a selection of Marx's early writings edited by David Easton and Kurt H. Guddat (1997: 93–5), who likewise attribute it to Marx. Luther is thus a key point of reference. There is now some dispute over whether Marx did actually write the article (Pr, CW1: xxxiii).

Nevertheless, one does find a pertinent passage in Marx's *Contribution to the Critique of Hegel's Philosophy of Law. Introduction*, where Marx did write about Luther. It is clear that the Feuerbachian notions of religious alienation, as well as religious exploitation, are at stake: '*Luther*, we grant, overcame the bondage of *piety* by replacing it by the bondage *of conviction* [...] He turned priests into laymen because he turned laymen into priests. He freed man from outer religiosity because he made religiosity the inner man' (CCHPLI, CW3: 182). In other words, the Protestant Reformation, although freeing northern Europe from the exploitative yoke of the Catholic Church and the priests, generated its own more subtle exploitation in individualism. Likewise, exploitation is evident in, for example, *The Holy Family* in which Marx and Engels see the Young Hegelians as leveraging belief in the idealistic sense of critique, as being the only possible means of change, in order to inflate their own sense of importance – and indeed, such intellectual exploitation is the main line of satire in the book.

This fourth version of exploitation thus serves Marx as an intellectual link back to alienation just as Marx employs Feuerbach's notion of alienation as an initial model to generate his own account of alienation under conditions of capitalism, he can employ Feuerbach's notion of exploitation (the misuse by one group of another, insofar as the latter are alienated) as an initial model in generating his own account of exploitation. Here, we need say no more about this sense of exploitation.

The fifth sense of exploitation will be the major contribution of the remainder of this chapter. Our aim here is to show that a *systemic* account of exploitation is operative in early Marx, and not exclusively confined to his later work. First though, let us return to Buchanan's taxonomy.

Now, Buchanan's first sense of exploitation is the most obvious and well known. As we saw right at the end of the previous section, Marx certainly did discuss a particular sort of exploitation as a feature of capitalist society, which reflects the peculiarity of capitalism, in which the mutable element of human nature became more individualistic than before. What makes capitalism so distinctive is thus highly significant, especially if one is to grasp his reason for being so concerned with exploitation in this economic arrangement, even though it had been a feature of previous historical epochs. The self-interested pursuit of profit had been such a feature in those earlier epochs too; but what made such pursuit distinctive in the capitalist era was its *systematic* quality. In capitalism, renewed profit is relentlessly pursued in a methodical way. Neither immediate consumption nor political objectives are the main reason for such pursuit. Indeed, political objectives under capitalism are guided by the main reason, which is to make profit, which in a continual process is used in the attempt to make more and more profit (Saunders, 1995: 5).

In other words, while the form that exploitation takes in capitalism is distinct (this is Buchanan's first sense), we argue that no less important is the systematic quality of exploitation under capitalism (thus our new, fifth sense). Moreover, the systemic aspect is important to Marx's theory of change which will be discussed in the next chapter, as it helps substantiate his argument that historical progress proceeds through the resolution of contradictions and the subsequent generation of new forms of human life. In that regard, Marx considered it necessary to conceptualize the transhistorical aspects of exploitation, which ran in close parallel to the formulation that later became known as the materialist conception of history.

The various sorts of exploitation with which the early Marx dealt can be identified, albeit in a very different way than Buchanan, with reference to Wolff's paper 'Marx and Exploitation'. Wolff too offers a discussion of Marx's view of exploitation which identifies examples from his writings at different periods. According to Wolff, Marx's definition of exploitation 'is limited to relations of economic exchange under conditions where there is no justified right to capital; that is, to earn money purely in virtue of one's property holdings' (Wolff, 1999: 105). For Wolff (1999: 108–19), to thus fix the definition of a term by identifying precisely things to which the term refers is rather different than to explain the meaning of that term, and to fix a fully general definition is different than fixing a definition within an assumed model. At first glance it seems therefore that Wolff is thinking simply in terms of Buchanan's conception (a): exploitation in the labour process in capitalism. (Wolff's initial definition may be terminologically accurate, but misses the broader picture. Marx certainly had no reason to collapse the various concepts of exploitation into one, for that would have hamstrung his analysis, but it is also vital to understand the interconnections between various possible usages of 'exploitation'.)

Wolff's treatment can also, however, on closer inspection be seen to bring systemic exploitation into the picture. As was discussed in the previous two chapters, Marx criticized means of production in which human nature is abused and people are in a condition in which the historical, changeable aspect of their nature is manipulated. This is a condition that arises when private property gives some people the ability to exploit others – and in some cases, as will be touched on in a moment, some people get the ability to exploit one another – and the institutionalization of such property legitimates the condition. Alienation is linked to such institutionalization, which allows exploitation to be sustained. Exploitation of a person, Wolff (1999: 111) stresses, 'only happens because that person has exploitable circumstances'. Exploitation can be considered wrong, he adds, and as we will note later, in the Kantian terms of the categorical imperative, to exploit someone is to treat that person purely as a means to one's ends, and thus not to treat her/him as an end in himself/herself (Wolff, 1999: 112). To ask what determines how well-off someone should be is too general a question, as this would apply also to cases in which exploitation was not a factor. Hence, he argues, it is necessary to restrict one's attention 'to how well-off someone should be with respect to the particular transaction under consideration' (Wolff, 1999: 113).

According to Wolff's interpretation of Marx's view of exploitation in such terms, therefore, exploitation can be seen in the economic exchange if this involves one of three things: unfairness, as Kantians would suggest; avoidable suffering as would be considered the relevant issue by utilitarians; or the interference with flourishing as would be suggested by Aristotelians. To illustrate how exploitation can take place without specific instances of unfairness or suffering, Wolff argues, with reference to Marx's notion of mutual exploitation in *The German Ideology* and to some related comments in the *Paris Manuscripts* of 1844, that this is likely to violate flourishing norms (through the notion of a species-being). The nature of each party to an economic transaction under capitalism is degraded. Wolff (1999: 115–16) summarizes Marx's view on this in the *Paris Manuscripts* as follows:

> Each person is treated simply as a means to the pursuit of self-interest, rather than a member of the same community with needs of his or her own, and the capacity to confirm their own standing in the world as a species being ... Each person is forced, by the circumstance that they live under capitalist economic structures which make room for only certain sorts of interaction, to make a trade which leads both parties away from a properly flourishing life.

In this case the structure of the system built on the institution of private property involves exploitation – one need not identify specific examples of unfairness in relations between individuals. Furthermore, if people in some cases exploit one another, even though we would not suggest this is unfair in a narrow sense, they are each making each other worse off because a life of purely self-interest does not allow one to achieve human flourishing as a member of the species-being. Systematic exploitation, where founded upon alienation, is thus difficult to identify – for example, as we shall see it disguises itself as 'common sense' – because it avoids categorization under the standard categories of moral infraction between individuals. Instead, exploitation qua some form of harm becomes an exacerbated alienation of stunted forms of human life from the full potential of the human.

Another, specifically humanist, way of grasping the significance of systemic exploitation as a form of harm, and as a problem that could be overcome, can be illustrated by looking at one of Marx's very earliest extant writings. Let us turn to an essay he wrote at the age of 17. In it one can detect the effect of the humanist education he had received at a high school in which the German Enlightenment, in particular the work of Kant, was hugely prominent (McLellan, 2006: 7–8). This influence appears to have shaped Marx's view. Kant was well aware of broadly utilitarian approaches to moral philosophy, particularly in Hume, as well as the so-called enlightened egoism tradition in moral thought; he argues explicitly against them both in the second section of *Grounding for the Metaphysics of Morals* (Kant, 2002: 53–62). Likewise, as we mentioned earlier, Kant's formulation of the moral law in terms of persons as ends in themselves is one essential ingredient in the general meaning of exploitation. However, more to our purposes, in one of his lectures on pedagogy, published as a collection in 1803, Kant (1900: 10) had expressed the following view:

> In times past men had no conception of the perfection to which human nature might attain – even now we have not a very clear idea of the matter. This much, however, is certain: that no individual man, no matter what degree of culture may be reached by his pupils, can insure their attaining their destiny. To succeed in this, not the work of a few individuals only is necessary, but that of the whole human race.

In other words, the perfection of the individual through education is fully compatible with, and indeed effectively equivalent to, the perfection of the fully met needs of humans as a whole. Marx expressed a similar view in the early essay just mentioned, the topic of which was the choice of a profession, as his mind was beginning to be made up regarding the ethics surrounding exploitation. The chief guide to that choice was, as he saw it, the perception of one's own perfection as being inextricably linked to the welfare of mankind. It should not, he elaborated, 'be thought that these two interests could be in conflict, that one would have to destroy the other; on the contrary, man's nature is so constituted that he can attain his own perfection only by working for the perfection, for the good, of his fellow men' (RYM, CW1: 8).

While he did not in his essay on a choice of profession mention exploitation by name, one can see that to exploit another would, given this view of converging interests, be a corruption of the fundamental, transhistorical aspect of human nature. This is consistent with his thoughts in the mid-1840s, as discussed in the previous two chapters of the present book, which conceive of the transhistorical aspect basically in terms of cooperation and a community that is not simply a subsequent aggregate of individuals. An act, regardless of its utility for the individual or even for its utility for the happiness of the many considered as individuals, that was not directed at least in part towards the furtherance of the good of the human community as a whole was morally wrong – we might think of it as an *indirect* harm – and thus exploitative in our broad and general sense. Marx was concerned with exploitation from his earliest writings and his first forays into political thinking. As was clear from our discussion of Wolff's analysis, this general meaning of exploitation can take its primary meaning either from moral concepts that are mainly applicable to individuals (such as unfairness or direct harm) or from the more Aristotelian notion of flourishing, which is less concerned with relations among individuals than with the growth of the human itself. Of course, the more specific senses of exploitation (those related to alienation or property) come later.

The systematic meaning of exploitation in Marx

Buchanan (1977: 130) comes closest to the systemic meaning of exploitation insofar as he identifies an implicit link in Marx's discussion of alienation in *On the Jewish Question* to the conditions for exploitation. The passage Buchanan cites does indeed suggest that only by means of alienation does the human being act and produce in an egoistic way – a way that is dominated by the institution of money (OJQ, CW3: 174). Acting and producing in a way dominated by money does involve exploitation, as other individuals and society are thus used for self-interested purposes even if the others and society become worse off as a result. Buchanan's discussion here is thoughtful; however, he elicits insufficient evidence to convince those who might be sceptical of the link.

We suggest that the most illuminating place to begin hunting in early Marx for such a meaning of exploitation is elsewhere. Seven years after writing his essay on the choice of a profession, having in the meantime completed his doctoral dissertation, Marx had begun to make his mark as a radical journalist. In this role he wrote a lengthy article, 'Debates on the Law on Thefts of Wood', which was published in the *Rheinische Zeitung* in October 1842. He discussed the consequences of a recent piece of legislation passed by the Rhine Province Assembly. The new law introduced an interpretation of the gathering of fallen wood as theft. Marx argued that this case was a clear example of the state failing to fulfil its purpose. He had at this time yet to adopt the view that political activity to bring about radical reform by means of the state was asking too much given that the state in the era reflected the dominance of the institution of private property (Megill, 2002: 57–122). He thus had yet to make a decisive break from Hegelianism, or rather was located in the camp of the Young Hegelians, who believed that with suitable reforms the state could be developed in order to achieve democratic legal, social and political reforms (McLellan, 1969: 22–6; Breckman, 1999: 275–8). Nevertheless, as we have seen before, in these early writings one can find important ideas that he would develop rather than abandon even after that break.

Marx insisted in his article on the theft of fallen wood that the state should be defending and securing the welfare of the poor. The poor should have both a customary right and importantly a legal right to a decent standard of living (DLTW, CW1: 230–1). Nevertheless, he was well aware of the problem that powerful interests used the state for their own advantage and that this involved harming poor people. Although Marx did not actually describe it as such in this case it can, given what he wrote later in the article (as will be mentioned in a moment) and elsewhere in his work, be seen in terms of *exploiting* the poor. In the case of the gathering of firewood, considerations of individual utility can be seen in the attitude of the forest owner. Marx said that in the particular case on which he was reporting the owner did not merely demand compensation from the thief for the general value, but also value for their own individual benefit. The forest owner thus gives the value an individual character. Individualism is considered to be in the general interest. The forest owner's ostensibly practical argument was, according to Marx, as follows:

> This legal definition is good insofar as it is useful to me, for what is useful to me is good. But this legal definition is superfluous, it is harmful, it is unpractical, insofar as it is intended to be applied to the accused on the basis of a purely theoretical legal whim. Since the accused is harmful to me, it stands to reason that everything is harmful to me that lessens the harm coming to him. That is practical wisdom. (DLTW, CW1: 229–30)

In other words, according to this line of reasoning, the law was merely institutionalizing something that common sense tells us should be done. With phrases like 'it stands to reason' or 'practical wisdom', what Marx is drawing attention to is the fact that the forest owner's acts, while certainly self-interested, are not necessarily consciously exploitative, but are part of what has become naturalized, what everybody knows. That is, what is at stake here is not an individual, isolated sense of moral harm. Whether this particular land owner is aware of exploitation or not is just not the issue. Rather, the owner's reasoning and his acts are simply in accord with the values of alienation and exploitation that have become normalized within capitalism. In brief, such reasoning is part and parcel of the system.

Marx argued that the logic of selfishness had turned 'the authority of the state into a servant of the forest owner'. What was more, the state had ruled that those individuals who stole the fallen wood should in return engage in labour for the forest owners. The very structure of the state and the purpose of the administrative authorities were, he went on, 'degraded into an instrument of the forest owner' whose 'interest operated as the soul governing the entire mechanism' (DLTW, CW1: 245). 'Interest' was the key word here. As we have already seen in the earlier chapters of this study, Marx's work in the early to late 1840s can be seen in terms of a critique of human society in which self-interest was a dominant norm that helped institutionalize the system based on the assumption that private property was a natural phenomenon. Marx (DLTW, CW1: 247) argued that morality and humane reason had become mere phrases. Interest invented such phrases and portrayed deeds as noble 'when the results are of considerable advantage' and 'yield it profit at the expense of others'. 'All of that, all of it', he went on, was 'exploited only in order to convert the infringement of forest regulations into current coin for the forest owner, to make the infringer of forest regulations into a lucrative source of income … for the wood thief has become a capital for the forest owner'. Although Marx said that it was morality and reason that were exploited, we have to remember that this exploitation was conceived for the purpose of taking advantage of human beings in a society. Exploitation thus took place as part of the system. Systematic exploitation occurs when a form of human life develops an economic, political or legal framework that locks alienation in place and allows one class routinely and 'legitimately' to exploit another, all behind the mask of appearing to act in the general interest or at least 'naturally' and with 'common sense'. Such a system is likely to grow incrementally rather than be the result of some grand conspiracy. Indeed, the general interest is even assumed in good faith by some theorists and supporters of the framework, rather than this necessarily being a malicious lie.

The criticism of interest as a driving force in the case of the fallen wood helps distinguish Marx from the utilitarian tradition of which, as mentioned earlier, he was so scathing. Even in the later work of John Stuart Mill, who sought to develop the tradition in pursuit of 'the permanent interests of man as a progressive being' (Mill, 1991: 15), self-interest was still considered worthy of defence. Mill's harm principle forbade both bodily harm and harm to interests. Mill (1991: 104–5) does frame this as interests the protection of which benefits society – the general interests. Nevertheless, embedded in Mill's individualist theory is the principle that invites the kind of manipulation of reason with which Marx was concerned in the case of the fallen wood. Marx's collectivism, as we have already established, can be described as anti-reductionism rather than radical holism because it does not dismiss or underestimate the significance of the individual. Comparing and contrasting Marx and Mill in this respect helps demonstrate that Marx's criticism of the earlier utilitarians is of interest because utilitarianism as a doctrine cannot devise a non-exploitative form of individualism, however far it is developed in the liberal individualist tradition.

The exploitation involved in the case of the fallen wood was broader than that which takes place at the hands of some individual human beings over others. People of a certain group (the forest owners) were exploiting the entire system which is built on human relations but becomes something more than an aggregation of them. While, of course, we are not concerned in this book directly with Marx's later writings, it is useful when discussing this case to note that the broad conception of exploitation can be found in them. As Buchanan suggests after analysing a broad range of Marx's work: 'Marx's criticism is not just that the capitalist labor process is exploitative – his criticism is that capitalist society is exploitative through and through' (Buchanan, 1979: 129). Marx's commentary on the case of theft of fallen wood in the forest indicates that he indeed conceived of exploitation in such terms in his early work.

Although the system itself exploits, capitalism or any society based on private property is produced by human beings. There are thus two levels within exploitation. First, the system exploits; second, people either (a) exploit the system in full awareness that they are doing so in order to benefit from the exploitation it generates or (b) benefit from that system unconsciously as they are simply better placed within it than those who suffer the exploitation. In some cases, a person or group of persons might sometimes benefit from systemic exploitation while at other times be the ones who are being exploited. In the case of the wood-gatherers the forest owners seemed to be fully conscious that they were exploiting the system or at least with a high degree of consciousness but, as we noted earlier, there will be other cases where the individuals who benefit from exploitation are not so aware or are even in some way exploited themselves.

In such terms one can see that, although to count as exploitation a particular transaction need not necessarily involve unfairness (i.e. direct harm), the particular transactions take place within a broader system of unfairness. As was discussed earlier in the present chapter, the forest owner exploited the entire system. Two years later, in an article on 'The Condition of England' in the eighteenth century, Engels (CE, CW3: 485) discussed a broader form of exploitation in which a class exploited an entire system:

> This revolution through which British industry has passed is the foundation of every aspect of modern English life, the driving force behind all social development. Its first consequence was … the elevation of self-interest to a position of dominance over man. Self-interest seized the newly created industrial powers and exploited them for its own purposes; these powers, which by right belong to mankind, became, owing to the influence of private property, the monopoly of a few rich capitalists and the means to the enslavement of the masses.

One can see that, rather than it being a case of Marx suddenly being influenced by Engels in forming a view of exploitation, or vice versa, the two authors were each arriving at similar views on the topic that enabled them to work together, leading to *The German Ideology*.

That Marx was thinking in systemic, anti-reductionist terms about the possibility of emancipation from the exploitative system can be discerned from a letter of September 1843 he wrote to Ruge, published in their journal the *Deutsch-Französische Jahrbücher*. 'The system of industry and trade, of ownership and exploitation of people,' he suggested, 'leads even far more rapidly than the increase in population to a rupture within present-day society, a rupture which the old system is not able to heal, because it does not heal and create at all, but only exists and consumes' (LDFJ, CW3: 41) In another example later that year, in *Contribution to the Critique of Hegel's Philosophy of Law: Introduction*, Marx compared the ability, on the one hand, of the bourgeoisie to take advantage of the revolution in France in order to cement its dominant role with the inability, on the other hand, of the German bourgeoisie to do likewise. Purported emancipation would, however, actually amount to domination. 'Only in the name of the general rights of society,' he argued 'can a particular class lay claim to general domination.' 'For', he went on, 'the storming of this emancipatory position, and hence for the political exploitation of all spheres of society in the interests of its own sphere, revolutionary energy and intellectual self-confidence alone are not sufficient' (CCHPLI, CW3: 184–5). To do so it was also necessary to portray another class as wholly responsible for the defects of society, the main stumbling block to change, and to portray one's own class as representing the interests of the whole. The French bourgeoisie were able to portray the nobility and clergy as such in France, whereas in Germany no class was able to present itself as the challenger, on behalf of the nation, to a dominant class. What is significant here is that a class was exploiting the system, which in turn involves exploitation of individuals. In France, the emancipatory role would pass down over time through the classes until general emancipation had been achieved. Germany, however, 'did not go through the intermediary stages of political emancipation at the same time as the modern nations' (CCHPLI, CW3: 183). It had not even reached in practice the stages which it has overtaken in theory. General emancipation would therefore be achieved directly by means of the proletariat, which Marx described as the class with radical chains, emancipating itself and all other exploited estates and spheres of society. Emancipation will be discussed in far greater detail in the chapter after next.

Another way in which the two pieces of Marx's work in 1943 that we have been discussing are important is that they illustrate a position that he could not have taken from the methodological individualist approach. Elster (1985: 166; 1986: 79) employs this approach in his analysis and implicitly attributes it to Marx. For Elster, the normatively relevant concept of exploitation, which co-exists with an explanatory concept in Marx's work, lacks motivational force, as workers may not recognize exploitation, may be mistaken about it or may have more pressing concerns. It is, however, necessary to recognize Marx's anti-reductionist standpoint in order to grasp his view that, as was discussed briefly in the previous chapter, workers need to escape their condition of exploitation in order to break free from the ethos of self-interested individualism and thus to perceive that they are also parts, however important that they also are in of themselves, of a collective body capable of challenging the power of the people and system who exploit them. Only collectively as a class or estate can people achieve emancipation and flourish. A lone individual or even a large number of individuals operating independently could not achieve revolutionary results to escape exploitation, thus achieving major social change. Individually, individuals could only achieve their own emancipation, which would involve exploitation of other people. Nevertheless, on Marx's analysis, the German and French cases were very different from one another. Hence, neither methodological individualism nor radical holism can account for this necessity. Furthermore, to achieve the social cooperation necessary for human flourishing, ultimately individuals would need to recognize that they were members of the human species-being.

The following passage in *The German Ideology* refers, in Marx's typically sardonic style, to exploitation taking place under capitalism:

> When the narrow-minded bourgeois says to the communists: by abolishing property, i.e., my existence as a capitalist, as a landed proprietor, as a factory-owner, and your existence as workers, you abolish my individuality and your own; by making it impossible for me to exploit you, the workers, to rake in my profit, interest or rent, you make it impossible for me to exist as an individual. – When, therefore, the bourgeois tells the communists: by abolishing my existence *as a bourgeois,* you abolish my existence *as an individual;* when thus he identifies himself as a bourgeois with himself as an individual, one must, at least, recognise his frankness and shamelessness. For the bourgeois it is actually the case, he believes himself to be an individual only insofar as he is a bourgeois. (GI, CW5: 229)

The passage is concerned with cases where a particular member of the bourgeoisie exploits particular workers. However, at issue is not some individual's concerns with communism, but rather the 'common sense' available to the bourgeois; so, in essence this passage is no different to the reasoning of the forest owner that Marx presents in 'Debates on the Laws on Thefts of Wood'. Both reflect the systemic quality of capitalism insofar as it naturalizes the values of alienation (in this case, alienation from any fuller sense of being an individual human being).

As was mentioned earlier in this chapter, in *The German Ideology* Marx and Engels criticized Holbach as an early utilitarian thinker. In the same work, they also criticized the famous utilitarians Jeremy Bentham and James Mill (father of John Stuart). Even before Bentham produced his contribution to such theory, political economy had, according to Marx and Engels, 'already given expression to the fact that the chief relations of exploitation are determined by production in general, independently of the will of individuals, who find them already in existence'. With the utility theory of Bentham, they went on, could be found 'the attitude of individuals to these important relations, the private exploitation of an already existing world by individuals' (GI, CW5: 413). This was clearly a view of systemic exploitation, with the two 'levels' discussed earlier. The following sentence on the same page indicates, nevertheless, that Marx and Engels still in *The German Ideology* conceived of particular cases of exploitation within the broader, systemic one: 'By taking into account the economic relations of rent, profit and wages, the definite relations of exploitation of the various classes were introduced, since the manner of exploitation depends on the social position of the exploiter' (GI, CW5: 413). What *The German Ideology* does is explore more fully the inner relationships between certain ways of conceiving of individual agents and systematic exploitation. Capitalism achieves the latter partly by way of the former.

According to Marx and Engels in *The German Ideology*: 'The complete union of the theory of utility with political economy is to be found, finally, in Mill' (GI, CW5: 412). This referred to James Mill. John Stuart Mill (1924: 151), who later declared that he 'never ceased to be a utilitarian', sought in the 1850s and 1860s to theorize a version of utilitarianism that would escape the cruder aspects of the ideas of his father and Bentham. As was discussed earlier in this chapter, the younger Mill thus attempted to build a theory of human flourishing. Marx, as we saw, had already in the 1840s anticipated insurmountable obstacles to any such project in the absence of a proper community reflecting human nature (Leopold, 2007: 224–54). Exploitation was a key feature of those obstacles.

This chapter has been discussing how, while he did conceive of exploitation as a feature of capitalism, this was part of a more complex view. Turning back to the *Paris Manuscripts* we find Marx discussing exploitation in a way that indicates that he of course recognized that exploitation took place in pre-capitalist modes of production, even though it was portrayed otherwise. In the epoch in which Marx wrote, wherein the bourgeoisie had challenged the dominance of the feudal mode, the paternalist disguise of exploitation as something of benefit to all was being lifted as capitalism began to dominate without the need for a mask. In the following passage, Marx described this process very clearly:

> It is necessary that this appearance be abolished – that landed property, the root of private property, be dragged completely into the movement of private property and that it become a commodity; that the rule of the proprietor appear as the undisguised rule of private property, of capital, freed of all political tincture; that the relationship between proprietor and worker be reduced to the economic relationship of exploiter and exploited; that … that the marriage of convenience should take the place of the marriage of honour with the land; and that the land should likewise sink to the status of a commercial value, like man. It is essential that that which is the root of landed property – filthy self-interest – make its appearance, too, in its cynical form. (EPM, CW3: 267)

Capitalism brings other forms of property into its orbit, 'monetising' it. Landed property *always was* exploitation of a general kind, clearly, although perhaps not of an exclusively economic kind and was masked by paternalism.

In the *Paris Manuscripts* one can also find a clear view of systemic exploitation. In this case because of increased rent that the landlord accrues from land, farm labourers, factory workers, tenant farmers and even capitalists are exploited. In this case 'the landlord exploits everything from which society benefits' (EPM, CW3: 262), but it was 'silly to conclude … that since the landlord exploits every benefit which comes to society the interest of the landlord is always identical with that of society' (EPM, CW3: 263).

In fact, in a system dominated by private property, the greater the interest that the individual has in society, the lesser is the interest of society in that individual. Although the landlord was interested in the welfare of society in terms of the increased wealth in it, and of the increased value of land, this did not mean that the welfare of each of the people in that society was increased. On the contrary, the growth of such 'welfare' bought about increased rent on that land property in order to keep pace with the growing wealth of the capitalists and increased poverty. The interest of the landlord was, Marx (EPM, CW3: 263) went on, 'just as hostile to that of the farm workers as is that of the manufacturers to their workers. He likewise forces down wages to the minimum.'

Clearly, in the writings of 1844–6, all five conceptions of exploitation are found in a complex but certainly not muddled mixture: a conception of exploitation in capitalism, one that refers to the pre-capitalist form of exploitation which was waning in competition with the latter, a general broadly moral conception, the conception of exploitation as it is linked to alienation and, importantly, a systemic and systematic one. In a later chapter, we examine Marx's thoughts on how people could achieve emancipation from their condition of exploitation. First, it is opportune to discuss the theory of change that he developed in his work from his doctoral dissertation to *The German Ideology*. It was this theory of change that led Marx to his confident view that emancipation was a real possibility in his own time and, moreover, a possibility that the exploited people would need to bring to fruition themselves.

CHAPTER FIVE

Change

We have already glanced at Marx's eleventh thesis on Feuerbach, which contains the following famous words: 'The philosophers have only interpreted the world in various ways; the point, however, is to change it' (TF, CW5: 5). Change thus, in 1845, became one of the most prominent elements of Marx's political thought. He was, however, not thereby declaring a thought that had suddenly entered his head. He was, rather, stating something that had been a present but less conspicuous element of his work since he began to air his youthful views in the 1830s. This was that philosophy or theoretical reflection has no point unless it is at least directed to achieving change, and that social change can only happen by means of the conscious action of human beings. Of course, those are rather broad generalizations which do not tell us much. Sometimes such human action will be of a proactive nature, while at other times it will be largely responsive to circumstances, for example, to previous social changes, or as reaction to natural phenomena such as natural disasters. Social change can, moreover, be major, minor or something in between. By the time Marx and Engels wrote *The German Ideology* of 1846 they had begun to think in terms of revolutionary change which will take place when workers develop their communist consciousness from *only* their place in the concrete class struggle, perhaps accompanied by progressive members of other classes, rather than from abstract theoretical reflection (Löwy, 2005: 114–16). As this chapter will discuss, the developments in Marx's thought over the previous ten years help illuminate this revolutionary position of 1846.

Initially, it is useful to focus on a very fundamental fact. The point is that human beings who take such change-producing revolutionary action consist, of course, of atoms or at least of *matter* of some kind, and they live in a material world. It is thus necessary for us to address Marx's *materialism* in relation to the notion of change. Crucially, though, some kind of volition is also required to make a significant number of those atoms move and as a consequence to collide with other atoms, to reorder the whole. In the case of the revolutionary action, which involves social change, this can only happen because of more fundamental actions on the part of human beings which produce changes. Those fundamental actions are human bodily ones and these happen due to what we normally call voluntary control. The action of raising an arm involves volition, or in other words willing. However, the change of situation that raising of the arm constitutes need not be the result of an action involving volition. Something else might have made my arm go up (McCann, 1974). Somebody else might have grabbed my arm and raised it against or at least without my will. Volition would, however, be a factor if I purposefully raised my arm, for example, if I did so in an activity motivated by dissatisfaction with something.

The account just sketched of the voluntary is deliberately brief: There is no need for us to get into the metaphysical questions of how matter could 'will', or whether within materialism there is anything like 'free will'. The key point for Marx (here following Hegel, who in turn follows Plato) is self-conscious awareness. An individual or a people can only be said to genuinely pursue their own interests (instead, for example, of acting as they are told, or out of habits) when conscious of the nature of those interests, and when it is this consciousness that in some way 'acts'. The minimum condition of something like volition, then, is self-consciousness; for only then could I, myself, be said to act, rather than something else acting *through* me. Revolutions take place when people are dissatisfied and *realize* that the origin of their dissatisfaction lies in something about the material social order that can be changed. Marx can be placed within the broad category of materialist thinkers.

Materialism

The category is broad because materialism has a long philosophical and scientific history, and Marx's relationship to that history is both subtle and important. Marx was, indeed, a sophisticated thinker in this respect. Marx tries, vis-à-vis both idealism and what we might call 'basic' materialism, to give shape to his own thought, and names his position in the *Paris Manuscripts* of 1844 'consistent naturalism or humanism' (EPM, CW3: 336). Wolff (2002: 21–8) discusses this clearly in *Why Read Marx Today?*, stressing that in his early writings Marx rejected basic materialism because it neglects the role of human activity in the historical development of the material conditions of the world. By 'basic materialism' is meant an ahistorical account. In early ancient atomism, such as Democritus, and in later materialism in the European tradition such as Gassendi or Hobbes, the 'rules of the game' so to speak are fixed, in some way transcendent to what matter does. That is, there are and have been since the beginning of time, natural laws; and human beings, no less than stars and stones, are subject to them. Things can change in such 'basic' materialism, according to these laws, but not the laws themselves; thus, it is ahistorical. Knowledge of the laws of nature can and must be acquired passively through generalization of empirical observation. In other words, basic materialism neglects the development of the ability to change the world *as such* and thus also for humans to change themselves individually and collectively. If we consider a key point discussed in the chapter on Production in the present volume, what is thus neglected is that humans thereby produce a historically varying form of life, which is always a more or less stunted version of human flourishing (full realization of species-being). Marx's sophisticated materialism is able to embrace this historical dimension and, not surprisingly, was thus crucial to his views on change.

Looking back in 1859, as he wrote his well-known and widely cited preface to *A Contribution to the Critique of Political Economy*, Marx recalled that when in 1843 he had undertaken to write his *Contribution to the Critique of Hegel's Philosophy of Law* and also to compose the introduction to this work which appeared in the *Deutsch-Französische Jahrbücher* the following year, his enquiry led him to an important conclusion. This was

> the conclusion that neither legal relations nor political forms could be comprehended whether by themselves or on the basis of a so-called general development of the human mind, but that on the contrary they originate in the material conditions of life, the totality of which Hegel, following the example of English and French thinkers of the eighteenth century, embraces within the term 'civil society'; that the anatomy of this civil society, however, has to be sought in political economy. (CPE, CW29: 262)

Marx was clearly not thereby simply making a statement of basic or crude materialism. As we shall see, by 'consistent' naturalism or humanism, Marx (i) is able to provide an account, within materialism, of production; (ii) does not surreptitiously assume the primacy of the idea over the sensual; (iii) does not misunderstand the distinction between activity and passivity; (iv) is able to account, again from within materialism, for the historicity of the human; (v) has an account of the possibility of change through 'volition' or the self-consciousness of one's conditions.

However, given that the terms 'naturalism' and 'humanism' have each been used in many different ways it would not be enough for our purposes to simply quote him and move on without elaboration. We can progress here by referring to Allan Megill's (2002: 3) description of Marx's thought in terms of 'embedded rationality', which captures very clearly Marx's view that actual underlying logical essences were not first created by means of generalization in thought from empirical data. There was, rather, a logic or reason inherent and embedded in the world, of which human beings and their social products are of course *a part*. Our power of reasoning is a material power and not something different from or merely representative of material nature. As a rationality in the world rather than a norm or standard, his was nothing like a theological conception; it did not perceive rationality to be embedded by God's design or indeed anything of a supernatural quality. Marx's rationalism was, moreover, based on neither a belief in intelligent design by a rational God nor a broadly Hegelian belief that God is the world and that everything in the world is thus God's rational spirit. Either of these is a species of the belief of the primacy of the idea over the sensual and material, the critique of which is the main point of *The German Ideology*. Marx was influenced not only by Hegel's belief in the progress and activity of rationality but also by the notion of predictivity he found in natural science. Progress could be predicted on the basis of natural science. The species-being was characterized by self-production, and progress in human life could be predicted by humans themselves. Hence, the conventional conception of materialism as an ontological view of the world as simply material and ahistorical does not apply to Marx's thought (Megill, 2002: 3–8). The development of nature for humanity and the subsequent development of humanity itself accordingly can, rather, be perceived in terms of the material ground of the human effectively changing *itself*, through the efficacy of material reason and thus through volition or self-consciousness.

When he thus concluded in 1843–44 that the legal relations and political forms had originated in the material conditions of life, which must be comprehended in terms of political economy, Marx meant that they originated in the productive relations of society. As was discussed in the previous chapter, he argued that self-production had, in his era, resulted in a stage of humanity during which one or more classes of person endured a particular, capitalist sort of exploitation by another class, and also by the class system itself. While it may indeed only have been in 1843 that Marx began to consider self-production in terms of a radical variant of political economy (and as was discussed in the Introduction to the present volume, the influence of Engels was significant in this respect), this was consonant with the distinctive materialist approach that he had begun to develop in several years preceding his production of *Contribution to the Critique of Hegel's Philosophy of Law* that year.

Indeed, this critique was developed over several years before Marx had even begun to make his mark as a prominent intellectual. When in 1837 Marx began to consider himself a Hegelian philosopher, this by no means meant that he accepted Hegel's ideas unquestionably. Taking a critical approach indeed led Marx eventually to insist that the concrete and the ideal were the wrong way around in Hegel's method. Nevertheless, in 1837 he was impressed by the latter thinker's recognition that the interaction between the concrete and the ideal were crucial to the understanding of the world (Seigel, 1973: 501–8). Roughly, Marx saw the term 'concrete' representing the interconnected material reality of the world, while 'ideal' meant either the level of ideas or thought, or (relatedly) the removal of something from its material context or relations. It was the dialectical relationship between the concrete and abstract (to be discussed later in the present chapter) which so impressed Marx even though, as mentioned earlier, he believed that Hegel was fundamentally mistaken about that relationship.

Epicurus and Hegel

Marx's critical approach to Hegel's philosophy became a significant factor in his doctoral dissertation, submitted to and approved by the University of Jena in 1841. In the dissertation, Marx (DD, CW1: 34–105) compared the atomic theory of the ancient Greek philosopher Democritus unfavourably with that of Epicurus. Democritus, writing in Greek about 400 BC, was the founder of the School of Atomism. He argued that the cosmos should be understood as reducible to a concatenation of indivisible things (a-tom, meaning 'not divisible'); everything observable was a result of the combination or interaction of atoms. Epicurus, again writing in Greek but about 100 years later, was a later adherent of this School. However, while Democritus assumed that all human activity is predetermined, Epicurus argued that atoms swerved rather than always taking a linear path downwards. Although Marx himself is quite wary of doing so, this new idea is usually interpreted as a way for Epicurus to introduce the possibility of free action into Democritus' determinism. In any case, swerve has important implications for how we understand change, obviously, for now the atomistic universe contained the possibility of either chance or free will. In addition, Epicurus developed as the primary practical goal that human beings should pursue, the notion of *ataraxia*, which means 'feeling at peace' or 'freedom from fear'. Specifically, for a materialist, there is no need to fear death, as the dissolution of the body must also mean the dissolution of the soul (and thus, for example, there is no 'afterlife' to be concerned about); and likewise no need to fear the gods, as they exist in the state of 'blessedness' and thus do not in any way interfere in human affairs. Although often accused of this, Epicurus was not atheistic or irreligious, but he certainly held that there was no direct interaction between human beings and gods, and that therefore we should not trouble ourselves by attempting to influence or appease them.

Marx's dissertation is a difficult work, because it is fighting contemporary philosophical battles through the lens of ancient thought. As we will see, several different interpretations of the work arise which are hard if not impossible to choose between. However, in all these interpretations we can see the first Marx's intention: a follower of Hegel, but not an orthodox one; insisting on materialism and positivity in the dialectic; agreeing whole-heartedly with Epicurus' critique of religion, but not with the specific ethical implications Epicurus draws; and seeking a way to reconcile a philosophy of historical human affairs (ethics and politics primarily at this stage) with the rigour expected of a science.

What Marx saw as a very significant distinction between the theories of Democritus and Epicurus in this respect is encapsulated very well by Franz Mehring (1962: 31) in his classical biography of 1918: 'What turned him against Democritus therefore was the lack of an "energizing principle" … And on the other hand, what drew him to Epicurus was the "energizing principle" which permitted this philosopher to revolt against and defy the crushing weight of religion.' The capacity for freedom that arises from the notion of 'swerve' is the 'energizing principle'; freedom especially to free oneself from fear (Brown, 2009: 179–96).

Mehring, however, recognized neither that Marx was critical of Epicurus on very crucial points, nor that Marx was *already* (in one at least of several ways) critical of Hegel in the dissertation. For example, Marx sympathized with Epicurus but could not accept his argument that, because all our information depended upon the senses, in some cases it might be difficult or impossible to determine the truth of a cause and effect relationship. The principle of *ataraxia* then suggests that, in those circumstances, the quest to establish the single right answer to some problem should be abandoned. Epicurus has in mind particularly celestial phenomena, what happens in the atmosphere or heavens, for which the true cause out of several possibilities may be impossible to reveal. However, arguably, the same notion of 'multiple explanations' may also apply in other areas of inquiry, especially concerning human affairs, and acceptance of this would have undermined young Marx's developing convictions concerning the effects of the political status quo.

There is more at stake, then, than simply the scientific understanding of some phenomenon. That Epicurus did believe his notion of multiple explanations applied to human affairs is indicated by a difference between his approach and those of philosophers such as Plato, Aristotle and the Stoics, who considered people to be naturally political. Epicurus recommended that, if a conventional system of justice was in operation, most people should steer clear of becoming involved in politics. They would thus avoid the disruption of *ataraxy*. Epicurus thus encouraged possessive individualism and reproduction of the status quo at the expense of the participative community that Greek political philosophy had helped promote (McIvor, 2008, 419). If human affairs could not always be thoroughly understood, they could also not be changed, and therefore a kind of political quietism arises. Obviously, Marx could not accept these conclusions.

Generally, there are two views on how Marx viewed Epicurus vis-à-vis Hegel. Either Epicurus was a kind of image of Hegel, or he was the philosopher who made Hegel necessary. Peter Fenves takes the first approach. He suggested using the contrasting scientific theories of the Greek atomists in a subtle way as a means to demonstrate that Hegel's philosophy constituted a marked advancement from that of Kant: 'Democritus occupies Kant's place while Epicurus appears as a proto-Hegel' (Fenves, 1986: 434). The place of Kant and Hegel in the history of philosophy has, along with Marx's view on it, been discussed briefly in the chapter on Production in the present volume.

At this point it is useful to quote Michael Evans' very useful summary which, while written in the 1970s, still serves to illuminate very well Hegel's stress on the significance of historical dialectic for the understanding of the world. 'What Kant took to be changeless and necessary categories are,' Evans suggested, in Hegel's view 'concepts subject to alteration and change, whose necessity can only be fully explicated in the light of the totality of historical experience' (Evans, 1975: 16). Democritus, with his rigid determinism, thus aligns to Kant, who argued that the categories of experience must be ahistorical; Epicurus, with the possibility of swerve, plays the Hegelian role, opening up the possibility of human self-production, and thus the historicity of the laws of human affairs.

Another view sees Marx's Epicurus as more akin to Kant, and thus setting up the conflicts that made Hegel necessary. It is often assumed that Democritus and Epicurus are basically agreed on principles, excepting only the infamous notion of 'swerve'. In the long introduction to his thesis, Marx is at length to point out that they are in fact opposites. Democritus was a natural scientist for whom the domain of human self-consciousness is a closed book; Epicurus, on the other hand, was essentially uninterested in natural science per se – he is indeed a materialist, but his atomism is in truth an account of abstract self-consciousness in the Hegelian sense. Marx insists that Democritus posited two basic types of movement of atom: natural falling in a straight line and 'repulsion' between atoms. Epicurus adds the third, 'swerve', and this in turn changes the meaning of repulsion. Falling in a straight line is the atom acting as mere inert material, in a universal manner (i.e. according to natural law). In swerving, Marx suggests that the atom is individualizing itself as self-consciousness; in this way it could be understood by others as something like willing or volition. Repulsion, rather than another universal phenomenon, is now the realization of this individualization with respect to other atoms. In adopting *ataraxy* as a basic principle, and high point of human flourishing, Epicurus is reinforcing his view that materialism is first and foremost an account of self-consciousness.

Rather than seeing Democritus as a Kant figure and Epicurus as Hegel, therefore, we might instead think of Democritus as essentially modern materialist physics (from Newton on), while Epicurus is Kant, with the latter's emphasis on the *activity* and *limits* of thought's relation to the world. This is why Marx hails Epicurus in terms of the Greek Enlightenment and, for example, why the conclusions reached in the chapter on 'Time' are basically Kant's. However, this self-consciousness, Marx repeatedly stresses, is 'abstract'. That is to say, it is thought of merely individualistically and isolated, and not as in a constituting relation with others. For that reason, it is not a fully realized consciousness in Hegel's sense. Since a not fully realized state must exhibit dialectical contractions, it follows that there must be contradictions in Epicurus that Epicurus himself cannot solve. These Marx discusses in the chapter on Meteors, where he insists that Epicurus is being consistent with himself *precisely by contradicting himself* in his account of meteors. Epicurus is aware that his own principles entail that natural science (at least in the full philosophical sense of science) is rendered impossible: a certain way of understanding meteors in nature is ruled out because of the principle of *ataraxia* on the side of self-consciousness. This contradiction, of which Marx sees Epicurus as entirely aware although unable to resolve, is the sign of a synthesis in thought that has not yet happened. This synthesis happens in Hegel, insofar as he brings an account of science together with, and indeed into unity with, an account of self-consciousness (in Absolute Spirit).

However, it is not the historical Hegel that Marx is thinking of at the end of his dissertation. For the dissertation does indeed contain a critique of Hegel, insofar as it begins with and *never entirely leaves* materialism. That is to say, Marx is anticipating a different kind of Hegel – it is possible that he has a philosopher like Feuerbach in mind already. For this reason, right at the beginning of the dissertation, Marx's very first mention of Hegel is backhanded. The great Hegel, he says, of course anticipated in his own history of philosophy the interpretation Marx is about to present. However, Hegel's exclusive focus on the highest forms of speculative thought meant that he did not fully realize the importance of Epicurus. As the second interpretation reads this, Marx is saying that Hegel simply could not accept that any account of self-consciousness could emerge from materialism per se.

So, then, there are two interpretative approaches: the one casting Epicurus as Hegelian because of the historicization of the laws of atomic motion, the other rejecting the first on the grounds that the contradictions Marx spotted leave Epicurus still awaiting a properly *materialist* Hegel. (Later in this chapter, we will come across another issue where multiple interpretations are possible.) Thankfully, the most interesting conclusions of both approaches are in fact compatible and very revealing of the directions Marx's thought was taking him: a materialist dialectical science of the laws of human affairs and the possibility of changing them.

In either case, Marx was doing something more than using the two Greek atomist philosophers to help stage debate among natural scientists, Kant and Hegel. He was also using the ideas of Epicurus as a means to show that, while indeed being an advance from the work of Kant, Hegel's philosophy *itself* needed to be critiqued, insofar as Hegel's thought still needs to be integrated with materialism. This is pursued in greater detail by Gary Teeple (1999: 64–5). Teeple argues that Marx wanted to highlight a distinction between the *duality* in Kant's philosophy (between the thoughts of the subject and the concept of the object) and Hegel's concern with *relations* (between concrete objects and subjects). Hegel was concerned with the progress of ideas and knowledge by means of self-consciousness of the subject regarding concepts; there was thus a dialectical relationship between subject and object which Kant did not fully appreciate. This is another way of stating that contrast with the changelessness of the categories in Kant. However, this new way of stating the difference also brings into play a new notion in Hegel: Hegel had sought to undermine the understanding of the actuality of a material world that is mind-independent; such a world was instead incorporated as part of the 'story' of the self-realization of absolute spirit. Because of this focus on ideas and consciousness, Hegel's resolution was for Marx insufficient for a full understanding of consciousness, the real material foundations of which it ignored. In other words, the Hegelian advance on Kant was one-sided, resulting in the illegitimate elevation of the status of the idea over the concrete and material.

Marx believed Epicurus had made an important contribution here, in understanding how consciousness relates to sense data. For Epicurus, sense data certainly were necessary to the understanding of the real world; however, on its own this was an insufficient account of such understanding. This was because the nature of the real world itself needed to be grasped (Teeple, 1999: 95–6). The problem with relying on sense data is the obvious, sceptical one: one person might have different sense data than another person when perceiving the same situation; indeed, the same person might sense differently at different times. So, despite this accumulation of data, the question remains unanswerable with certainty as to what is really going on. Materialism, as a 'basic grasp' of the nature of the real and of the origin of sense data, must come first. Only on that agreed basis could sense data be interpreted so as to arrive at one agreed explanation. However, this 'basic grasp' should not be understood as a prior concept or idea, in a broadly Hegelian or Kantian sense, which would put us again in the same trap just eluded. Epicurus was of course a materialist, not an idealist. Instead, this 'basic grasp' is itself just another configuration of matter, part of the whole that is the real world. For Marx, this meant that while the accumulation and interpretation of empirical data was the *method* of any science, the *basis* of that science first had to be rendered possible by the set of social and political conditions within which humans lived, and which they themselves had produced. Ideas (however understood) come from matter – they are the self-consciousness of one's material condition – and if they then *change* the configuration of matter, that is through self-consciousness of the configuration and through *material* production.

As was mentioned earlier, and to which this and the next chapter return, Marx saw problems with Epicurus' theory. Epicurus refused to explore the crucial implications of his own materialism, for fear of disrupting *ataraxy*.

Consistent naturalism or humanism

To appreciate the significance of the point just made, one should refer to the following statement by Marx in 1844 of his view of human nature:

[M]an is not merely a natural being: he is a human natural being. That is to say, he is a being for himself [*für sich selbst seiendes Wesen*].

Therefore he is a species-being, and has to confirm and manifest himself as such both in his being and in his knowing. Therefore, human objects are not natural objects as they immediately present themselves, and neither is human sense as it immediately is – as it is objectively – human sensibility, human objectivity. Neither nature objectively nor nature subjectively is directly given in a form adequate to the human being. (EPM, CW3: 337)

An apparently objective (crude materialist) view of the world would actually be no better than a subjective (crude idealist, if you will) view. To be fully human, the human being must apprehend itself and its world, immediately, as the world for species-being – a human world. In the dissertation, he criticized Epicurus for failing to grasp that rejection of a reliance on sense data in favour of a 'basic grasp' would be futile if one understood the state of things in terms of crude and ahistorical materialism, or if one understood that grasp idealistically (e.g. an a priori, and thus again ahistorical, concept). Epicurus came close but ultimately failed to appreciate the significance of the fact that humans were something more than bundles of atoms – of material – with 'swerve' added on but which simply existed *in the same sense as material nature*. Human beings can come to consciousness of their own material conditions and can act so as to change those conditions and, thereby, themselves. Humans could criticize accepted understandings and explore ways in which those understandings are inadequate. Humans, even and indeed especially when understood materialistically, could thus develop themselves and their society. In humans the swerve and also the repulsion of atoms were mediated by the particular composition of atoms that comprised the human being. Human beings are more than material things with the addition of freedom, for the latter ontologically transforms and individuates the nature of that being into a being for herself/himself.

That in turn though has further implications. We cannot glimpse these implications if we insist upon a fairly traditional account of activity and passivity – that is, that it is mind alone that acts and sensual matter is passive. To be sure, the active is founded upon passive, thought upon nature, idea upon matter. However, because, following Feuerbach the human is a species-being, each individual must see itself both as active and also as acted upon. Marx thus draws the conclusion that the human is both producing and produced. So, while as sensuously perceived, another human being is given (or is 'immediately presented') as just another instance of matter, nevertheless 'in a form adequate to the human being', that other must also be seen, no less immediately, as a being for himself, a co-worker and member of a community. Moreover, while the sensual natural object (a lump of coal, say) is immediately presented as an independent configuration of matter, nevertheless (in order that it be understood in a way adequate to the human situation), it is also that which is related to production, and therefore not simply independent. The lump of coal is produced as this kind of thing (i.e. coal) and as having this particular role in human affairs (e.g. as fuel). Genuinely human thought or perception is of the world as already human. Those things we do not transform through production are defined and thus produced negatively, as that which *has been protected or left alone*, and thus again become part of the objective realization of the human. Our senses too bear the quality of being for itself and cannot be thought of as merely passive. Marx clarifies this in writing:

> As a natural being and as a living natural being [man] is on the one hand endowed with natural powers, vital powers – he is an active natural being. These forces exist in him as tendencies and abilities – as instincts. On the other hand, as a natural, corporeal, sensuous, objective being he is a suffering, conditioned and limited creature, like animals and plants. That is to say, the objects of his instincts exist outside him, as objects independent of him; yet these objects are objects that he needs – essential objects, indispensable to the manifestation and confirmation of his essential powers. (EPM, CW3: 336)

Again, those independent objects outside of the human are also the very objects upon which his 'essential powers' will act in order to meet human needs, and are therefore not *simply* independent, for a properly and fully human sensibility. In this way, Marx presents his 'consistent' naturalism or humanism. Obviously, volition is significant. It is the *overlapping* so to speak of nature subjectively and objectively considered (or, if you will, humanly and naturally considered) that generates the possibility of change. The same material world that one would try to understand is, since the human is a part thereof, also the world that constitutes the human as able to understand it. Moreover, this world is in turn produced through human volition, meaning that (indirectly at least) the human produces in the world the very means it has of understanding that world. As an essentially productive being, humans realize themselves (come fully into being) by producing; in other words, humans exist by having a productive relation to material sensuous things. What is produced one way could in principle be produced another. Self-development takes place in the course of a willed change in the interactions with and thus production of the natural world. The following passage explicitly draws these conclusions:

> To say that man is a corporeal, living, real, sensuous, objective being full of natural vigour is to say that he has real, sensuous objects as the object of his being or of his life, or that he can only express his life in real, sensuous objects. To be objective, natural and sensuous, and at the same time to have object, nature and sense outside oneself, or oneself to be object, nature and sense for a third party, is one and the same thing. (EPM, CW3: 336)

The full conception of the human, then, requires a thought and a sense that is not alienated into thinking or sensing itself and its world in this or that limited way; rather, a thinking and sensing that immediately grasps itself and its world as both active and passive, subject and object, individual and community. Again, it is because of alienation that we hold these views of things to be incompatible. Note Marx's mention of vigour in the passage just quoted. Having natural vigour is significant in that it indicates that humans have a key role in changing the world in which they live, but also that volition stems from a natural condition.

We must understand the earlier discussion of the 'overlapping' of passive and active in the context of the Feuerbachian account of the sensuous that we provided in the chapter 'Alienation'. To the extent that I denigrate sensuousness with respect to the concept or the idea, then I (*qua* human) am alienated from my essence. Feuerbach was concerned particularly with the form of alienation found in theology, where the essence and perfection of the human was an idea distinct *from* the human. In Hess we found an analysis of what, for Marx, was a more immediately pertinent form of alienation: that in capitalism the senses treat activities as things to be possessed, objects of a possible 'having', and that thus mediate between us and our sense of communal activity. The senses are alienated under such conditions for they are constrained to apprehend the world according to an idea of a stunted humanity; the senses are no longer 'human'. Thus Marx discussed, in the *Paris Manuscripts*, the liberation of the senses. Marx writes, 'Private property has made us so stupid and one-sided that an object is only ours when we have it – when it exists for us as capital', and Marx means not only that we *think* of objects in this way, but that we *sense* them likewise. He continues: 'The abolition of private property is therefore the complete *emancipation* of all human senses and qualities' (EPM, CW3: 300). We will return to what it means to make the world and our sensing of it human, later and in the next chapter.

How exactly, though, are we to understand how Marx's view of the dialectical relationship of subject and object differs from Hegel's? Marx argued in the *Paris Manuscripts*, that

> because Hegel has conceived the negation of the negation, from the point of view of the positive relation inherent in it, as the true and only positive, and from the point of view of the negative relation inherent in it as the only true act and spontaneous activity of all being, he has only found the abstract, logical, speculative expression for the movement of history, which is not yet the real history of man as a given subject, but only the act of creation, the history of the origin of man. (EPM, CW3: 329)

Marx acknowledged that the conception of the self-creation of man as a process was an 'outstanding achievement' of Hegel's 'dialectic of negativity as the moving and generating principle' (EPM, CW3: 332). The dialectic as presented in Hegelian philosophy was nevertheless backward-looking, in that Hegel perceived the human being as the creation of abstraction, or self-consciousness, when in fact, for Marx, the latter was 'a quality of human nature, of the human eye, etc.; it is not human nature that is a quality of self-consciousness' (EPM, CW3: 332). In other words, the real human situation at any one time forms the human being who can then, as self-consciousness, either understand or change this situation. To be sure, the current situation was also produced in this way, but never from nothing or from the abstract idea, but always from human beings as they are and in their situation. There is an original positivity here, the givenness of human materiality, that Hegel sees arising only as an outcome, the negation of a negation. All the stages of the dialectic are materially positive in nature. Moreover, Hegel only sees activity as attaching to the function of negation; we have to grasp activity within positivity tout court as well. Specifically, as self-producing beings, the human situation is both a positive, material state *and* active. The mistaken contrast identified earlier as between passivity and activity is here found in Hegel, between positivity and negation. Only naturalism or humanism 'is capable of comprehending the action of world history' (EPM, CW3: 336).

Materialism and communism

One can appreciate more clearly the continuity in Marx's thought on materialism from the doctoral dissertation to his naturalist, humanist approach in the mid-1840s by considering an outline that he and Engels offered in *The Holy Family* of the historical development of materialist philosophy. Returning to atomism briefly, they summarized as follows the importance of English and French thought in this development:

> The metaphysics of the seventeenth century, represented in France by Descartes, had materialism as its antagonist from its very birth. The latter's opposition to Descartes was personified by Gassendi, the restorer of Epicurean materialism. French and English materialism was always closely related to Democritus and Epicurus. Cartesian metaphysics had another opponent in the English materialist Hobbes. (HF, CW4: 126)

Marx and Engels singled out Francis Bacon as a particularly important thinker in this process of development. Science must be based on experience, and the data thus produced should be subjected to a rational method of investigation involving induction, analysis, comparison, observation or experiment. For Bacon, though, this broadly empiricist epistemology went hand in hand with a materialist ontology: 'The primary forms of matter are the living, individualising forces of being inherent in it and producing the distinctions between the species' (HF, CW4: 128). Materialist philosophy evolved further with the work of Thomas Hobbes, who systemized what

Bacon had started by focusing on mechanical and mathematical motion. Marx and Engels summarized Hobbes' materialism as follows: 'My own existence alone is certain. Every human passion is a mechanical movement which has a beginning and an end. The objects of impulse are what we call good. Man is subject to the same laws as nature. Power and freedom are identical' (HF, CW4: 129). Bacon and Hobbes are significant because they had been key figures in the modern materialist tradition, and this allows Marx and Engels to differentiate their version of materialism from such important, but still 'crude' materialism. French thinkers such as Gassendi and then later eighteenth-century figures such as Holbach pushed materialism in important new ways that were ultimately inspired by the Epicurus that Marx too had found inspiring. 'The French', Marx and Engels stressed, 'imparted to English materialism wit, flesh and blood, and eloquence. They gave it the temperament and grace that it lacked. They civilised it' (HF, CW4: 130). French materialism, Marx and Engels suggested, leads directly to socialism and communism. They elaborated on this point in the following passage:

> There is no need for any great penetration to see from the teaching of materialism on the original goodness and equal intellectual endowment of men, the omnipotence of experience, habit and education, and the influence of environment on man, the great significance of industry, the justification of enjoyment, etc., how necessarily materialism is connected with communism and socialism. If man draws all his knowledge, sensation, etc., from the world of the senses and the experience gained in it, then what has to be done is to arrange the empirical world in such a way that man experiences and becomes accustomed to what is truly human in it and that he becomes aware of himself as man. (HF, CW4: 130)

Although often enough materialism came to be associated with liberalism and its celebration of individuals and their presumed basic egoism, in fact materialism has an inner relation to communism. A consistent materialism would be communism because it would recognize that such a strong set of influences on the individual meant that the individual was incomplete (or abstract) without such influences, and further that such influences required a trans-individual agency to recognize, understand and change them. Only a collective effort to modify the environment – so that it accommodates the human – can yield the fulfilment of the human.

Following the earlier passage, Marx and Engels went on to consider the notion of interest, in the sense of advantage or beneficial effects. It is useful to recall Marx's discussion of interests and exploitation, as examined in the previous chapter of the present book. As we discussed there, Marx suggested that the prominent political economists of the eighteenth and early nineteenth centuries had presented the present economic order as natural. Marx had argued that the present order was one of a number in history which had been built by humans and which served the interests of some by means of the exploitation of others. The species-being, which was productive and cooperative by nature, was thus stunted. In *The Holy Family*, Marx and Engels distinguished between private interest and the interests of humanity, stressing that the former must be made to coincide with the latter. This must not happen, though, simply as a contractual sacrifice of individual interest (as in, say, Hobbes or Locke). Merely individual interest is an abstraction and appears genuine to me only through the sleight-of-hand that is alienation. Instead, this change would require the arrangement of 'the empirical world in such a way that man experiences and becomes accustomed to what is truly human in it and that he becomes aware of himself as man'. This would thereby help bring about interest as correctly understood, which was 'the principle of all morality' (HF, CW4: 130). Marx and Engels announced that they were describing freedom as a 'positive power to assert his true individuality' rather than a 'negative power to avoid this or that'. The individual is realized only if given the positive social scope to do so, not just by negatively being permitted certain arbitrary and empty expressions of their individuality, as commonly found in the liberal tradition. One can see clearly here a concern for the development and realization of the cooperative and communal species-being which, Marx had argued in the *Paris Manuscripts*, would first require humans in the present society to recognize that they, both as individuals and even as a group, were in a condition of alienation. 'If man is social by nature,' *The Holy Family* continues, 'he will develop his true nature only in society, and the power of his nature must be measured not by the power of the separate individual but by the power of society' (HF, CW4: 131). As properly understood, an individual will no doubt have individual interests, but these will genuinely belong to that individual – the individual is 'free' – only if the individual grasps his or her being as species-being, which means also and originally social. It is not so much that private interests and those of humanity need to be brought together, nor that there are no individual interests at all. Rather that (in the unalienated condition of flourishing) they could be no more in contradiction than are my sense of something as both passive object and active part of a way of life. (See the discussion of alienated sense in the *Paris Manuscripts* earlier.)

Any interest that runs contrary to the social interest, such as that of a 'criminal', is ipso facto not free. Marx and Engels elaborated as follows on the reasons why the environment should be rearranged. 'If man is unfree in the materialistic sense,' which is to say, if the individual as a kind of isolated atom is an unreal abstraction, then 'crime must not be punished in the individual, but the anti-social sources of crime must be destroyed, and each man must be given social scope for the vital manifestation of his being.' A 'criminal' is more of an effect than a cause. Punishing the criminal is both unjust and, more importantly here, ineffective. 'If man is shaped by his environment,' Marx and Engels went on, 'his environment must be made human' (HF, CW4: 131).

Marx and Engels' section which we have been discussing in *The Holy Family*, charting the history of materialist thought, provides some useful detail which helps substantiate Marx's claim in the *Paris Manuscripts* the previous year that his consistent naturalism or humanism differs from both basic materialism and Hegelian idealism. It differs from both partly insofar as a human material way of life must be understood to have the capacity for changing that way of life.

In charting the history of materialism Marx and Engels were explaining how the developments progressed dialectically, as each new stage built on the last, ironing out contradictions. Furthermore, and crucially, for them it was not only thought that developed in this way. The acceptance of materialism would enable people to see how they could, communally and as members of the species-being, take control of their own lives, thus escaping the alienation that masks the processes by which people come to think in an individualistic, egoistic manner. In order to grasp his work on social, revolutionary change, it will therefore be useful to look more closely at his thought regarding the dialectic.

Dialectics

We introduced the idea of 'dialectic' in the chapter on Production; but now we need to examine the idea more closely. Marx thought in dialectical terms from the very beginning of his intellectual development. One can detect this as early as 1837 in the letter he wrote to his father shortly after beginning his studies in Berlin. He reflected on the change of attitude that he had recently undergone after reading Hegel approvingly for the first time. At such moments, he suggested enthusiastically, one becomes lyrical, 'for every metamorphosis is partly a swan song, partly the overture to a great new poem, which endeavours to achieve a stable form in brilliant colours that still merge into one another' (LMFT, CW1: 10). This is easily recognizable as an image of Hegelian dialectics, involving the development of ideas and thought, where a change is always in part a growth out of the difficulties encountered by a previous state, phase or condition. Nevertheless, later in the letter he discussed his work on the philosophy of law in a way that shows he was already beginning to think about the significance of material. Of course, Hegel too believed that material was significant, but as we have repeatedly seen, Marx following Feuerbach interprets Hegel as giving an illegitimate priority to ideas; material becomes a moment within the development of ideas. Marx seems already to have come to believe that material was far more significant than Hegel recognized. Marx conceded that he had divided the philosophy of law into the theory of formal law and the theory of material law, the first being pure form of the system in its sequence and interconnections, its subdivisions and scope, whereas the second, on the other hand, was intended to describe the content, showing how the form becomes embodied in the content. (LMFT, CW1: 15)

This, he conceded, had been an error, which stemmed from his 'belief that matter and form can and must develop separately from each other'. The concept, he now believed, was 'the mediating link between form and content', and most importantly, that 'the form should only be the continuation of the content'(LMFT, CW1: 15). He sought the idea in reality itself. 'If,' he elaborated in typical metaphorical style, 'previously the gods had dwelt above the earth, now they became its centre' (LMFT, CW1: 18). This is a statement that Hegel could have agreed with, except that by 'earth' Marx's metaphor becomes more literal – he means specifically *material* reality as the substance of 'gods' (i.e. ideas or spirit). If he had become a Hegelian, he was thus *already* a radical one.

In his doctoral dissertation Marx became still more critical of Hegel. Having since 1837 accepted the Hegelian dialectic, but very soon afterwards recognized that it did not take into account the precedence of material, he now in his critique of Epicurus combined materialism and dialectics. By inspecting the following passage, one can detect this combination by means of the three moments of the dialectic:

> The concept of the atom is … realised in repulsion, inasmuch as it is abstract form, but no less also the opposite, inasmuch as it is abstract matter; for that to which it relates itself consists, to be true, of atoms, but other atoms. But when I relate myself to myself as to something which is directly another, then my relationship is a material one. This is the most extreme degree of externality that can be conceived. In the repulsion of the atoms, therefore, their materiality, which was posited in the fall in a straight line, and the form-determination, which was established in the declination, are united synthetically. (DD, CW1: 52)

In repulsion, the atom is at its most material, for it is relating to what is to the most extreme degree external to it. But repulsion also involves the negation of that materiality (what is called 'declination' or form here). Repulsion, thus, is a phenomenon that is the synthesis of some situation together with its negation. That much is clear. However, what is also important about this passage is that Marx is indicating that in the repulsion of one atom by another, as is the case with relations between human beings, there is a material relationship. The synthetic unification of the form-determination and material happens *by means of* the material relationship. Material thus both starts and finishes the dialectical sequence.

As John L. Stanley (1995: 148) comments, although Marx had accepted Epicurus' concept of the atomic swerve, for Marx this concept does not begin the dialectical sequence of moments, but, rather, mediates them. It seems that Marx saw the conceptual atomic swerve as a means to contribute to the understanding of the actual phenomena of material in process, but nevertheless a contribution which did not get to the root of such phenomena – perhaps because Epicurus was in fact interested in the dialectical development of consciousness. The straight line of the falling atom and the repulsion of one atom by another mean, as we have just mentioned, that the material came first, before the concept (i.e. before the laws of their motion). The 'atomic swerve' is a concept which like any other concept is invented by humans. The movement of the atom is interpreted in this way. Referring to Marx's later, well-known suggestion in the 1873 afterword to the second edition of *Capital*, that with Hegel the dialectic was 'standing on its head' and 'must be turned right side up again' in order to 'discover the rational kernel within the mystical shell' (C1, CW35: 19), Stanley (1995: 148) suggests that Marx was already doing something like this in the dissertation. The kernel is the most important and central part of something. As Stanley seems to be implying, just as in Hegel's work the crucial material relationship (the understanding of which is the rational kernel) was obscured by the mystical idealist theory (the shell that covers up the kernel), in Epicurus' atomic theory it was the understanding of the relationship between actual material atoms that had been obscured by the notion of the swerve. This is because the straight line of the atom's fall represents the atom itself over time and the swerve is in fact repulsion caused by collision by another atom which means the first atom does not reach itself at the later stage further down the line. The atomic swerve could not be conceptualized without the existence of the first atom at the different places on the conceptual line and of the second atom, collision with which repulses the first atom. This is an instance of a concept trying to play catch-up, so to speak, with the material reality from which it arises; thus, Stanley's interpretation shows Marx anticipating his critique of abstraction and ideology in the years to come.

As we found earlier, however, Marx's dissertation sustains more than one reading. Alternatively, we could interpret the swerve as a production, at the level of consciousness, of new laws and forms of order. In other words, rather than seeing swerve as an illegitimate 'mystical' concept which needs to be put in its proper place, we could view it as Marx's first foray into the all-important notion of human material and historical self-production. In either case, it is clear that Marx was indeed *beginning* in the dissertation to turn Hegel's philosophy the right way up (as Marx saw it). Perhaps Stanley overestimates the extent to which this was the case. One has to remember that Marx was at this stage a Young Hegelian, albeit a radical one. Hence, he was seeking to revise rather than break fully from Hegel. This becomes evident in the notes to the dissertation (DD, CW1: 84–7). Bearing in mind this Young Hegelian standpoint allows one to appreciate more fully the links that Marx identifies between the philosophical weaknesses of both Epicurus and Hegel.

In fact, Marx's famous statement of 1873 is of broader significance, as it reflects a view he held circa 1843, when he *had* begun to break more radically from Hegelianism. At the beginning of the paragraph he stated: 'The mystifying side of Hegelian dialectic I criticised nearly thirty years ago, at a time when it was still the fashion' (C1, CW35: 19). Indeed, upsidedownness, inversion and so forth were common themes among the Young Hegelians. Marx had, moreover, criticized Hegel's dialectal method as follows in his *Contribution to the Critique of Hegel's Philosophy of Law* in 1843 (published the following year): 'The correct method is stood on its head. The simplest thing becomes the most complicated, and the most complicated the simplest. What ought to be the starting point becomes a mystical outcome, and what ought to be the rational outcome becomes a mystical starting point' (CCHPL, CW3: 40).

In his 1873 afterword, Marx had offered words that, as the remainder of the present chapter illustrates, echoed his criticism of that fashion in the 1840s:

> My dialectic method is not only different from the Hegelian, but is its direct opposite. To Hegel, the life process of the human brain, i.e., the process of thinking, which, under the name of 'the Idea', he even transforms into an independent subject, is the demiurgos of the real world, and the real world is only the external, phenomenal form of 'the Idea'. With me, on the contrary, the ideal is nothing else than the material world reflected by the human mind, and translated into forms of thought. (C1, CW35: 19)

Marx was thus in 1873 being quite accurate in his recollections. What is being asserted both in 1843 and, in the form of recollection, in 1873 is the same: Human beings in their material reality – that is, the historical condition in which we find ourselves, and the essence of human beings as self-producing species-being – are seen by Hegel as the *result* of both dialectical analysis and process, the outcome of the realization of the Idea; it should, however, be the starting point. On the other hand, any abstract ideal is not a mystical starting point, but rather just demonstrably a reflection of materiality in the mode of thought. So, for example, that Marx and Engels' fellow 'young Hegelians' did not make this *same* inverting move is why *The German Ideology* has the word 'ideology' in its title; for that book is a critique of those German philosophers who, despite being progressive or even radical in other ways, still follow Hegel in insisting mystically that the idea must be the starting point of any true or efficacious account of the social, political or economic order. Hence, turning Hegel's dialectic right side up again is a metaphorical statement that is very useful indeed for the understanding of the ideas of the first Marx. Although Epicurus was a materialist, his attempt to understand the movements of atoms relied on a conceptual swerve. If we accept Stanley's interpretation, this is an anti-materialist move. Hence, it would follow that, notwithstanding his materialism Epicurus was making a mistake with which later Hegelian idealism bore affinities. On our alternative interpretation, swerve is human productivity of new, historical forms of order, and thereby Marx is indicating the accord of Epicurus with Hegel broadly speaking, except that what is required is a specifically materialist Hegelianism. Just as one can understand Marx by turning Hegel's theory on its head, a similar metaphorical turning upside down which places material first can help one better to understand Marx's interest in Epicurus.

Epicurus' atomism was more radical in its historicality, Marx tells us, than it was normally interpreted to be. This was important in that it provided the foundation for Marx's own materialist but sophisticated dialectical theory of historical change. The relevant passage in the dissertation is as follows:

> Composition is the merely passive form of concrete nature, time its active form. If I consider composition in terms of its being, then the atom exists beyond it, in the void, in the imagination. Composition expresses merely the materiality of the atoms as well as of nature emerging from them. Time, in contrast, is in the world of appearance what the concept of the atom is in the world of essence, namely, the abstraction, destruction and reduction of all determined being into being-for-itself. (DD, CW1: 64)

Time is the form of material things which change in their environment; specifically, time is that which permits activity as the attempt to isolate being as being-for-itself, meaning avoid any disturbance of *ataraxy*. If we look back a few pages in the dissertation we find Marx stating that 'abstract individuality can make its concept, its form-determination, the pure being-for-itself, the independence from immediate being, the negation of all relativity, effective only by abstracting from the being that confronts it'. Abstract individuality had tried to isolate itself by idealizing the being that confronts it in order to overcome it; but such idealization was 'a thing only generality can accomplish' (DD, CW1: 50). Abstract individuality was failing to see that independence from the immediate being can only be achieved by generality, which was to gloss over the diversity and concrete interrelatedness of material phenomena. 'Being-for-itself' thus needed to be identified in non-individualistic terms, recognizing that humanity was something more than its individual parts, but without discounting that those parts still had significance. Wright, Levine and Sober's (2003) types and tokens distinction discussed in the chapter on Production in the present volume once again becomes useful to grasp what Marx meant. That he was considering 'being-for-itself' not only in regard to atoms but also and indeed primarily to humans can be seen in the following sentence where he suggests that for Epicurus: 'The purpose of action is to be found therefore in abstracting, swerving away from pain and confusion, in *ataraxy*' (DD, CW1: 50). In other words, action for Epicurus means to abstract oneself (to be clear, this is abstraction is its primary Hegelian meaning) away from that which threatens *ataraxy*. Marx thus implies that to define action as the maintenance of peacefulness in this way, however, is a mistake. One more step – to think of action as that which could alter the environment (to make the environment 'human' in the language we used earlier) – would have allowed Epicurus to integrate materialism and history.

Being-for-itself here, in the abstracted form of individualism, is the first Hegelian draft of Marx's account of human nature. Three years later, his conception of consistent naturalism or humanism in the *Paris Manuscripts* gets to the crux of what a being-for-itself actually is. That a naturalism should actually *also* be a humanism requires the agency of the human in the production of historical reality. Marx saw the development of humanity in terms of active self-production. He did not consider the role of such a being to be permanently as it was in his own time. Humanity would thus flourish by means of the transformation of the present society into a cooperative one.

For such a transformation to take place it would be necessary to resolve the contradictions of the existing society – a problem which Hegel had failed to address properly, Marx insisted. As Marx put it in his *Contribution to the Critique of Hegel's Philosophy of Law*: 'Hegel's chief error is to conceive the contradiction of appearances as unity in essence, in the idea' (CCHPL, CW3: 91). Marx believed that change was possible because the relevant contradictions were not at all like those which Hegel had considered to be constructions of the mind, and only reconcilable in higher concepts. The relevant contradictions were, rather, actual contradictions which were in fact features of extant societies; the resolution of the contradictions would have to be equally material and would have to occur in material practice, rather than through (or even under the leadership of) thought. Hegel's philosophy ignored these actual contradictions. These for Marx could be resolved, but only when those societies were abolished (Wilde, 1991). By reconciling the contradictions in the mind in the realm of ideas, Hegel had in fact *concealed* the actual contradictions, the most significant of which, in Marx's view, was that between civil society and the political state (Callinicos, 1983: 33). As an abstraction from civil society, the political state projected a vision of harmony and unity that transcended the divisions of civil society, and indeed which valorized the divisions in the latter as a domain of individual freedoms. This transcendence was false and the valorization warped. In fact, the contradictions were entrenched, irreconcilable in the existing society, the existing human way of life. Fundamental social change could not be avoided if progress were to be made.

Social change

Consistent naturalism or humanism and dialectics were together key to Marx's view of social, revolutionary change. A very brief summary of the main thread of the picture of Marx's thought of the early to mid-1840s as discussed in this book so far serves to illustrate that this is the case. If the point was, as he put it in his eleventh thesis, to change the world, then change must be the result of action on the part of those who could recognize the need to break free from their alienation and exploitation. They would understand that as members of the species-being they needed to produce cooperatively in order to achieve human flourishing. The mutable element of their nature would thus be transformed as the consistent, cooperative element was able to bring the individualist, egoistic one into consonance with it.

In the *Paris Manuscripts* of 1844 Marx argued that the new society would be a socialist, communist one. He considered socialism to be valuable in terms of positive self-consciousness, while communism would be still more important as the real characterizing feature of the society. For the socialist man, he stressed, 'the entire so-called history of the world is nothing but the creation of man through human labour, nothing but the emergence of nature for man, so he has the visible, irrefutable proof of his birth through himself, of his genesis'. This meant, for example, that mediations between the human and itself such as religion, and therefore also the negation of religion, were no longer needed. Socialism, he went on,

> no longer stands in any need of such a mediation. It proceeds from the theoretically and practically sensuous consciousness of man and of nature as the essence. Socialism is man's positive self-consciousness, no longer mediated through the abolition of religion, just as real life is man's positive reality, no longer mediated through the abolition of private property, through communism. Communism is the position as the negation of the negation, and is hence the actual phase necessary for the next stage of historical development in the process of human emancipation and rehabilitation. (EPM, CW3: 306)

Marx (EPM, CW3: 328–9) praised Feuerbach for his materialist development of dialectical thinking. To appreciate the point Marx was making about Feuerbach and Hegel we need to dwell for a moment on the Hegelian term 'negation of the negation', for this raises an aspect of Marx's version of dialectics that might otherwise be missed. It would seem that to negate the negation just gets one back to where one started, just as in grammar a 'double negative' carries the same meaning as a positive statement (e.g. 'I will not not do it' equals 'I will do it'). In Hegelian logic, as we have seen, negation is not simply to remove in that way. To negate the negation means to overcome the contradiction that had plagued that initial situation, but not simply by returning to that original situation – or indeed to any situation *before* it – but by continuing the development or advancement that it represented, but in a form that was not vulnerable to the contradiction it experienced. Marx is happily taking up this Hegelian (and Feuerbachian) idea. However, as we now know, he was doing so in a way that insisted upon the materiality and thus positivity of all the stages, the inefficacy of the idea, and thus ultimately the negation of the negation was not something that just happened in philosophy, but that it was a material-productive event.

Communism is the negation of the negation insofar as the abolition of private property removes the contradiction experienced within the current economic structure, wherein the human produces its own alienation, but does so without simply abandoning the advances in the modes of production previously achieved (e.g. the technologies of industrialization). Negation of the negation is a new positivity. The positive image of this new advance begins to emerge before communism has been achieved. This positive image is the socialist human being – the being who has been inspired by the initial goal of a socialist society. This course of development would continue as people recognize that the socialist society can be the basis of still greater human flourishing. Socialism is then turned into communism. Communism would allow humans to overcome fully the alienation experienced by the apparently 'natural' human being as conceived under the exploitative, alienating systems of the past. Marx discussed this process briefly, albeit quite clearly in the *Paris Manuscripts*. Humans would thus be enabled to realize their essence in the species-being. Humans would thus, as will be discussed in the next chapter, achieve their own emancipation. At this point, as we are concerned with the change that brings about emancipation, it is important to notice that Marx did not believe that communism would bring about a single, prescribed condition of emancipation. Communism would, as the condition of the negation of the negation, he suggested, be the actual phase necessary for the *next* stage of this process towards emancipation and rehabilitation. 'Communism', he went on, 'is the necessary form and the dynamic principle of the immediate future, but communism as such is not the goal of human development, the form of human society' (EPM, CW3: 306). Communism, insofar as it involves the activity of negation, is a necessary but not a permanent phase in the production of flourishing ways of life. Here again we see the type-token distinction, and another indication that the first Marx can, as was discussed in our chapter on Production, be considered as an advocate of anti-reductionist rather than holistic theory. Communism would provide the conditions in which through volition and action each person could achieve human flourishing, but would not prescribe the future developments of, or ultimate social or individual form of, the human.

A problem with Hegel's conception of the negation of the negation was, Marx argued, two-fold. First, most evidently, that it was uncritical of the latest resolution in the actual dialectical process that was being worked through by humans in their own historical development. That is, it was widely held by many Hegelians (especially, obviously, those on the right) at the time that the current form of the Prussian state was in fact the end point of Hegel's dialectical development of the state. Hegel thus neglected the continuing exploitation that characterized modern society. Here in the

Paris Manuscripts, though, Marx echoes a more general criticism made by Feuerbach. Hegel's negation of the negation was concerned only with thought and ideas, with the end point of the dialectic the only true positive – where by 'positive' is meant 'that which is posited, or said to be actually the case, without negation'. Hegel ignored the self-grounding 'positive' that is the sensual or material. The negation of the negation, considered as a positive, is 'still not sure of itself', Marx writes, and thus is constantly falling back into theological traps, positing the essence of man outside of concrete human existence. Thus Hegel had 'only found the abstract, logical, speculative expression for the movement of history, which is not yet the real history of man as a given subject' (EPM, CW3: 329). Feuerbach saw this problem in Hegel. 'Feuerbach,' Marx noted, 'conceives the negation of the negation only as a contradiction of philosophy with itself – as the philosophy which affirms theology (the transcendent, etc.) after having denied it, and which it therefore affirms in opposition to itself' (EPM, CW3: 329). As a materialist Feuerbach believed that so long as philosophers merely countered philosophy with more abstract philosophy, progress would not be made. The real, self-grounding positive was self-certainty, our sensuous relation to real, particular being.

Marx's interest in Feuerbach had led him to write to the latter in 1844 to say that his theories could serve as a philosophical basis for socialism and communism (LF 11/9/1844, CW3: 354–7). In the *Paris Manuscripts* that year, however, Marx's naturalism or humanism was already diverging sharply from the conclusions reached by Feuerbach. The following year, Marx arrived at the decision that Feuerbach's materialism needed to be criticized forthrightly. What is clear here is that Feuerbachian materialism is not wrong, per se, but just not radical enough – it does not draw the conclusions that its own premises and method yield. If sensuality is the only true positive, then a change in material conditions cannot come from ideas. We would still be countering philosophy with more philosophy. That is what these materialists are said to 'forget', in Marx's third Thesis on Feuerbach:

> The materialist doctrine concerning the changing of circumstances and upbringing forgets that circumstances are changed by men and that the educator must himself be educated … . The coincidence of the changing of circumstances and of human activity or self-change can be conceived and rationally understood only as revolutionary practice. (TF, CW5: 4)

Marx was aware that revolutionary practice does not stand alone, but is guided by some form of revolutionary self-consciousness or 'theory'. 'Critique' is the name that the young Hegelians typically gave to their political philosophy. But, on its own, critique is no more efficacious than any other philosophical analysis. As will be seen in a moment, in the *Theses on Feuerbach*, Marx used the phrase 'practical-critical' (*praktisch-kritischen*), which combines theory and practice. He seems to intend practical-critical as a gloss on his understanding of 'praxis' or 'revolutionary activity'. (Unsurprisingly, some translators leave Marx's word '*Praxis*' rather than render it as practice; both are just straightforward transliterations from Greek. Praxis means 'practice', and we must note that the Collected Works translates it that way. We will continue to use 'praxis', however, in order to indicate Marx's specific use of the term as practical-critical and revolutionary.) Marx's intent here has been interpreted by John Maguire (1972: 111) as 'the specification of the normative relation between thought and practice within the context of the problem of effecting social change'. Marx used the term 'practical-critical' specifically in the context of immanent possibilities for revolutionary social change. A problem with Maguire's interpretation is that it assumes the very distinction between thought and practice that Marx sought to transcend with the term practical-critical. One significant development in Marx's thought in the early to mid-1840s was an increasing inclination to demand not only that theory should be put into practice, but that theory which did not have an inner relation to practice was nonsense – revolutionary practice/praxis was needed (Löwy, 2005: 63–117). Hence, the term 'praxis' is often employed to refer to Marx's conception of consciously guided revolutionary practice (Fraser and Wilde, 2011: 166). We need now to pursue this notion of revolutionary practical-critical activity.

One can see this approach developing in Marx's mind as he wrote his two-part article 'Critical Marginal Notes on the Article "The King of Prussia and Social Reform by a Prussian"', published in the radical biweekly *Vorwärts* journal. This article dealt with the uprising of the Silesian weavers against exploitation and the violent response of the Prussian state to quell it. 'The Silesian uprising,' Marx suggested, 'begins precisely with what the French and English workers' uprisings end, with consciousness of the nature of the proletariat' (CMN, CW3: 201). While the English and French proletarians were more advanced than the German in terms of understanding economics and politics, respectively, 'the German proletariat is the theoretician of the European proletariat' (CMN, CW3: 201), thus employing German superiority in philosophy. The German proletariat was coming to realize that politics was important, but that this must be revolutionary rather than conventional politics; the German proletariat was the 'theoretician' in the sense that they were self-conscious of their alienation, exploitation and their status as the universal revolutionary class. The activity of this self-conscious class, the only possible revolutionary agency, is what Marx means by praxis.

In 1845 Marx made the necessity for revolutionary praxis very clear in the first of the *Theses on Feuerbach* which we quoted earlier. 'The chief defect of all previous materialism (that of Feuerbach included)', he wrote,

is that things [*Gegenstand*], reality, sensuousness are conceived only in the form of the object, or of contemplation, but not as sensuous human activity, practice, not subjectively. Hence, in contradistinction to materialism, the active side was set forth abstractly by idealism – which, of course, does not know real, sensuous activity as such. Feuerbach wants sensuous objects, really distinct from conceptual objects, but he does not conceive human activity itself as objective activity . . . . Hence he does not grasp the significance of 'revolutionary', of 'practical-critical', activity. (TF, CW5: 3)

Now, historically, the production of ideas, initially tied to and enmeshed within subsistence-level activity, gradually emerges into its own once subsistence is no longer a direct and pressing concern. Philosophy, for example, becomes possible as something that has a life and direction of its own, *apparently* separable from material processes. This apparent separation is not dangerous, provided thought does not believe that *in itself* it has any real power to change material reality, for thought is nothing but an *effect* of material reality or, better expressed, in fact itself just *another* type of material process. The danger is that a philosophy begins to believe itself *actually* so separated, and a kind of 'idealism' arises; specifically, an idealism believes itself to be the opposite of any materialism, and which gives priority to or takes as its point of departure the idea, concept or the abstract. It is here that Marx and Engels defer to Feuerbach, who provided the key critique of such idealism – Feuerbach's primary target was Hegel, but many other philosophers were also implicated – insofar as it embraced an elevation of the concept above the sensuous or the material.

However, Feuerbach neglected activity, and specifically did not recognize what on his own principles should have been obvious, that alongside sensuous passivity is a sensuous activity that can produce or change material conditions. By 'making history', what Marx and Engels meant was that it was humans themselves who made history by their very material actions. Now, as we have seen, under certain historical conditions, where the forces of production are already exhibiting a contradiction, thought can get 'ahead' of the existing social and political structure, in order to offer a critique of the current, and glimpse the next available, material form. That Marx held this view rather than a rigid determinism was suggested in a letter Engels sent to his fellow socialist Joseph Bloch many decades later – in 1890. Engels insisted that he and Marx had never asserted more than that 'the determining factor in history is, in the final analysis, the production and reproduction of actual life.' Anybody who twisted this into a doctrine that the economic is the *only* determining element transformed that proposition into 'a meaningless, abstract, ridiculous piece of jargon'. The various other elements which also exercised their influence included 'political forms of the class struggle and its consequences … forms of law and, the reflections of all these real struggles in the minds of the participants, i.e. political, philosophical and legal theories, religious views and the expansion of the same into dogmatic systems' (LB, CW49: 35).

With Engels' letter in mind we can get a better grasp of a point Marx had made a year or two before he wrote *Theses on Feuerbach*. Marx had suggested that, in terms of political history, the Germans were behind the rest of Europe, but at the vanguard in terms of the philosophical critique of politics (CCHPLI, CW3: 180–3). Likewise, in *The German Ideology*, we find discussed a historical stage when productive forces become 'destructive' ones, accompanied by the rise of the proletariat; within the proletariat arises a consciousness of the necessity of revolution which, they add, 'may, of course, arise among the other classes too through the contemplation of the situation of this class' (GI, CW5: 52). The German Young Hegelians such as Bruno Bauer had erroneously suggested that it was the critical thought of intellectuals that was the primary force in the making of historical conditions (GI, CW5: 56–7), and moreover that this critical thought was not itself dependent upon any materiality. That belief is what is called here 'ideology'.

Therefore, a simple rejection of philosophical thinking is not the true conclusion to be drawn here – although many have read the eleventh thesis in that way. Instead what is needed is a way of combining two things. First, a rigorous empirical analysis of existing reality, of the facts concerning how men live and produce; in other words, a real instead of an idealistic history. So, Marx and Engels write, 'The premises from which we begin are not arbitrary ones, not dogmas, but real premises from which abstraction can only be made in the imagination. They are the real individuals, their activity and the material conditions of their life' (GI, CW5: 31). The claim is that such a history is nothing other than the material conditions of production coming to consciousness, not mediated or distorted by alienation. Second, this is to be combined with the incipient revolutionary consciousness of the proletariat mentioned earlier. All this involves not a rejection of thought per se, but an embedding of thinking into material practice, creating what Marx called 'revolutionary practice' (TF, CW5: 4) or praxis. So, the material forces of production produce, by way of the detour of empirical historical enquiry and above all class consciousness, revolutionary change.

To be sure, some of the criticisms aimed at 'ideology' are disingenuous on Marx and Engels' part, forgivable only because *The German Ideology* is still at least in part a vicious polemic. Marx, not least from his own doctoral dissertation, would have been aware that the empiricism described here is itself a *theory* of knowledge – that is to say, a *philosophical* account of knowledge. Moreover, 'empiricism' is far from the only philosophical concept used in their supposed empirical account of the history of production, which is in fact swamped with post-Hegelian terminology. They draw attention to some of the far-fetched abstractions that might be made of the results of their empirical history (e.g. dismissing as 'nonsense' how Bruno Bauer might discuss the cooperation of individuals in production) (GI, CW5: 51–2). However, they can hardly avoid abstraction themselves (as in the Hegelian phrase 'world-historical', used just a few lines earlier). Likewise, in less polemical moments, they happily acknowledge the contribution of (rather than simply the mistakes of) Hegel and the Young Hegelians, especially Feuerbach and, to a lesser extent, Hess. They write: 'We fully appreciate, however, that Feuerbach, in endeavouring to produce consciousness of just this fact [that communism is not an idea but a revolution], is going as far as a theorist possibly can, without ceasing to be a theorist and philosopher' (GI, CW5: 58). That is to say, on this arguably the most important point, Feuerbach does not produce nonsense, but something of value (to the 'empiricists' that follow him), although of course not something that could of itself be efficacious. In brief, *The Holy Family* and to a lesser extent *The German Ideology* are both polemics and thus invoke a consciously exaggerated picture of Marx and Engels' dismissal of philosophy. Their empirical method – that is, the engagement with the current, real state of human beings and their social and productive relations – in fact yields something like philosophical 'theory'. Such 'theory' is legitimate only to the extent that (i) in its emergence it only follows the lines of the emerging self-consciousness of the proletariat (i.e. is nothing but the critical dimension of the practical-critical); and (ii) it avoids ideology (avoids assuming that the ideas came first, that ideas have efficacy over the material and, by being explicitly aware of the emergence of ideas from material practices, avoids imaginatively inventing new idealistic concepts), and thus knows itself to be nothing more than a moment within revolutionary activity.

In 1845–46, Marx and Engels were thus building on the more radical materialist position, which Marx had announced in *Theses on Feuerbach*. Their approach and terminology in *The German Ideology* written in those years will be recognizable to readers who are familiar with the 1859 Preface. The latter has come to be considered as almost the definitive statement of what Marx (CPE, CW29: 262) himself described as the 'guiding principle' to his studies – a guiding principle that would later come to be known as *historical materialism*. Although we do not intend to engage in the long-running debate regarding the extent of continuity between Marx's early and later thought, *The German Ideology* can be considered as a sort of fulcrum between those two phases. What distinguished the early work, including *The German Ideology*, was the left-wing humanist political philosophy that we are reconstructing in the present study – even though Marx sought to downplay the philosophical nature of the work. Humanist philosophy is concerned to understand, endorse and enact the worth and potential for flourishing of all human beings, usually based upon some positive view of the distinctiveness of human nature. From the late 1830s to the mid-1840s, Marx was such a humanist thinker. His philosophy revolved around his theory of the species-being, and this became particularly distinctive as he became more radical and began to advocate proletarian revolution in the 1840s. Although his work towards the end of this early period may appear to be concerned solely with the proletariat, one must remember that he considered that revolution would involve fundamental social change leading to a new communist society which would enable all human beings to achieve emancipation from previous, exploitative and alienating forms of society in which human productive capabilities had been stunted. While this constituted a development, most of his earlier ideas are still present and make an important contribution to this thought.

Marx's naturalist or humanist approach which built on materialist theory in a dialectical manner by considering the interaction of thought with matter is presented as follows: 'The first premise of all human history is, of course, the existence of living human individuals. Thus the first fact to be established is the physical organisation of these individuals and their consequent relation to the rest of nature' (GI, CW5: 31). Again, the inversion of Hegel is emphasized, for the 'starting point' must be human beings in their material reality. This is the 'positive' that Hegelian dialectic eschewed. A key point of his humanist approach, and thus Marx's rationalism, was that thinking about and organizing what human beings did with natural resources meant that they were producing their means of subsistence and flourishing, and that it was this that distinguished them from animals. Moreover, human beings came to see nature worked on, for the purposes of subsistence and flourishing, as a reflection of their own being, a confirmation in material terms of human existence. Nature is part of the world 'made human'.

Marx and Engels go on to argue that societies undergo change throughout history at certain points because they reach certain stages of development which they called modes of production. Such a mode, they argued, 'must not be considered simply as being the reproduction of the physical existence of the individuals. Rather it is a definite form of activity of these individuals, a definite form of expressing their life, a definite mode of life on their part' (GI, CW5: 31). It is a definite form because, as we have seen, the human is a producing being, and the realization of its full existence is in the production of objects, in a broad sense. Human beings realize themselves fully by producing and living in a 'way of life', which obviously includes individuals, their social relations, their practices as well as, for example, infrastructure and even nature. (We discussed this idea in the chapters on 'Production' and 'Alienation'.) The progress through these stages, or modes, is driven by productive forces, which develop as labour power, working with natural resources, becomes more advanced. They were, of course, writing as the industrial revolution was progressing at a great pace, and industrial development was their chief focus (a focus that, as we shall see in the Conclusion, might be a little misleading). Marx and Engels portray this development and the social changes that are thus brought about as follows:

[T]he whole internal structure of the nation itself depends on the stage of development reached by its production and its internal and external intercourse. How far the productive forces of a nation are developed is shown most manifestly by the degree to which the division of labour has been carried. Each new productive force, insofar as it is not merely a quantitative extension of productive forces already known (for instance, the bringing into cultivation of fresh land), causes a further development of the division of labour. (GI, CW5: 32)

Key here is the new idea of division of labour. To put this into the context of the first Marx's thought it is important to bear in mind that he believed human beings themselves – with their learning, skills and capabilities – to be productive forces, in addition to apparently external or separable things like tools, techniques, science and so on. More than a quantitative extension, the further development includes actual change in the human, which then involves differences in the alienation and exploitation that the division of labour encompasses. Marx and Engels went on as follows:

> The various stages of development in the division of labour are just so many different forms of property, i.e., the existing stage in the division of labour determines also the relations of individuals to one another with reference to the material, instrument and product of labour. (GI, CW5: 32)

The 'relations of individuals to one another' are the set of material relationships of a particular stage of human life – and recall from our chapter on Production that 'way of life' is the phrase Marx and Engels prefer in *The German Ideology* to indicate the nature of the human, both in its current form and in its future fulfilled form, in order to avoid the arguable abstraction in Feuerbach's 'species-being'. With each new division of labour, the relations of individuals are modified by new forms of property (ownership of these new and *particular* skills, materials, instruments or products), and thus also new varieties of alienation and possible exploitation. As we have discussed before, 'property' understood formally means that which some individual 'has', and which thus introduces a new mediation into social relations.

Taking up from where the eleventh thesis on Feuerbach had broken off rather abruptly, Marx and Engels suggested that 'in reality and for the practical materialist, i.e., the communist, it is a question of revolutionising the existing world, of practically coming to grips with and changing the things found in existence' (GI, CW5: 38–9). All this is brought together in the following passage:

> [This development of productive forces] is an absolutely necessary practical premise, because without it privation, want is merely made general, and with want the struggle for necessities would begin again, and all the old filthy business would necessarily be restored … . Empirically, communism is only possible as the act of the dominant peoples 'all at once' and simultaneously which presupposes the universal development of productive forces and the world intercourse bound up with them. (GI, CW5: 49)

In that passage, two ideas are brought together. The first is that the 'negation' of private property, which itself arises because of the current state of productive forces, must not be a *simple* negation that thus removes the development represented by these productive forces. Industrial, technological and other advances which meant that production was more than able to meet human material needs, are kept in this negation; otherwise, we end up as primitives, struggling to satisfy the most basic needs. The second point is that only insofar as these productive forces are universal – that is, are found in every nation – and likewise the institution of private property is communism indeed possible. Of course, one of Marx's most famous statements is, in capitals, 'WORKING MEN OF ALL COUNTRIES UNITE' (MCP, CW6: 519), at the end of *The Communist Manifesto*. This was not, however, an entirely new idea in 1848. Discussing the recent development of relations and meetings between radicals Engels made the following statement in 1845: 'The fraternisation of nations, as it is now being carried out everywhere by the extreme proletarian party in contrast to the old instinctive national egoism and to the hypocritical private-egotistical cosmopolitanism of free trade, is worth more than all the German theories of true socialism put together' (FNL, CW6: 3). The true socialists were those thinkers who he and Marx criticized at length in *The German Ideology* for regarding the ideas they adopted from the early English and French communists and radicals into their own theories as purely theory, neglecting the actual social conditions in which those ideas arose (GI, CW5: 453–539). Marx and Engels were working fully in cooperation in 1845 (Carver, 1983: 36–50). Engels' statement that year indicates that he was already beginning to contribute to the argument that he and Marx expressed in *The German Ideology*. Part of this argument, although not expressed as forthrightly as would be so in *The Communist Manifesto*, was that communist revolution must be international and simultaneous, even though it would be more advanced in some countries than in socially and politically less advanced ones such as Germany. Industrial advances and the development of world markets (such that each new industrial advance, each new commodity and each new 'need' was a world event) would be crucial to this process. As Marx and Engels put it in *The German Ideology*, the activity of separate individuals had been broadened into 'world-historical activity' under 'a power which has become more and more enormous and, in the last instance, turns out to be the world market' (GI, CW5: 51). This was a 'universal development of productive forces', which established 'a universal intercourse between men'. This produced 'in all nations simultaneously the phenomenon of the "propertyless" mass' and this made 'each nation dependent on the revolutions of the others' (GI, CW5: 49).

The naturalist, humanist approach by which Marx and Engels developed this theory of revolutionary social change soon became apparent in *The German Ideology*. The conception of history that they thus presented did not, they stressed,

> explain practice from the idea but explains the formation of ideas from material practice, and accordingly it comes to the conclusion that all forms

and products of consciousness cannot be dissolved by mental criticism, by resolution into 'self-consciousness' or transformation into 'apparitions', 'spectres', 'whimsies', etc., but only by the practical overthrow of the actual social relations which gave rise to this idealistic humbug; that not criticism but revolution is the driving force of history. (GI, CW5: 54)

Again, 'ideology' in the sense of the title of *German Ideology* must be rejected as superficial or ineffective. If ideas are merely reflections of social relations then ideas cannot, or at least not on their own, be expected to change those relations. Moreover, if the origin of ideas in material practices is not understood, then criticism is at liberty to invent 'idealistic humbug'. Truly efficacious philosophy, then, takes not the form of the analysis or critique of ideas, per se, but of the development of revolutionary self-consciousness – a practical-critical awareness of the nature and potential of the proletariat – from out of the material conditions of life.

Social change thus needed to be revolutionary change in order to emancipate ordinary people from their present condition of exploitation. As was discussed in the previous chapter, this would require people to escape from the alienation and exploitation that holds back the mutable part of their nature. As one can begin to appreciate, change and emancipation are thus inextricably linked together in Marx's early philosophy. The relevant change is dialectical change, and this would require people to recognize self-consciousness and take control of the processes of such change. They would thus emancipate themselves from the alienation and exploitation which stood in the way of their ability to develop as members of the species-being. Production would thereby take on a new form by which humans would liberate themselves not simply as individuals but, crucially, as members of their community. Having dealt with the concepts of production, alienation, exploitation and change in this and the earlier chapters, the next chapter of the present study will focus on Marx's views on emancipation. By changing themselves and their world humans would achieve emancipation for themselves.

CHAPTER SIX

Emancipation

The main argument of this book is that Marx was, in the early to mid-1840s, constructing an internally coherent, broad political and social philosophy in which a number of topics and concepts he discussed in his various writings of the period would come together. The topics and concepts examined in the earlier chapters of this book have each been leading to a key aspect of his political and social philosophy – that aspect being emancipation. Except for pessimists, one supposes, any political study that included concepts like alienation or exploitation would be expected to have by the end something to say akin to the notion of emancipation; so the word itself does not yet mean much in this context. 'Emancipation' is an unsurprising translation of the Latinate German word '*Emancipation*', but the concept shows up in other words and phrases, for example, those invoking 'freedom' [*Freiheit*]. This chapter aims to show in full the various dimensions of the distinctive notion of emancipation that may be ascribed to the first Marx.

Emancipation was a concern that began to develop in Marx's thought from an early age; while at the beginning he may have held a fairly vague notion of emancipation, it quickly became clearer and stronger. As a concern, moreover, which he never abandoned, emancipation was interwoven in various ways with the other key concerns of much of his work. Indeed, one of the most distinctive aspects of Marx's work not only of this period but also when considered as a whole was its combination of emancipation with both a view of historical change and a class analysis of society. This combination can be found throughout the different periods which have sometimes been identified in his intellectual development. Moreover, any of the later contributions to Marxism that have any genuine and credible claim to be interpreting or developing Marx's ideas have emancipation as one of their key ideas (Wright, 1993). Bearing this in mind, and following the terminology used to great illustrative effect by Erik Olin Wright (1993), in the next paragraph and later in this chapter we consider history, class struggle and emancipation as three crucial nodes of Marxism. This

conception of three interlinking nodes helps shed light on the crucial place
of emancipation in Marx's work of the early to mid-1840s. Although
class and history would become far more prominent in Marx's later work,
their less pronounced presence in the early work help one understand the
development of his views on emancipation in the early to mid-1840s. Our
analysis agrees with Wright's three nodes, provided that we recognize the
philosophical analyses that underpin them – which we have outlined using
the headings of production, alienation, exploitation and change.

Class struggle was a concern which developed gradually, coming to
prominence with the focus on proletarian revolution in *The German
Ideology*. The earlier concerns with alienation, production and the species-
being helped distinguish the developing interest in class in Marx's radical
humanist approach (discussed in the previous chapter of this study) from his
interest in class in the late 1840s and beyond. Marx did not of course invent
the concept of 'class'. What he did, though, was view class through the twin
lenses of (i) alienation and exploitation and (ii) the historical and specifically
material production of class. History had been important from the time in
the late 1830s when Marx came to consider himself a Hegelian. His views on
historical trajectory of course became very different when he disassociated
himself from Hegelianism, but nevertheless remained important to him.
Indeed, the radical nature of his humanism was driven by the belief that with
the overcoming of alienation, historical progress, and thereby emancipation,
could be achieved and the potential of the species-being realized.

Alienation links with emancipation in that the former was the very
condition from which, he believed, emancipation should be achieved – an
achievement to which he sought to make a contribution by means of his
writings (Comninel, 2010; Lukes, 1987: 80–6). However, emancipation was
a key concern for him even before he began his distinctive development of
the other nodes. Even though alienation has been the concept of his early
writings that has come to have the highest profile since the publication of
the 1844 Manuscripts in 1932, before 1844 it was emancipation that was
the most persistent node in Marx's development of a social and political
philosophy. It was a node that also featured prominently in the Manuscripts.
Indeed, the other nodes and their associated concepts developed in his
mind – influenced on some issues and at some points by Engels – as he
sought to theorize emancipation. As will be discussed in the remainder of
the present chapter, as he did so his thoughts on emancipation themselves
underwent significant development.

Emancipation from the doctoral dissertation to *On the Jewish Question*

In his very early writings, which we may very roughly say are the works
of the period until he submitted his doctoral dissertation, Marx held and

expressed a belief in the need for human emancipation which was rather indistinct and undeveloped. Indeed, he was, as a thinker in this early stage of his intellectual development, in the not uncommon position of knowing that the world needed to change in order for people to achieve human flourishing while being unclear what exactly was the problem and what such flourishing would itself involve. Marx was, of course, far better than most at expressing these relatively imprecise thoughts – that is one of the reasons why his writings have continued to hold our attention today. Nevertheless, evidence that these were not simply nebulous whims passing through his youthful mind, but rather deep-seated concerns, can be found if one turns once again to his doctoral dissertation.

Embedded within the dissertation was an argument for emancipation from suppression and an account of the ways in which culture and religion nurtured a fear of the unknown. This socially manufactured fear had for many centuries kept movements for emancipation at bay. Hence his interest in Epicurus, for whom fear generated by the power of the gods or the unknowns in nature were the key barriers to human flourishing. If, Marx (DD, CW1: 73) argued, 'that self-consciousness which knows itself only in the form of abstract universality is raised to an absolute principle, then the door is opened wide to superstitious and unfree mysticism'. Theological ideas (and political or moral ideas that are in turn grounded on them) that are in some way 'above' this material state are precisely what Marx and Epicurus had in mind by such mysticism. However, he could not accept Epicurus' broadly conservative argument that human flourishing meant simply *ataraxy*, or in other words calmness and peace of mind, which of course included disengagement from political activity and general apathy with respect to social and political conditions. For Marx, one might suggest, emancipation would require emotion rather than apathy.

As he worked to prepare his dissertation for submission Marx became aware of its subversive value in early-1840s Prussia, which was becoming an increasingly authoritarian state under the new king Frederick William IV. Hence, before submitting the dissertation to the University of Jena, Marx added a foreword which hinted at its radical potential. The mythical titan Prometheus was employed for this purpose. Prometheus, Marx (DD, CW1: 30) recalled from the classics, opposed both 'heavenly and earthly gods who do not acknowledge human emancipation as the highest divinity'. Within the dissertation is a philosophy of emancipation in response to philosophies which discouraged thinking that would break free from accepted wisdom. He was now making a bold statement in the foreword in which he meant that the earthly gods were the dominant ideas of the Prussian state, which seemed likely to suppress subversive political philosophies such as his own. He built on these early ideas over the next few years in some important thinking regarding the nature of human beings, the interrelationship of human beings and their connection to nature.

In the journalistic work he produced during the period following his doctoral studies Marx expressed his emancipatory aims from what was still a distinctly Young Hegelian approach, based on the belief that existing political states are far from the ideal – where that ideal is understood in Hegelian terms. Hegel distinguishes between the ideal, rational state and the political state. The latter refers to the constitutional state which is found in the empirical study of politics. Such a state does not match the ideal state which Hegel describes in his *Philosophy of Right* as follows: 'The state is the actuality of the ethical idea.' The state, he elaborates, 'is the actuality of the substantial will, an actuality which it possesses in the particular self-consciousness when this has been raised to its universality; as such it is the rational in and for itself'. In this state 'freedom enters into its highest right' (Hegel, 1991: 275). Young Hegelians thus employed their interpretations of this political ideal in order to criticize the relative shortcomings of the existing political order.

At Berlin Marx had come to develop political views which bore affinities to those of his Young Hegelian tutor at Berlin, Eduard Gans (Kelley, 1978). Gans was concerned with social conditions which meant that the working poor in Germany endured a standard of living amounting to impoverishment. The state could, Gans insisted, become more active in social welfare than Hegel (i.e. orthodox Hegel) considered appropriate. Living standards could thereby be raised. Gans also insisted that this would require greater democratic representation than Hegel was prepared to support (Breckman, 2001). Similar ideas to those of Gans were clearly held by Marx in the analysis of the legislation passed in the Rhineland against theft of wood, discussed in the chapter on exploitation in the present study. As Ralph Miliband (1965: 279) commented in an influential article of the 1960s, reflecting on this legislation, Marx considered the state in his own times to be, in effect, the servant of the rich. This was thus, for Marx, a perversion of the true purpose of the state, and amounted to what we have been calling 'exploitation'. One can express Marx's concerns in philosophical terms as follows. It would be bad philosophy to argue that poverty is natural or inevitable because the way society is organized today makes some people poor and others wealthy. This premise may be true but the argument would be invalid because it would need another premise to suggest that it is impossible to organize society in a way that would avoid the wealth/poverty division. We simply do not know if this second premise is true. Hence, it would be premature simply to accept that first premise. Evidently, Marx did not accept that premise; otherwise there would have been no point in his challenges – discussed in the present volume – to the exploitation of the wood gatherers, wine-growers or weavers of Germany and other countries. To all forms of human life limited or stunted by alienation and exploitation, there corresponds the realization of species-being, of cooperative production, by real individuals.

The Young Hegelian influence can be detected in an invitation Marx sent to Feuerbach in October 1843 to write for Ruge's radical *Deutsch-Französische*

Jahrbücher journal, based in Paris. Marx (LF 3/10/1843: CW3: 350) asked Feuerbach to criticize Schelling's zealous censorship of writing which opposed the authorities in Berlin and which might attract the attention of a wide readership. It would, Marx reasoned to Feuerbach, be a good idea to go beyond the German confines and expose Schelling to the French literary world in Ruge's journal. By drawing attention to Schelling's current role in the crushing of emancipatory writing, Marx stressed, Feuerbach's work would also serve as an attack on Prussian policy. Feuerbach did not accept the invitation.

Likewise, in August the following year, he told Feuerbach that, whether intentionally or otherwise, his works provided 'a philosophical basis for socialism' and that the Communists had 'immediately understood them in this way' (LF 11/9/1844, CW3: 354). Nevertheless, Marx had already begun to believe that a more radical approach was needed than that of any of the Young Hegelians. He began to focus more closely on emancipation and what this would mean for the present condition of humanity in the extant society in *On the Jewish Question* in 1843. Problems such as the suppression of the press in Prussia in 1943 and the timidity of the people of that country were, however, already leading him to appreciate the difficulties which the struggle for emancipation from the present situation would bring (Stedman Jones, 2017: 208). In other words, he was beginning to see the Hegelianism of his contemporaries as naïve, especially the beliefs (i) that an appeal to an ideal form of the state in and of itself could in any way bring about change, and (ii) that a change to the political order (in contrast to the conditions of civil society) would be sufficient. Nevertheless, the uprising of the Silesian weavers the following year indicated to him that a proletarian revolution was not beyond the realms of possibility (Stedman Jones, 2017: 161–4 and 210–11).

In the attempt to push the project of emancipation beyond the Young Hegelians, Marx distinguished between political emancipation, which could be achieved without substantive social change, and human emancipation which would indeed require such change. Human beings would have to produce not just a change in their political organization (as the Young Hegelians believed), but a change in their total material conditions and thus themselves, such that civil society too would be transformed. History, class struggle and emancipation had begun to draw together in his mind. As we saw earlier, in *On the Jewish Question* he discussed the concept of species-being which would be crucial to the *Paris Manuscripts* of 1844.

In *On the Jewish Question* one of Marx's various concerns was to outline the way in which the human species-being would need to develop in order to achieve human emancipation. Leopold (2007: 184–6) discusses this important development in Marx's thought very clearly, stating that Marx meant by a species-being 'an individual who has actualised – that is developed and deployed – his essential capabilities' (Leopold, 2007: 184). We saw earlier that Marx perceived two aspects of human nature. One aspect is mutable, the other constant within each member of the species, even if not yet realized or actualized. The essential capabilities are those in the second category; we have specified these as all that is involved in cooperative (i.e. social) production. Leopold's clear statement would have been more accurate had he extended it to say that for Marx the species-being should not be seen in binary terms of being realized or not realized, but instead in terms of a continuum. In other words the species-being can be lesser or further developed or, expressed negatively, more or less alienated from its full realization.

For Marx, the development and deployment of essential capabilities is what emancipation must involve. For the problem was that alienation and exploitation prevented the human being from actualizing her/his productive capabilities and fulfilling the species-being. To emancipate themselves humans would need to overcome this problem. Let us state this in a way that encapsulates the key topics of the previous chapters of the present study: an individual human being is a species-being if he or she is conscious of self, *both* as a part of the concrete totality of human life (this is the social and cooperative aspect) *and* as producing and product of that life (the essentially productive aspect). This would mean that he or she has consciously changed their way of living and of social organization such that work and thus production can occur – for the human being is *homo faber* – without alienation and exploitation. Full flourishing as species-being occurs accordingly, together with that of other members of the community. Importantly, even if one's ancestors had initiated the process and brought production under control, each person in each generation would still need to live and work as a member of the species-being. As Leopold (2007: 184) puts it in a very useful sentence: 'Marx suggests that only an individual actualising these essential capacities can be said to have developed in a healthy and vigorous manner, and that only an individual who has developed in such a manner can be said to have flourished.' Only when this has been achieved in the actual world, rather than in a society that supposedly reflects some ideal notion of a better world, the possibility of which was envisaged in Hegelian philosophy, will emancipation have been achieved.

In *On the Jewish Question* Marx was criticizing those who thought that to be free from any discrimination by the state regarding religious doctrine would be to have achieved emancipation. This would be to confuse political emancipation with human emancipation, and while some progress might be made by means of an approach focusing on the achievement of the former, this would nevertheless be to ignore *and indeed reinforce* the problems of the fundamental individualism and self-interest which were dominant norms in existing societies, notwithstanding their religious or political constitutions. He put it as follows: '*Political* emancipation is, of course, a big step forward. True, it is not the final form of human emancipation in general, but it is the final form of human emancipation *within* the hitherto existing world order. It goes without saying that we are speaking here of real, practical emancipation' (OJQ, CW3: 155). The distinction Marx thus drew between political and human emancipation can seem a little confusing because at first it appears to be a distinction based solely on religion – political emancipation being achieved when the state is not restricted by a state religion, leaving human emancipation yet to be achieved in a society dominated by religion. Religion, however, is not the only problem, and is in fact not the most fundamental one, although as we noted in the chapter on Alienation, it is Feuerbach's analysis of Christian theology that gives Marx his working model of alienation. Political emancipation had, by raising human beings above religion, nevertheless left religious power to continue in society. Something similar happened when the political form of recognizing private property was eliminated, as had happened in some North American states which abolished qualification for the right to elect representatives or be elected. As Marx put it, 'the political annulment of private property not only fails to abolish private property but even presupposes it' (OJQ, CW3: 153). That is to say, when democratic enfranchisement no longer recognized property as a criterion for political participation, it thereby assumed property was natural and inalienable in the civil domain, together with the principles of individualism and self-interest.

In order to achieve human emancipation people would need to recognize and organize their own powers as social forces. Social power would therefore not be separated from political power, and moreover would not be kept out of the hands of ordinary people (OJQ, CW3: 168). Political emancipation was limited because it assumed a division between the public and private human being. 'Only', he insisted, 'when the real, individual man re-absorbs in himself [*in sich zurücknimmt* – we might translate this as "takes back into himself"] the abstract citizen, and as an individual human being has become a *species-being* in his everyday life, in his particular work, and in his particular situation ... only then will human emancipation have been accomplished' (OJQ, CW3: 168).

It will be useful at this point to pick out a few key words in a passage from the sentence just quoted. First of all, 'reabsorb' or, less colourfully, 'take back' – Marx's point is that the distinction between political order and civil life is an illusion, meaning a material configuration of human life such that what originally belongs to the individual has been alienated from him, and must be 'taken back'. Let us also draw attention to ' a *species-being* in his everyday life, in his particular work, and in his particular situation'. Marx was thus voicing a concern that human emancipation can only be achieved by means of engagement in the sort of production applicable to the species-being (see the chapter on Production in the present volume). The individual in his particularity is species-being; species-being is the concrete, material form of human life itself, properly understood.

To explore this further, we need to remind ourselves that in *On the Jewish Question* Marx was tackling the basic assumption of liberal political-economy, which is individualism. For Hegel, civil society is the domain of free individual association; the State is that which binds people together despite the contradiction of individual differences. Liberal political-economy takes this distinction not as one made in thought for the purposes of philosophical analysis, but as something quite real and, indeed, a core definition of justice. In this way, alienation becomes systematic exploitation. It is the assumption that the distinction is real and just that Marx attacks, because it naturalizes a historically contingent form of alienation, namely individualism, and likewise restricts the scope of any possible change in human society to the political side. Whether the Jews are politically free matters little while they (and all humans) are exploited and, indeed, the very question of political freedom tends to obscure any recognition of the exploitation. We shall return to the question of in what way the 'individual' as such recognizes their role in all this later in the chapter, in discussing the corresponding passages in *The German Ideology* on the 'average individual' and their relation to 'class'.

Certainly, emancipation was crucial to his thought at this time and he had already begun to consider very carefully the exploitation from which people needed to emancipate themselves. We are nevertheless left to our own investigations to try to grasp what exactly Marx meant by human emancipation. Leopold's suggestion that, for Marx, emancipation involves the actualization of a human's essential capabilities gets us so far in this respect, but we are still left without anything like a substantial understanding. Marx emphasizes, understandably perhaps, *that from which* we must be emancipated so much that he leaves himself little room to explore what such emancipation consists of on its own terms. We can thus sympathize with Wolff (2002: 45) who is infuriated by Marx's lack of explicitness on this matter, conceding that for him this makes emancipation 'one of the most disappointing and frustrating aspects of Marx's Early Writings'. Perhaps if Marx had, as he hinted he might in the preface to the *Paris Manuscripts* of 1844, produced the series of pamphlets on the topics that contributed to his political and social philosophy and, probably even better, eventually wrote the special work that would bring it all together, we would not be in this frustrating position. Of course, we have to work with what we have. In no one place, and in no one piece of writing, does Marx make this notion clear; however, if we adopt our strategy of reconstruction, using a variety of texts from this period, it is possible (*contra* Wolff) to arrive at a picture of the early Marx's concept of emancipation, both what its nature and its conditions would be.

What is very significant is that production was coming to be another key piece in the jigsaw of his broader political and social philosophy of emancipation. Indications that this is the case can be detected as early as the late 1830s when he researched and wrote his doctoral dissertation.

As we saw in the previous chapter, Marx's dissertation is difficult to interpret. However, it does seem clear that Marx is broadly endorsing Epicurus' critique of a merely passive empiricism, as found in earlier materialists. If the 'swerve' introduces chance, freedom or individuation into the equation, then it also opens the door to human activity having a role in knowledge and perhaps even in the historical formation of human affairs. To assume that all phenomena are determined and thereby to rely, like Democritus, on essentially passive empirical observation and sensation would be to restrict the availability of knowledge, and thereby to inhibit both what one can know in the world and also what one tries to do in that world. As we have discussed earlier in this book, Marx later argued, in what would be the most fundamental element of his philosophy, that what humans do in their interaction with the world is to produce. They produce commodities, new forms of society and even new forms of the mutable elements of themselves. Eventually this would lead to human emancipation. The kernel of this idea is already found in the dissertation.

By the time Marx introduced the notion of the species-being in 1843 he had begun to insist that production is not something that is done independently by individuals. Some things at least are done collectively (and as we shall see in discussing the *Paris Manuscripts*, all acts of production are ultimately 'objective' – i.e. out there as part of collective human life). It is this collectivity that makes the highly developed species-being distinct from any abstract notion of 'the human'. As we saw earlier, he recognized the significance of this point in his report on the treatment of the Mosel wine-growers that year (JCFM, CW1). The notion of the species-being enabled him to articulate the view that humans could develop the mutable elements of their nature in order to achieve the permanent but immanent natural quality of interacting collectively with the world they inhabited in order to enable each to flourish as a member of the community. This development of mutable elements would involve the cessation of the conditioning of humans which, through alienation, makes the exploitation inherent to systems of private property appear to be a permanent feature of human relationships. By contributing to the termination of this conditioning, humans would be engaging in a production that would bring about their own emancipation.

In his *Introduction* to *Contribution to the Critique of Hegel's Philosophy of Law* which he wrote later during 1843 and the early months of the following year, Marx was already becoming aware that the exploited classes would need to work for their own emancipation. That is, such emancipation could not happen if led by intellectuals pursuing rational reform according to an ideal of the state, or indeed pursuing changes that relate to the situation of their class. Discussing the problems of political and social development in Germany, which lagged behind some of the more advanced capitalist countries, he offered the following assessment:

> It is not the radical revolution, not the general human emancipation which is a Utopian dream for Germany, but rather the partial, the merely political revolution, the revolution which leaves the pillars of

the house standing. On what is a partial, a merely political revolution based? On the fact that part of civil society emancipates itself and attains general domination; on the fact that a definite class, proceeding from its particular situation, undertakes the general emancipation of society. This class emancipates the whole of society but only provided the whole of society is in the same situation as this class, e.g., possesses money and education or can acquire them at will. (CCHPLI, CW3: 184)

The last sentence is a dig in part at the Young Hegelian socialists, who (Marx implies) had to imagine all humans having the education and leisure time for reflection – and thus money – in order to realize their own emancipation. To the above, Marx adds: 'No class of civil society can play this role without arousing a moment of enthusiasm in itself and in the masses' (CCHPLI, CW3: 184). Such a class can achieve political change, but only on the condition that civil society is held distinct from the political realm, so that another class can form, and that this civil society in its main features remains unchanged throughout. A swipe at the Young Hegelians and other reformers, we can also recognize these thoughts as a fragment of Marx's analysis of the French Revolution, in which the bourgeoise dramatically altered the political landscape, but left, and indeed had to so leave, the class structure of French civil society, and its economic interrelations, untouched. Any revolution begins with the 'particular situation' of a class. By this, Marx means that the resources for envisioning an alternative to the situation of some group emerge from out of the contradictions that the group experiences in that situation. So, the bourgeoise can bring about the political emancipation of the 'masses', but only insofar as those masses are *already* frustrated bourgeoise.

Where, then, Marx enquired, might one find what he called the 'the positive possibility of a German emancipation?' The answer, he went on, was as follows: 'In the formation of a class with radical chains, a class of civil society which is not a class of civil society, an estate which is the dissolution of all estates.... This dissolution of society as a particular estate is the proletariat' (CCHPLI, CW3: 186). The word 'radical' here and in most instances elsewhere does not mean 'extreme' or descriptive of some particularly revolutionary activist group. Rather it means 'from the ground up' – the Latin means 'root' (as in 'radish') – that is to say, these chains are *comprehensive* in the way they bind, binding *in all ways*. 'Estates' in this sense are particular groups with interests in society. This reflected the institution of the estates of the nobility in Germany; but Marx was extending the use of the term to any group with interests. The notion of a class of civil society which is not such a class is rather strange; the clue to what Marx meant lies in the notion of an estate which is the dissolution of all estates. To be sure, the emancipation of the proletariat would bring about and indeed require a society in which there would be no class division and thus no particular estates. It would be, as was discussed earlier, human emancipation, in which humans would realize the species-being and enjoy collective self-flourishing which would not require any group in society to undergo alienation or exploitation. More than this, though: even prior to this revolution, the proletariat is *already* such a dissolution. As Marx put it, the proletariat was a sphere in society

> which has a universal character by its universal suffering and claims no particular right because no particular wrong but wrong generally is perpetrated against it; which can no longer invoke a historical but only a human title; which does not stand in any one-sided antithesis to the consequences but in an all-round antithesis to the premises of the German state; a sphere, finally, which cannot emancipate itself without emancipating itself from all other spheres of society and thereby emancipating all other spheres of society, which, in a word, is the complete loss of man and hence can win itself only through the complete rewinning of man. (CCHPLI, CW3: 186)

The estates are, or rather are *supposed to be*, the complete set of the 'spheres' of society. The proletariat is the universal class because it does not occupy this or that position within the society or state, but exists as the 'all-round antithesis' of that society. In other words, it exists as the class that is not a class, insofar as the set of estates are thereby revealed as necessarily incomplete. The proletariat stand as humanity itself, in the condition of utter alienation (i.e. 'complete loss of man'), not as one estate would have it suffering a particular wrong but suffering all wrongs. 'Wrong generally' is not some historically specific type of wrong, but all wrong and thus bears a 'human title', that is, covering all historical forms of wrong committed by man against man.

The proletariat was coming into being in that country, Marx went on, 'only as a result of the rising industrial development' (CCHPLI, CW3: 186). It was this development which would provide the infrastructure and resources to make human emancipation and thus collective self-flourishing possible, but *also* exacerbate the 'radical chains' of the proletariat to the point where these chains are both recognized and unbearable. Once again one can detect the three nodes of Marx's thought: the theory of historical trajectory, the class analysis of society and the argument for emancipation.

Now, in the *Paris Manuscripts* later that year Marx's analysis took on a different focus, the class analysis became very prominent while emancipation was seemingly of much lesser significance. The Manuscripts are actually best known for Marx's groundbreaking work on alienation, which we dealt with at length in an earlier chapter and which permits groups to exploit others. Importantly, however, the private property of the dominant class was the fundamental alienating problem that needed to be faced. Emancipation, as the way of addressing this problem at its deepest level, is therefore implied throughout even when not named in the Manuscripts.

Emancipation in Marx's works of the mid-1840s

In the *Paris Manuscripts* Marx addressed the relation of alienation to private property, which was basically the reason why some in society exploited others. Or perhaps more starkly, the institution of private property simply is exploitation in its most general, modern form. As he put it, the implications were as follows: 'From the relationship of estranged labour to private property it follows further that the emancipation of society from private property, etc., from servitude, is expressed in the political form of the emancipation of the workers' (EPM, CW3: 280). This mention of the political form of the emancipation of the workers may be confusing, especially as the manuscript breaks off a few pages later without Marx having elaborated on 'political form' in this context. To grasp what he was thinking it is useful to remember that in the same year (1844) Marx had suggested in his 'Critical Marginal Notes on the Article "The King of Prussia and Social Reform by a Prussian"' (CMN, CW3: 206) that for the proletariat revolution would be a political act – how could revolution not be? But, in accord with the analysis of the distinction between the political and civil, it could not be *only* a political act. In its upending of the relations of production, 'there socialism throws off the *political* cloak'. It was not, Marx went on in the *Paris Manuscripts*, that the emancipation of the workers alone was at stake, 'but because the emancipation of the workers contains universal human emancipation – and it contains this, because the whole of human servitude is involved in the relation of the worker to production, and all relations of servitude are but modifications and consequences of this relation' (EPM, CW3: 280).

Marx was thus linking human servitude with the institution of private property. He argued that there was an assumption among political economists that private property – and indeed the accumulation of more of it – was something that people almost naturally seek to acquire, and indeed formed the foundation of any sense of justice in the economic arena. This assumption permeated the beliefs of people in society, including the alienated workers themselves (EPM, CW3: 270–9). Alienation disguises itself under headings such as 'natural' or 'necessary'. Those who thus suffered alienation and exploitation did so in order to serve such seemingly natural property accumulation. Human emancipation would thus involve the abolition of private property. He put this as follows:

> The abolition of private property is therefore the complete emancipation of all human senses and qualities, but it is this emancipation precisely because these senses and attributes have become, subjectively and objectively, human. The eye has become a human eye, just as its object has become a social, human object – an object made by man for man. (EPM, CW3: 300)

Marx could have been clearer here regarding his reference to the human senses. He would thus have made more understandable the way in which he was suggesting that emancipation would involve the overcoming of alienation and the realization of the human species-being. Nevertheless, it is clear that Marx was adopting Feuerbach's work on the senses, which we have discussed in the chapter on alienation. As we saw there, the basic point is that even the alienated senses 'see' the world in terms of property, something that 'has' its 'properties' (e.g. blue, round, soft) and which circulates independently of the human sphere and specifically independently of the subjective sphere. This could be 'owned', but this does not affect them in their pure objective independence of subjective activity. In contrast, the emancipated senses 'see' things in the world immediately as integrated into that world as *objectively* human. Objects are objects of human 'essential needs' or 'powers', not free floating. The thing is still blue, round and soft but (we might extrapolate from Marx) these are apprehended immediately as meaningful within the human social sphere: the blue is this or that known shade, the roundness is useful, the softness comfortable. The world of sensual objects is nothing other than that material way of human life, where humans have taken back control of production and can flourish or fulfil species-being.

To be sure, Marx's thinking here goes beyond Feuerbach already, in a manner specified a year later in the fifth thesis on Feuerbach: 'Feuerbach, not satisfied with abstract thinking, wants [sensuous] contemplation; but he does not conceive sensuousness as practical, human-sensuous activity' (TF, CW5: 4). Feuerbach had countered the idealist Hegelian identification of thought with reality by insisting that the crucial factor was sensibility, or sensation. A general notion of alienation, then, was the subordination of sensuality to thought. A problem with Feuerbach's response was, however, that it did not take into account the concrete material reality on which sensation was based, nor did Feuerbach think of sense as active (i.e. ultimately as production). It thus ignored the interaction of the active human being and their surroundings (Hook, 1994: 294); that is to say, Feuerbach's sensuous world made human is not also the world as produced and productive, the objective realization of human activity.

A few pages after the passage of the Manuscripts just quoted, Marx stated that 'Sense-perception (see Feuerbach) must be the basis of all science' (EPM, CW3: 303). Marx argued that 'true science' required sense-perception to 'involve both sensuous consciousness and sensuous need'. The human sensuous powers could, he suggested, writing from his radical materialist perspective (which, as we discussed in the previous chapter, Megill's notion of embedded rationality helps one grasp) 'only find their self-understanding in the science of the natural world in general, just as they can find their objective realisation only in natural objects'. Recapping on 'the social reality of nature', he stressed that this and human natural science, or the natural science of man, are identical terms (EPM, CW3: 304). In other words, Marx believed that humanity could not be properly understood in terms of a collection of individuals, with social phenomena simply reflecting the results of their interactions, like isolated atoms bouncing off each other. Rather, those interactions and relationships made society what it was. Social reality could not be reduced to the individuals, and any effort to account for humanity scientifically in purely individualist terms (e.g. individual psychology) would fail comprehensively, just as would any account of human social relations without considering humans as self-producing agents.

The theory of historical trajectory comes into the picture of the *Paris Manuscripts* when Marx talks about emancipation in communist society. It is useful at this point to repeat part of a quotation we included in the previous chapter of the present study. Communism, he suggested, 'is the position as the negation of the negation, and is hence the actual phase necessary for the next stage of historical development in the process of human emancipation and rehabilitation' (EPM, CW3: 306). We discussed the concept of negation of the negation in the previous chapter. Communism would be such a negation as it would abolish private property and thereby resolve the situation whereby humans produce their own alienation. This negation of the negation would be achieved without abandoning the advances already accomplished in the modes of production.

Although it is well known that Marx said very little about the communist society into which human emancipation would take people, it is quite clear that he did not have in mind an authoritarian regime in which individuality would be devoured by a collectivist form of despotism. Eagleton (2011: 238) outlines the case for this individualist element in Marx's thought very graphically: '[he] did not dream of a future in which we would all wear boiler suits with our National Insurance numbers stamped on our backs. It was diversity, not uniformity, that he hoped to see.' As will be discussed in a moment, this approach can be seen very clearly in *The German Ideology*. First, however, it will be useful to stress once again a point made in earlier chapters of the present study. This is that one should not try to understand this key individualist element of Marx's approach by means of methodological individualism, which holds that any macro social type is reducible to another level which consists of an explanation referring to individual people and the relations that happen to pertain between them. In a note at the end of the section on materialism in *The Holy Family*, Marx and Engels quote Bentham's criticism of the notion of general interest in a passage which serves as a useful example of what we now know as methodological individualist thinking:

> The interest of individuals ... must give way to the public interest. But ... what does that mean? Is not each individual part of the public as much as any other? This public interest that you personify is but an abstract term: it represents but the mass of individual interests ... If it were good to sacrifice the fortune of one individual to increase that of others, it would

be better to sacrifice that of a second, a third, and so on ad infinitum …
Individual interests, are the only real interests. (HF, CW4: 134)

As he quoted this passage we can be confident that Marx was fully aware
of the sort of method which would come to be known as methodological
individualism. A problem with this method was that it could not account
for the significance of the relations between human individuals *to* those
individuals. As mentioned earlier, the relations make society what it is; those
relations make society something more than an aggregate of those relations.
The relations, for example, help produce class dominance, which is far more
powerful than a collection of individual cases of dominance. A class that is
united in some ways notwithstanding divisions of its members in other ways
can control institutions in a way that cannot be achieved by an aggregate
of individuals who are dominant over the other humans with whom they
engage. The tradition of utilitarianism in fact itself suffers from this problem,
insofar as it tries to maximize human happiness, and thus individuals only
get factored into the sum (this is sometimes called the 'trolley' problem).
Marx's reply to Bentham's insistence on only individual interests is akin
to his reply (which we discussed in the chapter on Alienation) to Stirner's
radical individualism: that of course individual human interests count, but
the most important human interest is in *being a human* who achieves the
characteristics of the developed species-being, which is something that does
not happen to us merely insofar as we are individuals. Only as a species-
being can I *then* be an individual in any genuine sense. Bentham's initial
distinction between levels of interest is a mistake from the beginning. Insofar
as they are fully human, and aligned with the conditions under which others
too can attain to their full humanity, the individuals' interests are sovereign.
Moreover, those interests genuinely belong to them, rather than part and
parcel of their alienation. Importantly, however, the 'public interest', just
like species-being itself, is not something that is or belongs somehow to an
abstraction, but is rather just those social and economic conditions within
which an individual could be fully human.

The ideas of the first Marx can be understood in terms of a different
analytical method which employs the terms of types and tokens. Such a
method is offered by Wright, Levine and Sober, whose anti-reductionist
method has been mentioned and discussed in several places in the earlier
chapters of the present volume. As an example of the anti-reductionist
method we can, as they suggest, 'define the capitalist-worker relation as a
type of relation among individuals, while the relation between the owner of
a particular firm and the employees of that firm would constitute a token
instance of such a relation' (Wright et al., 2003: 62). As will be discussed in
the present chapter, this sort of approach was taken by Marx, and so one
would not fare any better either adopting methodological individualism or
trying to understand his views on capitalism in terms of radical holism,
which discounts the significance of individual agency.

Wright et al. (2003: 59) suggest that radical holists perceive relations among individuals to be 'essentially epiphenomenal with respect to social relations'. In other words, the operation of the whole generates those relations. According to Wright, Levine and Sober (2003: 59–60) the holistic approach has been taken by a range of Marxist writings including teleological accounts of history which see individuals as agents of forces working towards a given end; arguments which stress collective agency, suggesting that the bourgeoisie does this, the proletariat does that and so on, and those which present extreme accounts of structural causality, such as Louis Althusser and his followers. More significant for us is the claim by Femia that Marx himself worked on the basis of a holistic ontology. According to Femia (1993: 8), holism can be defined as follows: 'The assumption that the social whole takes priority, both methodologically and morally, over its individual human components.' This attributes to Marxism a rather less radical ontology than the one that Wright, Levine and Sober attribute to some later Marxists. Femia's argument obscures the individualist element retained in the type–token distinction. Femia (1993: 3) quotes the words 'ensemble of social relations' from the *Theses on Feuerbach* and argues that the holistic ontology collapses the distance between the individual self and that ensemble, thus overlooking that the human subject is a sovereign agent of choice.

The anti-reductionist method presented by Wright, Levine and Sober has far greater applicability than holism to the thought of the young Marx, including, importantly, his view on the requirements for emancipation (we will not be concerned in this study to estimate its applicability to Marx's later work). In order to draw on this method most constructively, it will be useful to outline what is, for our purposes its most relevant point. The anti-reductionist method draws a distinction between two sorts of possible reduction. One is token–token reduction and the other is type–type reduction. Consider capitalist society as a type. Two tokens of that type may be US capitalist society in 2017 and Canadian capitalist society in 2017. Already we see two tokens of the type. The two tokens differ from one another and so capitalist society does not reduce to another type, but instead to the two tokens (along with the many other tokens in the history of the world). Now, it *might* be possible for each of these tokens to be reduced to other tokens: US capitalist society in 2017 reduced to all the individuals and the relations between them at that time. Even were this possible, however, it does not account for what makes US capitalist society in 2017 a token of capitalist society. For this we need to focus on the type with the many different tokens which come into its domain. As the example in the previous paragraph illustrated, types of behaviour are represented in real life by tokens of each type. The macro-type cannot be reduced to any one example from the range of tokens, as there is something distinctive about it, and vice versa. The nature of capitalism itself cannot be reduced to any one, or any set, of specific instances of ownership and employment;

moreover, no one or set of instances are necessary under conditions of capitalism, nor provide a definition of what capitalism is. Hence, the anti-reductionist method is useful because, as Wright et al. suggest (2003: 62), 'we would want to explain why specific instances of capitalism emerged when and where they did but also explain what capitalism is'. That is to say, we would want to provide explanations at both token and type levels, rather than assuming the one explanation simply follows from (because reduced to) the other.

The same non-reductive relationships would pertain also in communism: no specific forms of life (e.g. this or that mechanism for collective decision making) are made necessary by communism, and none uniquely illustrate the nature of communism. The implication is that tokens of communism need not follow a strict pattern: the individuals of one communist society may flourish in different ways than in another, and perhaps indeed from each other. Marx's communist theory was thus not a strict doctrine, and thus Marx's writings about communism and emancipation in this early period must be understood to have such open-endedness.

Marx's views on emancipation were not devised exclusively with capitalism in mind. As we saw earlier, Marx similarly discussed exploitation in relation to other types of society as well as capitalism. He was indeed concerned to find a way to achieve emancipation from all kinds of exploitation. His earliest writings are particularly significant in this respect as they illustrate the way in which over time his focus shifted from the broad range of exploitative societies to a more specific concern with ones we today recognize as capitalist. The key point here is not that capitalism is the only systemic exploitation, but rather that all other forms of exploitation (e.g. religious exploitation) are *also* found in capitalism, and it is the proletariat that is exploited in all these ways. 'Wrong generally', is how Marx put it in his Introduction to the *Contribution to the Critique of Hegel's Philosophy of Law* (CCHPLI, CW3: 186). That is why the proletariat can be universal. Hence, we need to build on the work of Wright, Levine and Sober to consider a broader macro-type than capitalism. While not at all imaginative, the label 'exploitative society' serves this purpose. Perhaps a better label for his work in the *Paris Manuscripts* and *The German Ideology* would be 'class-divided society'. This is because while in the very early writings he was not thinking primarily in terms of class, those writings helped him to formulate his work of the mid-1840s in which he was referring specifically to class. Class-divided societies were, for him, exploitative ones, because class divisions are the contradictions within a given political and economic situation that are experienced as alienation.

Löwy summarizes very concisely the developments in thought which led Marx to both his specifically class analysis and his thought on emancipation in the mid-1840s. Reflecting on the rapid advancements of the Industrial Revolution, with the growth of towns, concentration of the workers and the various movements that sought the emancipation of the masses,

Löwy (2005: 20) argues that Marx 'was able to grasp the common feature of these experiences...'. Thus inspired, Marx was able 'to develop into a coherent theory the more or less vague and fragmentary tendency towards communism and self-emancipation, and he could grasp and give expression to the real movement of the proletariat'. Marx was then concerned from 1843 with explaining how the workers could discover the meaning of their own actions and the nature of their conditions, and thus how those workers could become conscious of their own emancipatory capabilities.

Note that Löwy uses the term 'self-emancipation'. Actually, in the early to mid-1840s Marx was at a rather early stage in developing the notion that the workers themselves should be at the forefront of their own emancipation, rather than rely on leadership and inspiration from others. For example, in his article 'Communism and the *Augsburg Allgemeine Zeitung*' in October 1842, alluding to recent workers' activity in England and France, he used the term estate rather than class but was clearly thinking of self-emancipation in the following sentence: 'That the estate that today owns nothing demands to share in the wealth of the middle classes is a fact which ... is obvious to everyone in Manchester, Paris and Lyons' (CAAZ, CW1: 216). By 1844 the uprising of the Silesian weavers was, as mentioned earlier in the present chapter, leading him to express the belief that the German proletariat could soon take revolutionary action (CMN, CW3). As Hal Draper (1971: 84) suggests, it would not be until 1864, in the general rules for the First International, that Marx actually offered what might be considered 'the classic formulation of the self-emancipation principle' which held that emancipation of the working class must be done by that class itself. Nevertheless, Löwy's statement helps draw attention to the development of that idea which, as Draper charts in detail, took place in the thought of Marx' thought throughout the 1840s and which was in fact essentially complete by *German Ideology*.

That the reasoning leading to this development of the self-emancipation principle originated in Marx's critique of Hegelianism can be appreciated by focusing for a moment on his eighth thesis on Feuerbach of 1845: 'All social life is essentially practical. All mysteries which lead theory to mysticism find their rational solution in human practice and in the comprehension of this practice' (TF, CW5: 5). Marx was not, as was discussed in our previous chapter, working from a crude or basic materialism, but rather a more sophisticated radical humanist position which does not simply negate the value of thought. Hence, the eighth thesis mentions both human practice *and* comprehension of that practice. This is consistent with his work in the *Paris Manuscripts* on alienation. In their alienated condition people would not fully comprehend their situation. With the eighth thesis, we return to the practical-critical – or more specifically, revolutionary practice or praxis – which we discussed in some depth in the chapter 'Change'. Up to this point, we have established several basic principles of praxis. Praxis must contain an element of 'theory', the 'critical', or 'comprehension' (as Marx puts it here).

But this element must emerge on the same grounds and along the same path as the self-consciousness of the proletariat, meaning that it relates directly to the contradictions within real material conditions. In other words, it does not come from some mystical ideal, but emerges from out of, and has its meaning and truth only in, human practices. Moreover, it must emerge in such a way as to never be abstracted from social action (i.e. from what we have been calling 'production', and especially those aspects of production that directly relate to non-alienating forms of social organization), nor thought of as independently efficacious (as in ideology). What the eighth thesis now entails is that the truth of this comprehension lies in the relation to practice. This idea is still more clear in the second thesis, which reads:

> The question whether objective truth can be attributed to human thinking is not a question of theory but is a practical question. Man must prove the truth, i.e., the reality and power, the this-worldliness of his thinking in practice. The dispute over the reality or non-reality of thinking which is isolated from practice is a purely scholastic question. (TF, CW5: 5)

Truth is not originally to be understood as the correct correlation of something about a subject and something about an object (i.e. my thoughts and the world) – for a materialist, these are just two different states of matter, after all. Rather, truth exists as a world achieved practically (i.e. produced). Marx explores this idea in the *Paris Manuscripts*, in that portion of the manuscripts devoted to a critique of Hegel. He writes that, 'the *externalisation of self-consciousness* posits *thinghood*' [note that, to avoid confusion, we have here translated 'externalisation' rather than 'alienation']. That is, consciousness grasps the world around it as a world of things, possessing and enclosing their properties independently of consciousness, in the way abstract consciousness possesses and encloses its thoughts in isolation. In Hegel, the highest form of self-consciousness is the realization of this, and absolute knowing is the grasping of the object in its identity with spirit. Marx, though, interrupts Hegel long before that stage. For such 'thinghood', Marx insists, is and must remain abstract in Hegel; this is no 'actual thing'. '[T]hinghood is thus without any *independence*, any *essentiality*, vis a vis self-consciousness' (EPM, CW3: 335). It is only 'a semblance of' an independent, actual nature. It follows that Hegel's manner of overcoming truth as the correlation of subject and object, in absolute spirit, is a sham, for self-consciousness and object were never actually distinct. Marx insists therefore that, instead of following Hegel's path here, all this must be re-conceived on materialist terms, in order for the end aim (emancipation) to be genuine and not just another surreptitious form of alienation.

'Real, corporeal man' is not an abstract subject (self-consciousness) that 'falls' from its 'pure activity' to some creation of an object (EPM, CW3: 336). Instead, actual corporeal man is *materially productive*. His world is independent of him only to the extent that he as an objective being (i.e. as a part of nature) produces it as such – indeed, to the extent that the human being realizes himself as a productive being through production. The 'subjective' is from the beginning 'objective' – that is, what we think of as the mere innerness of consciousness is already a natural object, and what we think of as mere 'thing' must be understood also to be active – because the human is a part of nature, and produces/is produced by material conditions. Mere or pure conscious activity, and mere or pure having of myself (individuality in Stirner's, or indeed the liberal economic, sense) always was an abstraction. 'Real, corporeal mean' – man emancipated from conditions of alienation – understands this, and his flourishing as an individual occurs accordingly.

Truth is a practical question: the old, 'scholastic question' of the truth of thought is now only an isolated moment within truth, what Marx there in the 'Theses' is calling 'comprehension'. For a human being, whose essence lies in production, mere comprehension – comprehension understood ideologically – is a form of alienation. So, praxis, emerging as a kind of empiricism (this point is stressed in *The German Ideology*) thus arises out of practical life itself, as a capacity to identify and reflect upon contradictions, alienation and exploitation; and moreover, as an envisioning of an alternative, this alternative is a collective organizing *of production* (communism as the abolition of private property), which is achieved through the *production* of new forms of social life (in revolution). No other class than the proletariat can achieve such praxis. (An intellectual like Marx has a valuable role in the revolution, to be sure, but *qua* intellectual is always teetering on the edge of *mere* 'comprehension'.) It follows that self-emancipation by the proletariat is the only available path.

Interestingly, it follows from the earlier analysis that nature is 'independent' in some sense because it is *produced as independent*. Thus, in *The German Ideology*, Marx and Engels argue that the world is always 'historical': 'the world surrounding him [i.e. the German idealist, and especially here Feuerbach] is not a thing given direct from all eternity, remaining ever the same, but the product of industry and of the state of society' (GI, CW5: 39). The example given is the cherry tree, originally imported from another part of the world and cultivated. Even the most distant and wild tracks of nature are in this sense 'cultivated' (Marx and Engels' example is 'a few Australian coral islands'); we can only think of them as original nature if we first posit that human beings are *not* natural beings. Human activity would thus mediate between the subject and object distinction, which from the beginning was alienation, resulting in human wholeness (Eccleshall, 1975: 98). 'Human wholeness' refers to what we have been calling 'flourishing', or the emancipated fulfilment of species-being by individuals.

Note that throughout the period from 1843 to 1846, 'nature' has these multiple meanings: (1) Nature as that which was assumed to be distinct from the domain of the human (e.g. from 'history'); (2) Nature as inclusive of the human, thus humans as natural, material beings; (3) Nature as part of the humanized world, that is, nature as cultivated or produced; and (4) Nature can also be used to mean 'essence', although this is less relevant here. In any one passage, the meaning is to be deduced from the context. The key point, though, is that nature in the third sense must be understood to be primary, and thus the other meanings are conceptions within a more or less alienated consciousness. For further discussion of this notion see the chapter 'Change'.

As Robert Eccleshall (1975: 98) has commented, Marx was of the view that, by demystifying Hegel, a practical mastery of the world would be achieved, and the dehumanized world would be overcome by means of radical transformative action. Importantly, 'practical mastery' does not mean human *domination* of nature. Domination assumes the original separation of the subject and object, such that the latter can be possessed in its totality. Possession, most obviously in the case of private property, is part of the problem and not the solution. Rather than domination, then, 'mastery' implies the overcoming of a distinction between human and nature, as well as between owner and worker.

A natural world confronts the human being, prior to industrial techniques and forms of organization, but alienated from his essence by the projection of that essence into a deity, as in some way belonging to that deity and thus inscrutable, alien and overpowering. Even then, nature was 'produced'. As we have seen, such an experience of nature finds its critics both in Epicurus and in Young Hegelians such as Feuerbach (and it is clear that there is something of Kant's account of the sublime here). Industry, developments of the forces of production and division of labour, makes possible instead the domination over nature. But, for workers, this simply replaces domination (meaning alienation with the emphasis on power) *by nature* with domination *by capital*. Nature is now understood either as the ultimate objective opposed to human subjectivity, and that which could be, but is not yet, owned; the raw material of production that is just as alienated from the workers in its raw state as the commodity subsequently is. Or else, nature is understood as the human sphere, but as alienated from me, where the products of my alienated labour lie alongside one another. In other words, 'practical mastery' must mean the 'humanization' of the world: neither the immediate social sphere (the relations of humans with each other, and the produced objects that sustain them) nor nature (what is supposed to lie beyond the human sphere) will any longer embody, for either thought or sense, and as if original and necessary, human alienation. This, of course, is 'emancipation'.

In discussing the products of labour as an alien power confronting the worker, Marx writes:

And what a contradiction it would be if, the more man subjugated nature by his labour and the more the miracles of the gods were rendered superfluous by the miracles of industry, the more man were to renounce the joy of production and the enjoyment of the product to please these [alien] powers. (EPM, CW3: 278)

Three things are being said in this passage. First, if it ever was, the alien power could not now be nature or a deity, but must be 'man himself'; second, the terrible historical irony of all this industrial progress replacing one alien power by another, one domination by another; third, renouncing joy and enjoyment means alienation from fulfilment through labour – but also renouncing it would amount to renouncing the emotion necessary for emancipation.

Man knows nature insofar as, through practice, nature has been made 'human', in the sense that we have elaborated earlier. As Terry Eagleton (1997: 3–4) has suggested, this is an action-orientated theory of the sort 'sometimes known as "emancipatory knowledge"'. Although he does not say who knows the action-orientated theory as such, Eagleton has in mind Jürgen Habermas and other critical theorists of the Frankfurt School. Their critical theories aim to provide reflective guides for emancipatory human action. Those who engage in action will produce their own emancipation as the knowledge they develop enables them to reflect on their frustration (Guess, 1981: 1–2). Frustration begins to emerge when people begin to question their own alienation and become increasingly conscious of its genuine nature. Emancipatory knowledge, which is thus the sort of self-understanding a group or individual needs in order to know themselves, changes their own situation and moreover to alter themselves, indeed serves to summarize the sort of knowledge that Marx believed people could gain in the process of overcoming alienation. Emancipation thus involves the development of the mutable aspect of human nature discussed in the earlier chapters of the present study. The implications of this for human flourishing in the future communist society were explored by Marx in *The German Ideology*.

Emancipation and *The German Ideology*

Marx made some points in *The German Ideology* which, while not mentioning emancipation directly, clearly illustrate his thought as it had developed by the mid-1840s. 'In short,' Steven Lukes (1987: 80–1) suggests, '"alienation" is the name for what is distinctive of the Marxian view of capitalist unfreedom, and for what, according to that view, makes capitalism distinctively unfree.' Now, there has been much discussion whether alienation continued to be as prominent in Marx's thought after the mid-1840s (Cowling, 1989). Moreover, alienation is a broader concept than Lukes suggests, having, featured, for example, in Judeo-Christian beliefs of the fall of man and Feuerbach's thought in relation to religious projection (Breckman, 1999: 100–103; Mészáros, 2005: 28–33). Nevertheless, Lukes' statement does encapsulate the way in which alienation and emancipation are inextricably linked in Marx's early thought. This is because alienation suppressed human development. Free development could never be achieved while their conditions of life, work and indeed existence were extraneous and out of their control – conditions which alienation fostered. In the following passage, one can detect a significant stage in the development of the stance in which he and Engels would insist upon self-emancipation by the workers. The 'communal relation into which the individuals of a class entered', Marx and Engels wrote, referring to previous and existing consciousness of belonging to a class,

> and which was determined by their common interests as against a third party, was always a community to which these individuals belonged only as average individuals, only insofar as they lived within the conditions of existence of their class – a relation in which they participated not as individuals but as members of a class. (GI, CW5: 80)

To belong to a class means to share certain common interests with others, which in turn are only common because of the shared conditions of existence. Since it is argued (by previous economic thought) that an individual and his or her conditions are quite distinct and separable – they must be, since the individual under other circumstances would be the same person but belong to a different class – class membership is not something that individuals qua individuals participated in, but only as 'average'. My 'real' individuality could take or leave happening to belong to a class, just as I 'choose'. Marx and Engels thus provided an example of the problem of attempting to reduce a collective entity to the level of individuals, or vice versa. In this example the situation of each individual may have particular features, but to list each individual and their features would not capture the general situation. The entire group of people (the class) just happens to share the same socio-economic circumstances, but to list those circumstances does not capture each as an individual. Significantly, however, they are nonetheless capable of recognizing these similarities and identifying themselves as a class. Perhaps more importantly, this class as a collective can achieve something that individuals challenging the system to which they belong cannot – genuine change. But this change is still the merely political revolution that Marx talked about in *On the Jewish Question* and the *Contribution to the Critique of Hegel's Philosophy of Law*: it is not yet change at the level of civil society. The latter, as the domain of individuals and their voluntary associations, remains untouched because class identity kept itself distinct from individual identity. The French Revolution is the most commonly referred to example of this. This served the bourgeoisie in France well. As was mentioned earlier in this chapter, it seemed that Marx recognized this to be the case.

Marx and Engels went on as follows to compare the previous and existing consciousness with the alternative that, they considered, the workers could develop for themselves in a new community once the existing social conditions had been abolished: 'With the community of revolutionary proletarians, on the other hand, who take their conditions of existence and those of all members of society under their control, it is just the reverse; it is as individuals that the individuals participate in it' (GI, CW5: 80–1). The proletariat do not identify themselves against some 'third party', another specific class, which in principle they could join were their circumstances different, but against alienation as such. Now, this comment on the revolutionary proletarians portrays them in terms of individuals. On Marx's part, at least, what is written here is a direct continuation of *On the Jewish Question* in which it is asserted that the individual is emancipated 'as an individual human being has become a *species-being* in his everyday life' (OJQ, CW3: 168). *The German Ideology* thus clarifies what was meant there. (We discussed this passage earlier.)

Since there is no separation of state and civil society, to be an individual is no longer defined in terms of sovereignty over a merely private sphere, which is whatever happens to be *left over* after determination by the economic and political system. Marx and Engels elaborate on this point: 'Up till now association ... was simply an agreement about those conditions, within which the individuals were free to enjoy the freaks of fortune ... This right to the undisturbed enjoyment, within certain conditions, of fortuity and chance has up till now been called personal freedom' (GI, CW5: 80–1). 'Personal freedom', though, is born from alienation, from a deeply dehumanizing *lack* of freedom for two reasons. First because it arises out of 'conditions which were previously left to chance and had acquired an independent existence over against the separate individuals precisely because of their separation as individuals'. Second, 'because their inevitable association [i.e. class], which was determined by the division of labour, had, as a result of their separation, become for them an alien bond' (GI, CW5: 80). In the revolutionary proletariat, individuals belong to a class, now *as* individuals. This represents a change in the meaning of both class and individual. An individual no longer sees his or her interests as separated from those of the whole (i.e. civil society as distinct from the 'interests' of the economic and political system), nor as in original and defining conflict with those of other individuals. Marx and Engels write, 'it is the association of individuals (assuming the advanced stage of modern productive forces, of course) which puts the conditions of the free development and movement of individuals under their control' (GI, CW5: 80).

Bearing in mind Marx's concerns in the *Paris Manuscripts*, emancipation although not named is clearly at stake in the passages from *The German Ideology*. Moreover, it is clearly the end point of a sequence of thought that has led through production, alienation, exploitation and change, which we considered in the earlier chapters of this study. Each fit into the picture that Marx and Engels drew in *The German Ideology*.

Marx and Engels were concerned there with both macro social types and tokens of those types. They were interested in both the social situations which cannot be reduced to any particular token thereof, but also of the contributions of people and the relations between them. For example, let us look again at the passages quoted earlier concerning the relation of individuals and class. In the summary of the previous and existing sort of consciousness the focus was on the type, and the tokens were the sphere of alienated 'personal freedom'. Whereas, in the discussion of the developing situation of the proletariat, tokens of the type, including people and their relations, were emphasized. In each case Marx and Engels recognized the importance of types and tokens to a fuller understanding of the issues in question. Importantly, for the revolutionary proletariat, the type–token distinction remains a useful one, but its nature changes. Whereas previously the tokens (specific instances of capitalist relations, or specific types of individual behaviour within capitalist system) were understood as essentially arbitrary (not determined by type, but in no meaningful sense 'free'), now the tokens are consciously chosen modes of fulfilled life.

George Comninel argues that there is a dialectical character to emancipation from alienation. As Comninel (2010: 75) put it: 'Unless the state's defence of property is overcome, there can be no overcoming the alienation of labour. At the same time, without overcoming the alienation of labour there can be no transcendence of the political form of the state.' In this explanation Comninel may appear to be offering a paradoxical statement which seems to suggest simultaneous causation. We can grasp the dialectical character of the argument when we realize that, for Marx, the distinction between these two levels (the state, and the market for labour) is an illusion, itself a form of alienation. Dialectical means that contradictions – here, the contradiction between state and civil society, and between capitalist and labour – are *actually present* in the material conditions. They are not ideas, derived from pure theoretical contemplation of the nature of the human or of the state. Because of this, dialectical synthesis and thus revolution look hopeless. The conditions of alienation seem naturalized, everywhere and eternal; it is as if reality *just is* contradictory; so, where could revolution begin? The self-emancipation of the proletariat, then, occurs when the falsehood of this distinction is recognized. This collapse of apparently natural distinctions echoes what we said earlier about the revolutionary proletariat and class: class-consciousness is not something different from individual consciousness. The state cannot be excused from its responsibility for labour alienation; and the latter must be seen as productive of the state; they belong together as a system.

On this point, Marx and Engels are clear:

Communism differs from all previous movements in that it overturns the basis of all earlier relations of production and intercourse, and for the first time consciously treats all naturally evolved premises as the creations of hitherto existing men, strips them of their natural character and subjugates them to the power of the united individuals. (GI, CW5: 81)

Social phenomena do not just happen, and certainly human ways of life do not just drop from the sky (with the exception, as we have discussed, of certain 'immutable' features of the human). By 'premises' are meant what, at any one point, we think of as the basic character of the human or of society, what is considered natural. Although they certainly evolve, these premises do so not independently, but precisely through the productive activities of humans. To criticize these premises is at the same time to subjugate them to the 'power of the united individuals'. That means to see them as produced, to view them precisely as *not* natural, certainly but *also* to take the conscious decision either to carry on producing them or to produce other premises. Theory is nothing separated from practice.

The passage continues:

> Its [communism's] organisation is, therefore, essentially economic, the material production of the conditions of this unity; it turns existing conditions into conditions of unity. The reality which communism creates is precisely the true basis for rendering it impossible that anything should exist independently of individuals, insofar as reality is nevertheless only a product of the preceding intercourse of individuals. (GI, CW5: 81)

Communism is essentially economic because it concerns the organization of the powers of production. (Since production is part of that essential or immutable characterization of the human, however, this should remind us that 'economics' has to be defined very broadly. We will return to this point in the Conclusion.) Whereas 'existing' conditions are conditions of the separation and alienation of individuals and the conflict of classes, communism creates the 'conditions of unity'. This is because communism will have removed all the material contradictions that alienate individuals, and pit them against both other individuals and the whole. This removal of contradictions is here summarized by saying that communism creates a new reality (which is the same as the conscious recognition that reality never was truly anything but a product) such that individuals no longer experience a dominating power against them. With the removal of these contradictions, the removal of the premises must also happen, those premises that made the alienation and conflict seem inevitable. We can see then that Marx and Engels were already in the mid-1840s of the belief that, after a campaign of self-emancipation by the workers – or proletariat – the institution of communism would help consolidate and indeed further the process whereby human emancipation would be achieved.

This emphasis on communism rather than socialism was somewhat more than a choice between two words to describe collectivist radicalism. In much of *The German Ideology*, part of the subtitle of which was 'Critique … of German Socialism according to its Various Prophets', Marx and Engels criticized the German philosophers who styled themselves as 'true socialists'. Following the German Hegelian tradition these socialists focused on the abstract 'man', evaluating abstract social and political forms, professing the universal love of mankind. They thus ignored real human beings and their social divisions. Without any real party interests they had abandoned any revolutionary enthusiasm (GI, CW5: 456–7). More fundamental than this critique of 'true' socialism, however, was a leaning that Marx and Engels had towards communism more generally. As was discussed briefly in the Introduction to the present study, by the mid-1840s communism and socialism were widely considered to be quite distinct from one another. Socialism tended to represent association and cooperation while communism stood for egalitarianism and sought confrontation to overthrow the existing order. Thinkers and activists tended to affiliate to one or the other, with Hess being a notable exception. Marx and Engels, considering socialism to be the weaker doctrine, had begun in the mid-1840s to build their own version of communism. This would not be the austere, authoritarian levelling communism of old, but an entirely new one that would result from emancipation and involve freedom and flourishing achieved collectively by people who had released themselves from alienation.

We have already established that Marx understood emancipation as the transformation of the institution of private property to one of collective responsibility for the production of reality. Nevertheless, some substantiation will help clarify the matter further. That emancipation was indeed in the minds of Max and Engels can be seen clearly in the following sentences of *The German Ideology*.

> In reality, of course, what happened was that people won freedom for themselves each time to the extent that was dictated and permitted not by their ideal of man, but by the existing productive forces. All emancipation carried through hitherto has been based, however, on restricted productive forces. The production which these productive forces could provide was insufficient for the whole of society and made development possible only if some persons satisfied their needs at the expense of others, and therefore some – the minority – obtained the monopoly of development, while others – the majority – owing to the constant struggle to satisfy their most essential needs, were for the time being (i.e., until the creation of new revolutionary productive forces) excluded from any development. (GI, CW5: 431–2)

The point Marx and Engels were making here is that previous, pre-capitalist modes of production did not have the means to produce enough resources, and therefore some group would of necessity be left out. However, elsewhere, they make clear that this is not the full picture. The majority may have had to have been exploited in the early stages of each epoch in order for one or more class to assert its power. This was because at that point there were not enough resources for a satisfactory distribution. In the later stages of the epochs, however, the problem for the dominating class was precisely that there *was* the capability to produce enough to go around. The productive forces had to be held back so that the dominant class could retain its power regardless. Marx and Engels use the notion of 'fetter' [*Fessel*] in this regard. For example, summarizing the rise and entrenchment of capitalism earlier in *The German Ideology*, Marx and Engels wrote that competition

> produced a mass of productive forces, for which private property became just as much a fetter as the guild had been for manufacture and the small, rural workshop for the developing handicrafts. These productive forces receive under the system of private property a one-sided development only, and for the majority they become destructive forces; moreover, a great many of these forces can find no application at all within the system of private property. (GI, CW5: 73)

A few pages later, Marx and Engels stress that the evolving productive forces were taken over by each new generation. The history of this evolution 'is therefore the history of the development of the forces of the individuals themselves' (GI, CW5: 82). Very importantly for the purpose of illustrating this point about the obstruction of productive forces, Marx and Engels wrote that 'this development proceeds only very slowly'. Various stages of development emerge as the different interests of groups and sections of society come into relation with one another. These stages and interests, 'are never completely overcome, but only subordinated to the prevailing interest and trail along beside the latter for centuries afterwards'. 'Thus,' Marx and Engels went on, later in *The German Ideology*, 'society has hitherto always developed within the framework of a contradiction – in antiquity the contradiction between free men and slaves, in the Middle Ages that between nobility and serfs, in modern times that between the bourgeoisie and the proletariat' (GI, CW5: 432). Productive forces generate contradictions such as these insofar as now forms of alienation and exploitation are produced, and the domination of a particular class becomes 'naturalised'. Revolution can happen when the forces are sufficient to provide for all needs but, because of the failure of stages of productive relations to keep pace with productive forces, the development of human beings remains fettered.

The German Ideology also helps shed light on the notion of specifically 'human' emancipation discussed earlier in the present chapter. In a passage that follows immediately after the one just quoted Marx and Engels offered the following thoughts. The historical process of contradictions 'explains, on the one hand, the abnormal, "inhuman" way in which the oppressed class satisfies its needs, and, on the other hand, the narrow limits within which intercourse, and with it the whole ruling class, develops' (GI, CW5: 432). They continued thus:

> Hence this restricted character of development consists not only in the exclusion of one class from development, but also in the

narrow-mindedness of the excluding class, and the 'inhuman' is to be found also within the ruling class. This so-called 'inhuman' is just as much a product of present-day relations as the 'human' is; it is their negative aspect, the rebellion – which is not based on any new revolutionary productive force – against the prevailing relations brought about by the existing productive forces, and against the way of satisfying needs that corresponds to these relations. (GI, CW5: 432)

What Marx and Engels were suggesting in this rather opaque passage was that the human was the positive product of the relations (the human, even that in it which we have called 'immutable', is still *produced*). That is, the current state of the human is produced by the current state of relations of production.

Marx and Engels went on as follows:

The positive expression 'human' corresponds to the definite relations predominant at a certain stage of production and to the way of satisfying needs determined by them, just as the negative expression 'inhuman' corresponds to the attempt to negate these predominant relations and the way of satisfying needs prevailing under them without changing the existing mode of production, an attempt that this stage of production daily engenders afresh. (GI, CW5: 432)

The 'human' is whatever fragmentary state of human flourishing (that ensemble of human relations within which individuals can be cooperatively productive) was achieved thereby. The 'inhuman' is whatever resistance is put to the existing state of things, through recognition of 'narrowness' or of the 'exclusion' from development. However, this resistance occurs without changing the existing mode of production (e.g. it is seeking reform or partial revolution). It can be found among the ruling class both because that class too experiences alienation as a result of the contradictions and also in the persons of intellectuals who recognize something of the condition of exploitation. The 'inhuman' therefore is consciousness of the negation of the human (thus the prefix), without the material resources (and the forms of consciousness they make possible) to achieve some new revolutionary form of the organization of production. This new form means the way of satisfying essential capabilities in a way which brought about collective, human flourishing for all. This required emancipatory action which would overcome the existing relations characterized by the domination by the excluding (ruling) class. The maintenance of this domination, on the other hand, was inhuman as it denied members of both the dominating and dominated classes from achieving change in the mutable aspect of nature and thereby fulfilling the role of the collectivist species-being. It channelled and thus dissipated any revolutionary energies into mere reform. The existing form of the 'human' is limited by the 'inhuman'. Emancipation, judging from Marx's thoughts on it since the late 1830s, would involve the transition from the relations corresponding to some limited form of the human, one that gives rise to its own negation, to those relations wherein the human no longer presents a negation. This point is what, in Marx's earlier Feuerbachian language, called the individual realizing itself, or flourishing, as species-being.

The German Ideology helps one appreciate how in the early to mid-1840s Marx was developing a philosophy which started with emancipation and also featured the topics covered by the earlier chapters of this book: production, alienation, exploitation and change. If one thinks in terms of types and tokens and bears in mind the three nodes of class analysis, theory of historical trajectory and an emancipatory normative theory, we can better understand the philosophy which, unfortunately, he never presented in a relatively concise book or series of pamphlets.

The first Marx never wrote at length about emancipation, and generally did so with specific issues in mind. Thus it is easy to sympathize with those who like Wolff find emancipation a frustratingly 'thin' concept. Nevertheless, a substantial, wide-ranging but by no means disparate account can be reconstructed. We have identified above a series of elements of emancipation that combine coherently and arise from the linked set of analyses given in earlier chapters. These elements are: (1) Emancipation as a freeing from institutions that suppress human flourishing, insofar as these are taken to be grounded in something above or beyond the human (as in Epicurus or Feuerbach's accounts of religion); a state could also be such an institution insofar as it uses religion or some political ideal (as in the right Hegelians) to justify itself. (2) Emancipation as a freeing from ideology, meaning those practices of thinking that take thinking in itself (or critique) to be efficacious with respect to social or political reform, and to be original and independent of that which is 'critiqued'. Thought and action thus become praxis. (3) Emancipation as a freeing from political institutions that distinguish (as 'natural' or as 'just') the political from the civil order, and thereby open up both a false (abstract) domain of individual freedom and a no less false order of community, and thus also confuse reform with revolution. (4) Emancipation as the becoming conscious of the historical basis of one's way of life, the alienating or exploitative contradictions woven into it which might previously have been viewed as 'fair' or 'necessary', and thus also of the capacity for radical change so as to overcome those contradictions. (5) Specifically, emancipation of the proletariat from that alienation and systematic exploitation which forced them to identify themselves as, regardless of circumstances, individuals forever 'distinct' from their class. That class must then self-emancipate, in the sense that only it is sufficiently universal in regard to the wrongs done to it, so as to be able to liberate all of humanity which otherwise also remains (however dominant the class) in a state of alienation. (6) Still more specifically, emancipation as the overthrow of the institution of private property, the stunted ways of life and the stunted forms of human thought, action and sense that it generates, and finally overthrow of the systematic domination of some particular class by way of that institution. (7) Emancipation as that way of life in which human beings understand the original objectivity (i.e. productivity) of all their activity, and thus recognize the public, material world (including 'nature') as the realization of their full humanity. (8) Emancipation as the recognition that the proper relation of individual and community is a reciprocally conditioning one, by way of a material form of life. From this it follows that tokens of alienated forms of life are arbitrary, while tokens of emancipated forms of life are voluntary. (9) Emancipation as that form of life in which human individuals can realize themselves as cooperatively self-productive beings (i.e. flourish as full species-being).

This is the first Marx's emancipatory normative theory. We might express this in a less jagged and formal manner, as the following narrative. In the previous and existing divided societies the powerful vested interests maintained their dominance by means of relations of production which the dominated classes came to see as natural or normal. People accepted their fate, so to speak. They thus existed in a condition of alienation (in all the various forms which we outlined in a previous chapter) which enabled not only the dominant class and its vested interests but also the socio-economic system itself to exploit the dominated class. The system also ensured, moreover, that members of the dominating classes exploited one another and that they too suffered alienation, as they were dehumanized and thought that their situation was normal. Emancipation was required for all to flourish by realizing their human species-being. The vested interests could not see this and, moreover, would not want to be enlightened as they jealously guarded their wealth and power. The role of emancipation thus fell to the proletariat. They would need to take revolutionary action, guided by emancipatory knowledge (praxis). The proletariat must self-emancipate. No independent critical investigation can instigate revolution, but at best accompany and help clarify the self-consciousness of the proletariat. Praxis is this self-consciousness insofar as it is active and collective (i.e. shared), conscious of their alienated condition and its real grounds, and conscious also of the not limited or restricted possibilities for humans in their societies. Self-emancipation would thus bring about a collective society. The communist revolution would enable each as an individual to flourish in such a society. There would no longer be a dominant class and thus everybody would benefit from emancipation led by the proletariat. Such a society would be purposely planned by the individuals who would comprise it. Hence, it would not determine their condition. Nevertheless, together they would be able to achieve flourishing lives that could not be enjoyed as isolated individuals. Collective society is thus a type of which there could possibly be various tokens. The emancipation from alienation that would by this time have been realized would help make that collectivist society one in which there was no place for exploitation. All humans would view their essential productive activity as fulfilling.

CHAPTER SEVEN

Conclusion

The chapters of this book have discussed the period from the late 1830s until 1846, in which Marx considered himself to be primarily a philosopher who worked critically first with an Hegelian and later more a Feuerbachian set of methods and principles. Thereafter, so the story typically goes, he (now with Engels) broke decisively with philosophy and became the more familiar materialist economist and historian. When scholars of Marx look at the early period, the temptation is to see it primarily as a ragged series of premonitions of and developments towards this later thought, and the philosophy as a kind of unnecessary baggage soon to be dispensed with. Far less common are studies which take the first Marx seriously as a philosopher, on his own terms. His thought certainly developed during the period in question, but his writings towards the end of that period incorporated many of the ideas he had expressed at the beginning as he began to consider the revolutionary implications of the need for human emancipation. It is the emancipatory philosophy he thus formulated that the present study has constructed from his various writings of the period.

Emancipation was the topic of the last chapter before this conclusion for a good reason. It was a topic which almost all of Marx's work touched upon either directly or otherwise. Emancipation has, indeed, been described as one of the nodes around which all his work – early and late – revolved. Even before he began to publish in the 1840s, his youthful writings and doctoral thesis on Epicurus and Democritus were concerned in various ways with emancipation. In the course of the first seven years of the 1840s his theories regarding production, alienation, exploitation and change were all conceived with emancipation in mind.

One of Marx's major theoretical developments of the early to mid-1840s was the formulation of the view that emancipation must be achieved by the working class for themselves. As was discussed in the previous chapter, this was a view that Marx had come to hold firmly by the time he and Engels abandoned the manuscript of *The German Ideology* to the mice. Although this view of *self*-emancipation was not in his mind at the end of the previous decade, or even in the early years of the 1840s, he arrived at it on the basis of the development of his political philosophy throughout this period. Perhaps, therefore, more than any other concept, the concern for emancipation was the driving force of his revolutionary thought during the later stages of the period.

As has been stressed at several places in the chapters of the present volume, Marx's method was to work at both individual and collective levels, as to work at only one level would produce inadequate social explanations, and would instead result in the necessary falsification of one or more levels. As a collective of individuals, he believed, the people of the world could achieve human emancipation, which was something that each as an individual could not. This would involve the realization by individuals collectively of what, in *On the Jewish Question* in 1843, he had begun to refer to as the species-being (OJQ, CW3: 154–68). On the other hand, and especially in conditions of alienation, it is in the experiences of individuals that this realization begins. As he went on to discuss in his *Paris Manuscripts* of 1844, the fully developed species-being would achieve fulfilment collectively, free from exploitation by both individuals and the social system they had produced, and free from the alienation that had held them back (EPM, CW3).

Continuity and change in the first Marx

One gets an indication of the development in Marx's mind of this belief in the importance of self-emancipation, and of the significance of this belief for his political philosophy in general, by focusing on a letter he wrote to Ruge in September 1843. His thought in the letter focused on political and social change. Although unmentioned in the letter, the significance of emancipation can easily be determined. Marx criticized the Hegelian aim of 'raising the representative system from its political form to the universal form' (LDFJ, CW3: 144). Although, he elaborated, the old order is thus challenged, nevertheless the party by making this move goes beyond its own confines, exposes its own weakness and defeats itself. A political party, he seems to have been suggesting, would fail in its emancipatory aims if, in trying to go beyond the role of encouraging, educating and initially leading, it claimed to represent by means of working in a political, representative system. Such a system would achieve only limited changes. To achieve a thorough, human form of emancipation the exploited people would need to engage in informed direct action on the basis of a critical understanding of their own plight and the possible alternatives. Emancipation, he seems to have been suggesting, cannot be achieved by representatives, but only directly by human beings for themselves. As Alex Callinicos (1995: 20) has observed, in this passage from his letter to Ruge in 1843 can be found 'the origins of Marx's later attitude towards the working class'. The theorist, in Marx's view, does not tell the workers what to do, but rather makes sense of the struggle, of what is being fought for, suggesting what that class should do to achieve its own goals. Marx, indeed, went on as follows:

> Hence, nothing prevents us from making criticism of politics, participation in politics, and therefore real struggles, the starting point of our criticism, and from identifying our criticism with them. In that case we do not confront the world in a doctrinaire way with a new principle: Here is the truth, kneel down before it! We develop new principles for the world out of the world's own principles. (LDFJ, CW3: 144)

In mentioning in his letter to Ruge the development of new principles for the world out of its own principles, rather than trying to formulate and apply a new principle, Marx was thinking with a materialist dialectic. Change occurs not through criticism of an existing order from the point of view of some separate idea. Rather, it occurs insofar as a new synthesis is arrived at through recognizing and then overcoming contradictions that are found in the actually existing system. Marx went on as follows: 'We do not say to the world [i.e. all human beings]: Cease your struggles, they are foolish; we will give you the true slogan of struggle. We merely show the world what it is really fighting for, and consciousness is something that it has to acquire, even if it does not want to' (LDFJ, CW3: 144). The anti-idealist stance is again clear, and we are not at all distant from the empirical method that Marx and Engels follow in *The German Ideology*. Furthermore, we are also not very far from Marx's famous eleventh thesis on Feuerbach: 'The philosophers have only interpreted the world in various ways; the point is to change it' (TF, CW5: 5). The world, which as always is seething with discontent because of the contradictions it embodies, must itself become conscious of its exploitation, and of its proper goal.

The concern with emancipation, gradually becoming a belief in the importance of self-emancipation by the workers, thus links together the various writings and themes of the first Marx. The chapters of the present study have illustrated the way in which a substantial political philosophy can be constructed from those various writings. Importantly, moreover, Marx was not unaware of these links. Nevertheless, while emancipation constitutes an element of continuity across the period, some of the developments in Marx's thought in the early to mid-1840s were substantial. An anecdotal but nevertheless very illustrative indication of one of the major developments can be found in a letter Engels wrote his comrade Franz Mehring in September 1892. With reference to an allegation that Marx had read 'the historico-Romantic works ... between 1837 and 1842', and become aware that the materialist conception of history had been presented in those works, Engels reassured Mehring that

> Marx was then a Hegelian to whom that passage would have been downright heresy; he knew absolutely nothing about political economy and thus could not have made anything at all of a term such as 'economic system'. Hence the passage in question, even if he had known of it, would have gone in at one ear and out of the other without leaving any noticeable trace in his memory. (LM 28/9/1892, CW49: 549–50)

Engels added that he doubted that Marx could have been able to find the materialist conception of history in the literature in question anyway for a simple reason: it was unlikely that allusions to the conception were there to be found, rather than being the product of hindsight, so to speak. The important point is, however, that Marx was barely if at all concerned with political economy and the economic system in the late 1830s and early 1840s. The very young Marx's first emancipatory themes were indeed political issues, including political links to religious authority and to various conceptions of law. By the time he wrote the *Paris Manuscripts*, of course, these economic themes had come to prominence within Marx's thought. As we mentioned in our Introduction, this occurred because of the collusion of several factors, including the influence of Engels, Marx's own experiences as a journalist and 'the Jewish question' which introduced the all-important distinction between change in the political and civil domains. Importantly, Marx indicated that he intended to pull together the significant content of his earlier critical work on law, ethics, politics and so on with his thought on political economy in a connected whole, in which the interrelationship between the parts would become evident.

Not content to understand the world, Marx, as we stress so often in this book, became more concerned to change it. Hence, he never found either the time or inclination to construct the broader philosophy from the fragments. In undertaking the task for him this volume has uncovered a passionately committed political philosopher with a distinctive rather than merely derivative voice.

For this to be more than a scholarly exercise of reconstruction and thus to do justice to that distinctive voice, it remains for us to consider briefly how well the different parts of the philosophy of the first Marx hang together. To do this, we will perform a construction by sketching out in simple terms what Marx's interlinking thoughts would look like if pieced together into a theory. We ask the reader to consider the implications of Marx's view of human nature; of the place of humans characterized by such nature in a society dominated by private property; and their likely attitude and course of action once they would recognize such dominance and its effects upon them. As will be seen, the various fragments of Marx's writings of the late 1830s to the mid-1840s flow together. Although there were, as mentioned earlier, changes and developments in his thought during this period, this meant not that the early ideas were abandoned, but that they were altered as a result of his experience of the social and political developments of the times in which those ideas took forms which fitted together with the others in the theory. What this construction will demonstrate is that, although Marx may not necessarily have been entirely correct in all his views of human beings and their world, those views taken together form a coherent philosophy which warrants consideration by anyone who seeks to both understand and change the relationships between humans in their world.

A *précis* of the first Marx

What follows is a presentation of the bare-bones of the first Marx, stripped of argument, evidence, detail, explanation or evaluation. Our claim is that at any point from about 1844 to 1846 – the culmination of the period we are analysing – Marx would have recognized this *précis* (privately, if not necessarily publicly, given the importance he attached to polemic).

First of all, the first Marx is a materialist. This means that there are no basic differences between human beings and the world they inhabit, and moreover that there is nothing beyond that world. As such a materialist Marx is an ontological monist, although not deterministic or reductive. This is already clear in his dissertation on Epicurus. He is attracted to Epicurus for several reasons. The most obvious is the atomistic materialism. For Marx, though, Epicurus is not really an atomist in the sense of a natural scientist; Marx sees the infamous 'swerve' as the moment of self-consciousness and individuation. Marx is attracted to Epicurus also because of the latter's critique of religion (and, for Marx, politics also insofar as it claims a transcendent ground). Epicurus advocates *ataraxia* – calm or indifference in the face of powers that are beyond our understanding and control. Although the Dissertation does not carry this out, Marx appears to propose a quite different solution, which is a Hegelian synthesis of that which remains contradictory in Epicurus: namely, the philosophy of self-consciousness on the one hand, and natural science on the other. This synthesis would permit a thorough understanding of, engagement with and change of the political world. A plausible name for this synthesis that Marx envisions here, and indeed would do so for several years to come, would be 'materialist Hegelianism'. All negations are in fact positives, in the sense of being real forms of material life. He thus assumes a dialectical account of change (contradiction as negation; synthesis as negation of negation) – but again these movements are not found at the level of idea, but rather at the level of the material forms of human life. Marx insists that even matter has a history. *Contra* Feuerbach, the 'sensuously given' is not in fact ever *simply* given but always at least in part produced. It is clear, therefore, that Marx at this early point is by no means an orthodox Hegelian, but (at least) one of the 'Young Hegelians'.

The first Marx accepts the Feuerbachian critique of Hegel. Hegel's exclusive focus on development at the level of idea obscures a prior positivity at the level of the sensuous contact with the material. Having from the beginning chosen to ignore its proper foundation, Hegelian thought always remains hopelessly abstract. Hegelian thought is ultimately theological in nature, and consequently perpetuates the alienation of human beings that is also found in the history and practice of religion. However, Marx goes beyond Feuerbach. For Marx the main alienating factor is political and economic life (i.e. the actual material conditions within which production occurs), rather than philosophy or theology. Both philosophy and theology, however important they may be in other ways, are ultimately just echoes of the facts of political economy. From this follows the idea of 'embedded rationality'; that is, Marx's sophisticated materialism does not dispense with reason, for example, but also does not allow it to be considered an intellectual function that lies outside of matter and history. Reason lies within material history, although human beings can become conscious and take charge thereof.

The first Marx thus also advocates a curious kind of Kantianism that we may call 'transcendental materialism': the material conditions of political and economic life form the conditions of possible modes of human life and human self-consciousness. To borrow a phrase from Foucault, this is the 'historical a priori'. A further conclusion to be drawn from this starting point is that the first Marx is staunchly anti-idealist. Again, thought in general has its origin in the material conditions of life; thus he refutes the 'critical' thought of the Young Hegelians, which he argues always understood thought or the idea as separate, higher or more efficacious than material action. From this follows a critique of abstraction in both its senses. These are, first, a separation of the concrete particular from its conditions. The most important example of this kind of abstraction is classical liberal thought of the individual in distinction from its social life and world. Second, the abstract is that which is general, applying to many different instances (the idea or ideal, the concept).

Thus, Marx insists that political change cannot come from our comparing and correcting the current state of things according to some ideal, for the latter always has only a subsequent existence. Marx also argues that this position leads to an empirical methodology. No ideologies – in the sense of theoretical preconceptions – are permitted; analysis can therefore extricate itself from anything that claims to be 'natural' or 'necessary'. Analysis must remain within existing states of affairs, and indeed must remain on the path of self-consciousness that the proletariat will follow.

The first Marx is a humanist. This means that the origin of all moral or political value lies in human beings (and not for example in a Deity, or in some abstract principle). Marx had a theory of human nature or human essence. That essence is materially 'within us'; this human essence is understood not as prior, nor an ideal, but as a form of life for real, material human beings. This essence has two elements, the mutable and immutable. The single most important immutable, but immanent, element within human is cooperative production. The mutable element changes according to one's environment; in other words, it is historically produced. The immutable element he calls (after Feuerbach) 'species-being'. Marx and Engels abandon that term in *The German Ideology*, but the replacement ('human life') serves the same purpose. Species-being is being for itself, where the 'itself' is not considered as originally separate from other individuals or from nature. Species-being does not mean some giant super-individual organism, and certainly not an 'idea', but rather is the total collection of individuals together with their social and material relations such that there is a harmonizing of the interests of individuals with those of the collective. At any given time, because of the prevailing conditions of production, the existing type of human life will be 'alienated' with respect to full species-being. That is, it will be unfulfilled or stunted with respect to its full development. For Marx, the issue of human flourishing towards fulfilment of its essence is central to the concept of emancipation.

As a material, objective being, the human realizes itself only in the production of objective things, including itself, or equivalently in the transformation of its environment. As species-being, humans produce their world as a human world. The original meaning of 'thing' or 'object' is not 'that which is external to me' or even 'that which I have made to be external to me', that is, something essentially not part of what is human. That conception leads to an illusory subject–object dualism, where the real human being is the isolated, perceiving and possessing, subjective individual. It thus also leads to false (alienated) conceptions of philosophy, science, truth, labour and so forth. Rather, the original meaning of thing or object is something produced, as it is, in order to be part of the complete objective form of the self-realization of humans. The human world (including human beings) and nature too are produced so as to constitute a fulfilled form of human life. Species-being will be realized when individuals self-consciously realize, in a mode of life, cooperative production. Where philosophers previously have sought merely to understand the world, the point is rather thereby to change it.

Anything in human self-conception or organization that limits human flourishing is alienation. This notion broadly speaking comes from Hegel. For example, in the master and slave dialectic, when self-consciousness cannot fully realize itself without recognition through the other; or generally, where the subject remains merely subject insofar as it does not recognize its own exteriorization in its object. Equally important is Feuerbach, specifically the alienation found in theological forms of religion (which for Feuerbach includes most of philosophy), where the perfection of the human is projected outside itself, and sensuality subordinated to the idea. Marx, at around the time that Hess was formulating a similar analysis, considered the specific alienation of labour as property (or as money), which is seen as the alienation of human activity or change in the form of a false and mediating permanent. Most forms of liberalism involve the alienation of the individual from its communal nature, that is, assume to be primary that which is derivative possibility (this is most obviously found in Bentham, and in economists such as Smith and Mill, and gets exacerbated in a Young Hegelian form by Stirner). Alongside such liberalism is the Hegelian idea of the distinction between the political domain and civil society, where the former is the collective and the latter the sphere of individual freedom. This idea is alienating, Marx argues, as it encourages reform rather than revolution. That is, it prevents the realization that individuation, the economic system and the political order are all of a piece. Alienation becomes exploitation when it provides an opportunity for one group or class to advance its own interests at the expense of another; exploitation is systematic when the whole economic-political situation is one that natively involves exploitation. The need for emancipation is a driving force for all the rest of Marx's ideas. (There is a précis of Marx specifically on emancipation at the end of the chapter of that name.)

Private property, and especially within the systematically exploitative type of economy that is industrial capitalism, entails alienation of the human in several senses. The first sense is alienation from the product (through labour, rather than producing the human world, I produce something that belongs to another, a commodity). The second sense is alienation from oneself (my labour becomes abstract in the form of money; I identify myself with an industrial role; and the only thing of value to me is leisure). Third is alienation from one's fellow humans (I am a merely abstract individual, with my labour and my needs understood to be essentially in competition with others). Finally, there is alienation from the species-being (from my self-consciousness as human, and thus from my objective fulfilment in cooperative production). Even the human senses, to the extent that they remain in a condition of alienation, are 'stupid', only able to grasp things as 'property' or 'having properties'. That is, objects of sensation are to be understood not as alienated resource or commodity, nor as abstract matter, but rather in their real relationship to human flourishing, part of the produced human world and with respect to my harmonized needs.

Only because material conditions exhibit contradiction (i.e. internal differences) can a critical element arise in thought and in practice, meaning consciousness of alienation and the envisioning of a more complete form of human life. The proletariat is that class whose condition incorporates all the alienation also experienced by other classes; it is the universal class. The proletariat is not defined over against some other class; in fact, it is not so much a class as simply 'the human'. Economic events are now world events, meaning that the proletarian revolution occurs internationally; there must be simultaneous revolution. Revolutionary praxis can occur when the proletariat becomes self-conscious of its own exploitation as the stunting of the human per se, and thus acts towards not reform but revolution. Because productive forces are now able to meet the needs of all individuals, there is no necessity to class; revolution becomes possible, such that the means of production are assumed by the collective. Part of exploitation is the attempt to disguise this fact and this possibility, by evoking the idea that the existing ownership and class relations are 'natural' or 'necessary'. The result of revolution will be a change in the mutable essence of human beings, such that they no longer consider necessary the forms of alienation. Communism is a type of the organization of production such that its tokens (forms of life for individuals and groups) are not alienating, and are consciously chosen.

Now Marx's challenges to exploitation focused on a common way in which advantage is taken of some humans by others in relationships wherein the former have worked to produce either material things or experiences for the others to enjoy while the exploited themselves neither benefit nor gain any satisfaction. If we accepted this situation as natural, then we would be in a condition which Marx called alienation. This would involve the misunderstanding of and thus alienation from the things and experiences we produce, from ourselves as the producers, from our fellow exploited and alienated human beings, and from the species-being itself. Assuming that we are among those exploited by private property, once we were to begin to question the premise that it is impossible to organize society in a way that would avoid the wealth/poverty division we would recognize that actually we had been mistaking our situation for normality. We would, moreover, subsequently no longer be accepting, perhaps unconsciously, as natural the exploitation and domination by others who benefit from the situation. Of course, this would involve thought, volition and action to challenge the existing material circumstances. This raises the following question: which has primacy – material or ideas?

Marx was no *simple* materialist. For him, the material world is experienced by human beings who have the capacity to form an understanding of themselves as having the potential to enjoy fulfilment as active and cooperative members of society. But this becoming conscious, having potential to be fulfilled and having some cooperative agency in change are all material processes (and not acts of a mind, soul or spirit!). In a reciprocal process we both produce and are affected by our environment, but we do not always simply respond to events that harm us or produce other unpleasant feelings in us by way of reflex. Rather, we react through volition. There is a will at work between the experience we have and the action we perform in response. As we have the capacity to understand our situation and condition of alienation, we might at some point realize that capacity. When we begin to recognize that our condition of alienation is not in fact a natural one, we are likely to become dissatisfied and possibly, by volition, decide to take action to try to change our situation. If we recognize, furthermore, that we have been misled or that we have misled ourselves, our thoughts form or change in a particular way.

Once we have recognized that the existing situation is unnatural and that there must be a better social arrangement, we are, Marx's theory goes, likely to realize that another group, or class, of people in society are exploiting us, or perhaps that the system which characterizes our society is exploiting us. If the latter, we seek to change the system, rather than *only* to prevent particular people from exploiting us any longer. When we have decided to take some kind of action to change our situation of exploitation, we have undergone change. Furthermore, we then seek to produce changes to our environment which, once again reciprocally, change us some more as we develop ourselves. Specifically, we are beginning to modify our 'form of life', meaning the current state of the human. As we do so we begin to work towards our own emancipation. We do so of our own free will, even though we may need some initial encouragement to do so from people like Marx. Once thus encouraged that it is our own responsibility to work for our own emancipation in cooperation with our fellows we free ourselves from alienation and exploitation and we determine our own development, acting on the basis of our own will. In the case of action to emancipate humanity, once we recognize that we have the same purpose this is a collective will. We thus resemble in some but not all ways the kind of human beings that existentialists claim to recognize.

Marx and existentialism

In a number of ways, Jean-Paul Sartre's famous existentialism of the late 1930s and 1940s is an echo of Marx's thought a century earlier. Both were Hegelian, but not orthodox by any means. Both were fascinated by the prospect of emancipation, and both for similar reasons suspicious of idealist or theological paths to emancipation. Both took as their starting point the notion of self-production in its relation to a very broadly Aristotelian idea of flourishing. Both employed transcendental methods that could be traced to Kant (in Sartre's case, the phenomenology of Husserl and Heidegger), and likewise the basic structures of their ethics were also Kantian (we refer to the concepts of autonomy and of the human as end in itself). And last but not least, what both wrote clearly reflected contemporary struggles against authoritarian and profoundly reactionary political movements.

In his essay *Existentialism and Humanism* of 1945 Sartre spelled out his reasons for combining existentialism and humanism in a single philosophy. This was several years before he began to argue that existentialism and Marxism were compatible with one another. Sartre came to argue that the Communist Party needed to act for the proletariat, before changing his mind once again and seeking a less authoritarian solution as the road to emancipation (Khilnani, 2003: 304–10). Nevertheless, we focus on *Existentialism and Humanism* because its focus on the human means that the significant affinities with the philosophy of the first Marx are clear to see. In the essay Sartre (1973: 26) described his existentialism in terms of a belief that in the case of human beings 'existence comes before essence – or, if you will, that we must begin from the subjective'. This well-known slogan is a somewhat skewed reading of Heidegger's analysis of human existence in *Being and Time*, published in 1929 (Heidegger, 1962). (We will return later to the somewhat uncomfortable gloss on his own idea as a beginning 'from the subjective'.) Sartre's point is that there is no pre-existing or even immanent essence to the human being, but only one generated through existing, which here means through production. Although humans produce things for use according to some conception, plan or formula, nobody has similarly produced humans – there is no God as creator of mankind and therefore there is no essence of mankind. Hence, there is no human nature. Humankind must exist before there is a conception of it. 'Man' is in the beginning nothing. 'He will not,' Sartre (1973: 28) went on, 'be anything until later, and then he will be what he makes of himself.' Sartre (1973: 56) stressed that his existentialist position should be described as existential humanism because 'it is not by turning back upon himself, but always by seeking, beyond himself, an aim which is one of liberation or of some particular realisation, that man can realise himself as truly human'. Sartre thus believed emancipation to be possible.

'But has not Sartre contradicted himself?' a reader of the first Marx might comment. Not to have an essence prior to self-production is *precisely* to have that *as* its essence. This provides the essential differentiation of human beings from animals or plants who, as we have seen, reproduce but do not self-produce. Human beings are essentially productive. What in Marx we called the 'immutable' aspect of human essence is by no means dissimilar to what Sartre might term the ontological condition of human beings. This condition, Sartre argues, frames all human existence but does not determine the way of life, the 'who I am', developed through self-production. So, is the difference between them on this point just a matter of terminology, with the first Marx calling 'essence' or 'Species-being' what Sartre would call 'ontological condition'? Not quite, for at least two reasons. First, since the kind of radical freedom that Sartre's human existence possesses can reject even this limited sense of essence, for example, through a radical act such as suicide, one could eliminate even existence. Marx would have opposed this belief that suicide and thus the elimination of existence is rational, but not in the way Sartre's critic Albert Camus (2005: 1–9) would suggest: that one should be courageous, face up to the absurdity that is an essential feature of life and endure it. Rather, for Marx, the absurdity is a feature of the existing way of life which people in their condition of alienation do endure. The point, for Marx, is to change it! More importantly, however, for Sartre my emancipation means something like explicit autonomy. I must recognize that I am radically free, and that my existence is prior to my essence, and if I do so, then whatever condition I am in is emancipated provided I have endorsed it, and continue to do so, with my freedom. Let us imagine (this example is deliberately a very Sartrean one) an example of two nuns in a convent, living lives that for all practical purposes are identical, having had backgrounds that were likewise. The first, however, has 'fallen into' convent life, partly out of a faith inherited from her family and her culture, and partly out of a sense of helplessness in her prior life. The second, however, having had the same experiences, nevertheless understands that the choice is hers and hers alone, and that if she has faith it is because she has chosen to have faith, and if she feels helpless then she has chosen to feel helpless, and with all this awareness has chosen the convent. That is, she has in full freedom chosen to have a ready-made essence. The events of her life are the same, but the meaning of her actions is different. Within Sartrean existentialism, the first is living 'inauthentically' and the second 'authentically', that is, is emancipated.

In contrast, the 'immutable' essence in Marx does to some extent act as a restraint on what forms of life could be called emancipated, instead of alienated or exploited. So, the condition of a worker in a factory, exchanging labour for wages, is exploitative *even if the worker consents to it*. In fact, that consent is precisely what is seized upon by liberal economics as entailing that no moral harm is done, that is, such economics tries to claim that this is not and could not be a condition of exploitation. To be sure, Marx did not really consider the Sartrean situation; for him, the idea that someone could be conscious of their exploitation and *not* feel aggrieved about it and at least desirous of change would be mad. Alienation is tantamount to 'misled in some way, but unaware of it'; both the misleading and the lack of awareness are what make exploitation possible. Nevertheless, a stunted realization of human fulfilment is indeed stunted even if, for some reason, it really was consensual.

For Sartre, in saying humans were responsible for what they are, this means not only that they are responsible for their own individuality, but also that they are responsible for all other humans. 'For in effect,' Sartre (1973: 29) went on, echoing Kant on universalization, 'of all the actions a man may take in order to create himself as he wills to be, there is not one which is not creative, at the same time, of an image of man such as he believes he ought to be.' By attaching value to a way of living, one might elaborate, I am advocating it as a way of living. It is impossible consistently to will one way of life for me and a different way for you, without acknowledging the legitimacy of your judgement of me as unfree, as a mere object. This is of course Sartre's version of the Hegelian dialectic of recognition that we have seen previously in both Feuerbach and in Marx. (Sartre (1992: 320–4) most fully discusses such issues in the chapter 'The Existence of Others' in *Being and Nothingness*.) The Sartrean individual, then, is not alone but necessarily carries with it consciousness of being with and for others. Sartre here treats this as a kind of 'burden': the full weight of my free responsibility is revealed when I understand that it is not merely my own essence that is at stake, but that of all humanity. My self-production is always already a production of a human essence.

The first Marx, however, sees self-production as never simply 'mine' from the beginning. Emancipation includes the consciousness that I exist as a social being. Thus, the meaning of all my actions is immediately social (something Sartre grasps too) but more, that the conditions under which I could be emancipated are, at least in part, always a gift of others in a collective act of production. An individual is free by way of and towards the collective; specifically, she is so from out of the historical grounds of collective human self-production and in recognizing the destination of human flourishing as cooperative production. This is why Sartre's gloss 'begin from the subjective' is so important. Individual freedom is and must be an absolute origin for Sartre. It has no conditions, or certainly no conditions that would in any way determine or even enable that freedom. Sartre seems uncomfortable with the gloss, we noted earlier, precisely because he knows that the distinction between subjective and objective had received one of its definitive critiques in phenomenology, especially in Heidegger. Nevertheless, it indicates a core truth about Sartrean existentialism, namely this absolute origin of freedom in individual existence. Marx cannot concur.

Now, Marx one may recall had argued in the 1840s that humans produce things to use, themselves, their society and their environment. In his view as their social environment changed, largely because developments in productive forces brought about conditions in which one class could capture the dominance upon which a declining class had lost its grip, human thought changed accordingly. The thoughts that humans have and the actions they take change according to their situation. This can in one respect be seen in terms of subjectivity because their existence does not mirror some external or timeless essence that determines their entire nature. Such subjectivity is not, however, understood as abstract individuality, but as originally social. As a materialist he understands freedom as grounded in conditions that no individual could encompass or control.

Nevertheless, as we have seen, Marx's philosophy is one concerned with freedom and by no means dispenses with the individual, and certainly not in the radically holistic fashion that some critics have claimed. Marx held that there was such a thing as human nature, and that this nature was divided into changeable and permanent elements, but that neither was deterministic of the individual, at least not in the condition of emancipation. For him, there was a human essence, and this was that of the species-being. Humans did not always, and indeed had rarely, recognized and still more rarely realized this essence. Nevertheless, once they had overcome the condition of alienation they would, by means of emancipation, be able to do so. This would not only free humans as a collective, but also individuals who were no longer shackled to the stunted, abstract sense of individualism of liberal capitalism. Hence, the subjective–objective binary opposition does not feature in the first Marx's philosophy; one could not experience being, as Sartre says however reluctantly, from the subjective, for that is always already an abstraction. His philosophy was thus richer and potentially more emancipatory than that of Sartre, as the emphasis is not entirely on each individual to somehow find that their willed existences would all meaningfully coincide. Rather, for Marx, there was something in particular to overcome – the alienation by means of which they accepted their exploitation, which is to say a real, trans-individual material condition, and thus a material system that foisted alienation upon individuals – and also a minimal sense of species-being to realize before emancipation could be achieved. If they come to recognize these things *in their life activity* (what Marx called 'praxis') then this would be beneficial to them all in cooperation.

The first Marx today

Now that 200 years have passed since Marx's birth, it might be supposed that his thoughts as a young man in the late 1830s and early to mid-1840s are merely of interest to historians of political and social thought. There are some prominent issues today, however, to which his work continues to be resonant. One such issue is consumerism. Why do people buy things the primary purpose of which is to have been bought, when often they have meagre disposable income? A second issue is helplessness. Have we become individuals who, driven by what C. B. Macpherson (1962) famously called 'possessive individualism', are unable to look after ourselves and our fellow human beings qua human beings – beings that naturally live together in groups? A third issue concerns ecology. Do the first two issues have implications for ecological problems today? We will be looking ever so briefly at such questions, guided throughout by the conceptual tools developed by the first Marx.

In 1990, Sartre's former existentialist disciple André Gorz (1994: 51–2) posed the following question:

> By dint of monetizing, professionalizing and transforming into jobs the few remaining production and service activities we still perform for ourselves, might we not reduce our capacity to look after ourselves almost to the point where it disappears, thus undermining the foundations of existential autonomy, not to mention the foundations of lived sociality and the fabric of human relationships?

Let us gloss, and expand upon, Gorz's idea here. There is a kind of division of labour in how the contemporary individual produces their own life. In some cases, the division arises due to identity encouraged by discrimination, exploitation and disadvantage of groups – such as people who do not match what is considered as the norm in a society regarding race, ethnicity, sex and sexuality. As writers such as Iris Marion Young (1990) have discussed, in response movements of oppressed groups can sometimes assert a positive meaning to group difference and identity. This can help cultivate the rejection of stereotypes that mark groups as inferior and so on. Such groups can become motivated to engage in political struggle rather than just accept exclusion and subordination. Moreover, people who do not belong to these groups can support policies and rules that attend to group difference positively. In other cases, the division is manufactured by means of an array of gadgets for this and services for that which encourage us to believe that we can create our own way of lives on the basis of choice. The division is, however, contained within a hegemonic order in which the stereotypes just mentioned develop. In the 1960s, Marcuse discussed the latter situation in terms of false needs. As he put it: 'Most of the prevailing needs to relax, to have fun, to behave and consume in accordance with the advertisements, to love and hate what others love and hate, belong to this category of false needs' (Marcuse, 1986: 5). This was, for Marcuse (1986: ix), a feature of an irrational society in which 'productivity is destructive of the free development of human needs and faculties'.

Fifty years on from Marcuse's irrational Western society, the situation is not substantially different. Features of our being such as sexual orientation, our particular specialization of interests and competencies, and the ever-expanding typologies of character subtypes with which we can identify provide us with a ready to wear identity, perfectly suited to an era of social interaction dominated by social media. Corresponding to this is dizzying expansion of the number of businesses or franchises offering specialized products and services, increasing along the way opportunities for mediation, alienation and exploitation. Turning back to the passage quoted from Gorz, one can appreciate that he was raising issues which deem the thought of the first Marx to be remarkably resonant.

Our first step to grasping such resonance is to understand what meaning 'proletariat' might still have in contemporary society. As was discussed in the present study, in the 1840s Marx became increasingly convinced that social change would need to be the result of revolution by the proletarian class. Only that class could, by means of emancipation of itself, abolish the need for any exploitation in society. Proletarian emancipation would thus bring about human emancipation. Of course, since the 1960s there have been many reminders from thinkers of the left that proletarian emancipation would not mean the abolition of all kinds of oppression, domination, discrimination and exploitation. Various thinkers have, in their different ways, stressed that the left needs to move away from its traditional emphasis upon the emancipation of the proletariat. The New Left philosopher Marcuse (1986) made such a case in the 1960s. Gorz (1982) said 'farewell' to the working class in the 1980s, and in that decade the post-Marxists Ernesto Laclau and Chantal Mouffe (1985) argued that the emphasis on class identity served to take attention away from other antagonisms involving other sorts of identity. There were others in addition to these well-known writings.

It is necessary to ensure that attention is not paid only to class and proletarian struggle. Emancipation which left discrimination or exploitation on the grounds of, for example, race, colour, sex, gender and sexual orientation in place would be wholly inadequate. As long as one bears in mind that these other issues need to be dealt with the works of the first Marx are still of value, including the emphasis on proletarian self-emancipation. What is nevertheless important is to develop the concept of proletariat or working class in today's social conditions which are very different from those of Europe in the 1840s.

The notion of proletariat or working class needs to cover all people who are exploited in their work. All these people are involved in production of goods, of services, of society, of themselves and of what Marx called the species-being. This would be the many. The few who gain and enjoy great wealth and luxury may exploit one another, and they may be enduring alienation, but if they are to learn that a better, cooperative, emancipated life can be had in a new society, this is unlikely to happen without human emancipation brought about by self-emancipation of the very extended majority. How must the notion of 'proletariat' be expanded, without losing the inner link Marx discovered between the proletariat and production, alienation, exploitation or emancipation?

Marx, as we have seen, came gradually to the idea of the proletariat as the universal class. For the first Marx, the notion of emancipation neither begins there, nor is emancipation only about the proletariat, defined narrowly. One example of a wider interest in emancipation concerns the status of women. There is a discussion of marriage in the *Paris Manuscripts*. Marx is in fact here criticizing crude forms of communism for imagining that women would be sexual property held in common. But, his argument assumes that the status of women is *already* that of private sexual property (EPM, CW3: 294–5). It is worth also looking at how he cites the data on prostitution (EPM, CW3: 244). Exploitation of women is a part of the contemporary political-economic system, without women necessarily being members of a narrowly defined proletariat (or only in some industries, such as cloth mills). In other words, we are missing something in the analysis of capitalism if we take the proletariat simply or even mainly to mean industrial workers, that is, the traditional 'working class'.

There were of course good reasons why in the 1840s industrial workers were a key group – competition among workers for job opportunities, working 'hand to mouth' and alienation through labour were most visible here. Moreover, recent labour movements, strikes or revolutionary activity had emerged from that group. Even in saying that the proletariat are the 'universal' class, whose emancipation would lead to general human emancipation, though, it is already clear that Marx was aware of other alienated and exploited groups. In turn, this means that notions like alienation and exploitation are not *only* found in industrial workers.

Social and economic conditions have evolved, meaning that today's 'proletariat', in either a narrow or an extended sense, find themselves in a different position. Already in 1899, Bernstein shocked the Marxist movement when he argued that social relations had *not* intensified in the way depicted in the *Communist Manifesto*. There had been an enormous increase in social wealth, and rather than a decrease in the number of capitalist magnates there had been a rise in the number of capitalists of all grades. As he put it: 'The middle classes are changing in character, but they are not disappearing from the social spectrum' (Bernstein, 1993: 2). In other words, workers have become increasingly 'middle' class, diminishing those who are working only for bare sustenance, as had been common much earlier in the century. 'Working class' had become more of a social category than an economic one. Part of the reason for this was the evolution within capitalism of a means of defusing effects of alienation. The minimum acceptable pay equals what is needed to be a consumer, to participate in global consumerism. Alienation and more subtle forms of exploitation are masked by consumer products.

Naomi Klein (2000) in her book *No Logo* discussed at length the way in which the big companies had identified that the most profitable way forward was no longer to produce things but instead to produce brands. Consumers were encouraged to consume brands. Things could be produced anywhere in the world very cheaply – due to the exploitation of those who made them *there*. The value they had was determined by the brand that was attached to them. Marx's early work enables us to add another feature to Klein's ground-breaking work. Alienation has reached a new level. It is no longer things that appear to have a life outside of the labour that producers had given to them. Now brands had assumed a similar character and had become still stronger than the things to which they were attached. The producers, meanwhile, are alienated still further from those other humans who consume them. Those others appreciate only the brand. The product to which the brand is attached is barely considered. Producers are exploited and consumers are happy to be hypnotized by brands. Neither producer nor consumer approaches the human nature of the species-being.

With contemporary consumerism in mind, one might notice that the capitalist emphasis on paid work exacerbates four things that the first Marx had already noticed. Quickly: (1) The human being is the animal that possesses and uses money and property. (2) Property comes to mean that which is exchanged for money. (3) Production is defined solely in terms of property and money. (4) Production is thus confined to various kinds of discrete artefacts or services. Discussing these will be the penultimate task of this concluding chapter, before turning very briefly to the ecological consequences.

So, to the first of these points about paid work in capitalist society. Consumer capitalism seeks to gradually redefine the human as the animal that owns property, where work is (with the exception of luck) the only way of obtaining money and thus property. There is an inner link here to the well-known concept of possessive individualism which, Macpherson (1962: 3) argued, is driven by a 'conception of the individual as essentially the proprietor of his own person or capacities, owing nothing to society for them', and by implication expecting to receive nothing likewise. If property and especially money come to mediate between human beings, then the only role or relation I have to others is a narrowly economic one; we are either consumers or competitors, or else I am nothing.

From this feature of contemporary capitalism arises the modern version of a very old view of the poor and unemployed: your condition is your fault. The modern version takes the form: you have no right to consume unless you work. Now, out of the goodness of our hearts we won't let you starve, but we also will not simply give you money. Instead, have food stamps and so on. In part, this follows from mainstream, historical liberalism: economics is not in the political sphere. There is also a widely known Protestant value system in play. But in addition, a subtext of the modern version is that you are the kind of sub-human that would starve your children for a branded pair of shoes, but who can't be bothered to *work* for either. The social conditions here are, of course, in many ways very different from those of the 1840s, but nevertheless we have seen Marx study similar attitudes in his accounts of the wood-gathering laws, and the Mosel wine-growers. Workers and non-worker alike very clearly experience a version of alienation in the first Marx's sense: property and money become a mediator between human beings, and thus also a barrier to any realization of their cooperative human essence. Humans who do not work and own property are thus not considered fully human, when it is precisely this view that prevents us from understanding the true productive nature of the human.

Among those who do work in that conventional sense, the situation is different but no less alienated. We have a 'disposable income', and can join the club that even the rich inhabit: we can purchase and consume. The product we end up trying to produce, through economic activity, is human wholeness – which that economic activity rendered partial or stunted in the first place. As consumers we continually seek through consumption to make whole our condition alienated by private property. By having things, we hope to make up for what is essentially lost *by having things*. We literally are trying to buy (back) our humanity. Moreover, in initially mentioning Gorz earlier, we described how self-production had become specialized, franchised and splintered. Contemporary consumer economy has 'industrialized' self-production by humans. This means that, as specialized individualists, our consumption is *also* devoted to making us *distinct* from others, fracturing our social groups into 'special interests'. Sociality, cooperation and concern for our fellow humans are considered as secondary matters – if indeed they are considered at all. In terms of our capacity to flourish as humans and fulfil species-being, we become helpless.

The second implication of consumer capitalism concerns how property is understood. The emphasis on working for money and property seeks to constrain our definition of 'property' to that which is subject to voluntary exchange *using money*. This reveals to us another remarkable metamorphosis of capitalism since the mid-nineteenth century. Capitalism remains entirely focused on property, but only partly on property that is normally exchanged in monetary terms. It *serves* capitalism for the focus of critique to be on money, and thus on the wages of labour, for thereby its metamorphosis goes largely undetected. What other market for property is there, than one whose primary mechanism is money?

The answer is power and privilege. In *On the Jewish Question*, Marx famously analyses the distinction between political and civil societies. This includes an account of the French Revolution as a revolution only in the political sphere, such that the bourgeoisie obtained (indeed, for a time, eclipsed) the political privileges formerly confined to the aristocracy. Because the distinction between social domains is an illusion, such revolution was and had to be incomplete, leaving out those in civil society who remained subject to exploitation. Marx now emphasizes revolution at the level of the economic. But this does not mean – indeed, it would be self-contradictory nonsense if we thought so – that Marx did not care about specifically political forms of exploitation, such as the disenfranchisement of many groups from any political voice. With the elimination of the distinction between political and civil must also go the idea that a genuine emancipation would leave one or the other untouched. Likewise, for us to continue, today, to talk about the proletariat in narrow terms is to leave these other markets unexamined.

Power means 'control of opportunities' both for oneself (the best schools, the right contacts – this is what normally falls under the heading of 'privilege') and for others (e.g. sexual exploitation in exchange for roles, as has been practiced by a famous mogul in the film industry). Because of possessive individualism, the humanism of the mere ego, opportunity becomes competition. Because of the enormous variety of products and services and their production sites, possible markets for power and privilege have exploded in number. Every business and every service-provider has such a market as a more or less unconscious part of its 'business plan'. Opportunity granted by power or privilege becomes a crypto-currency, functioning as a means of exchange but below the 'radar' of financial accountancy, or any other public form of scrutiny. 'Expenditure' of such power does not lessen it, but rather enhances it by normalizing and reinforcing its conditions. Power thus accumulates like capital, while exploitation becomes universalized beyond the traditional 'working class'. Protection of these markets, one suspects, is a key reason why, in more recent political history, there has been a definite convergence of socially conservative and economically conservative political interests. No doubt abuse of power and privilege has always happened, but it is an extraordinary thing that capitalism should in recent times make them its own. This too permits us legitimately to expand the notion of 'proletariat' far beyond what Marx himself likely imagined.

For reasons that go all the way back to Marx's use of Hegel, the exercise of this power especially in the second sense, as an 'exchange' of opportunities with others, is alienating for both parties, though exploitative only for one. Using power to elicit consent is only at the merest remove from slavery or rape. The victim feels helpless, objectified, without recourse (for the exchange was never entered on any accountant's slate) and certainly also alienated from any fulfilment that ought to accompany production. On the other hand, the power broker's actions become compulsive, each time trying finally, hopelessly to produce a bridge across the alienation between consciousness and the realizing recognition of that consciousness by the other. Hopeless, of course, since both the alienation and the accumulation of power occur *through* the existence and exercise of power.

The third consequence of the focus on paid work has to do with how production is defined. In fact, there is at no point a state of non-production, or non-activity of the human. Human beings are essentially productive, of their own being, of social relations, of an overall 'form of life' in which they and others participate. All human activity is to be understood as productive; accordingly also, the concept of 'economics' must be dramatically expanded. Only within the frame of some configuration of productive forces – and thus a set of interests concerning what is produced and how efficiently – could one say 'he is not productive'. That is, these interests determine what counts as genuine production. If an employee is labelled 'not productive', this only has meaning within the employer's interest in profitability; if someone unemployed is also 'unproductive', then that is possible only within a framework where employment (exchanging work for wages) is the norm. If we come to consider *ourselves* unproductive, then we have internalized these contingent perspectives. One could be *mis*productive, perhaps, for example, criminality, destructiveness or even genuine laziness, but even this depends upon the frame; in any case, one could never not produce. The baseline definition and value of a human being does not depend upon *what* or *how* they produce. The unemployed are sometimes labelled as 'scroungers', 'undeserving poor' and are scapegoats for the exploitation that 'ordinary' people feel. Ironically, in this the unemployed are being *very* productive, performing an essential service for capitalism by allowing exploitation to be felt but for the real source to be mis-identified. The same holds for immigrant populations.

The fourth consequence of consumer capitalism is the manner in which it dramatically reduces our sense of what we produce. We have just seen one aspect of this, since unemployment, for example, is defined as unproductive. Let us now follow the first Marx in expanding upon this point. Humans produce the realization of themselves. The complete, flourishing human is not a mind, or a mind and a body, or an individual agent – these are all abstractions. Rather, the human is a being within a community and at the same time within a material form of life that they have produced, freely, for themselves. Neither the lived environment (buildings, streets, factories, power cables) nor *nature as such* can be excluded from this 'material form of life'. The natural world, the wider environment, is thus produced as part of a human, material form of life. This production of nature happens in several senses. Certainly, aspects of nature are changed through human activity (as we saw, Marx's examples were domesticated species of plants and animals). Concepts of nature are produced likewise. Concepts of nature were not just 'there' in some sense prior to human beings, and these concepts have histories. Such concepts include the competing ideas of nature as industrial resource, nature as some kind of 'spiritual' resource where human beings can be renewed (thus natural parks) and nature as the object of study for the production of scientific knowledge. We live in nature according to the concepts of nature we have produced. There is also nature as a regionalist or nationalist symbol. Finally, we produce nature as the diminishing source of raw materials and energy, and the not-infinite final resting point of our by-products or waste. Pollution and climate change are just the most obvious, widespread instances of this. The danger is that the longer this continues, the greater will be the problem of helplessness and, moreover, resolution of that problem may be too late.

As humans' natural environment deteriorates largely as a result of their present activities, emancipation from the exploitation involved in the capitalist system will only be short-lived if this is achieved by means of measures that continue to bring about global warming and the exhaustion of the world's resources. Recall, as we mentioned in the chapter on Change, that for Marx in his doctoral dissertation, time is the active form of concrete nature. The concept of time refers to the changeability in an environment, the possibility of the reproduction of what is or the production of something new. As humans produce their things, their selves and their world, change takes place. Change could be for the better or the worse. As Susan George puts it in *Another World Is Possible If . . .* , capitalism treats nature as simply a source of raw materials and a dumping ground for waste. The market thus 'functions within a time framework contrary to the reality of natural time'. She continues as follows: 'Production (of goods) and reproduction (of species or natural systems) are different processes and do not obey the same temporal rules' (George, 2004: 39–40). Marx's theory of alienation once again becomes relevant and can be further developed. In the contemporary world the emancipation from alienation needs to consider that the species-being can only flourish if the temporal rules of nature are respected.

Broadly, we argue that the temporality of capitalism is one-directional: towards accumulation of wealth (or power and privilege), 'progress' and 'growth'. The temporality of cooperatively productive (including self-productive) human beings, though, is *circular* – in the sense that the impact of human productive activities is felt *within the human*, rather than lost without a trace as waste and then replaced also without a trace from out of infinite resources. It is this circular structure that must be emphasized, that human production is not concerned with individual things, or even with individual bodies, but with the sustaining production of a whole, social and material way of life. The latter is the 'frame', to use again the term we introduced earlier, for evaluating the what and how of production.

One might wonder whether this problem can be resolved within the capitalist system. As Terry Townsend suggests, it would seem that shifting, for example, to more energy-efficient production would be in the interests of the capitalists, as would the replacement of dirty fossil fuels with cleaner, more efficient renewable sources. Townsend (2007: 19) elaborates as follows:

> Many in the environmental movement argue that with the right mix of taxes, incentives and regulations, everybody would be winners. Big business will have cheaper, more efficient production, and therefore be more profitable, and consumers will have more environment-friendly products and energy sources. In a rational society, such innovations would lower the overall environmental impact in terms of materials and energy used per unit of output, when substituted for more harmful technology.

However, as he reminds us: 'Unfortunately, we don't live in a rational society' (2007: 19).

Humans continually produce their natural environment and if the extended working class we have just conceptualized is to continue to produce nature for long in the future then the new human relations that emancipation brings about will need to reflect the need for change in the relations between humanity and nature. As Alec Loftus (2009: 159) has put it: 'If nature is produced through everyday practical activity, the environmental challenge is to restructure productive activity and to transform the relationships through which environments are produced.' For him, the *Theses on Feuerbach* 'provide a wonderful springboard for a political ecology of the possible'. As Loftus (2009: 160–1) suggests, the statement in the first thesis that previous materialist thought, including that of Feuerbach, had failed to understand that reality is constituted by sensuous, practical human activity serves as a foundation for an ontological argument that such activity produces nature. This is activity both between humans and by humans using resources while operating within the constraints of their environment. Loftus also focuses on Marx's third thesis, which stresses that the coincidence of the changing of circumstances and the human activity of self-changing can only be understood in terms of revolutionary practice. This, Loftus (2009: 163) argues, serves as an epistemological ground for the argument that: 'Knowledge claims about environments are rooted in the process of making and changing those environments.' The ontological and epistemological grounds together, he suggests, form a foundation for a political–ecological praxis (Loftus, 2009: 164). This amounts to an argument that 'change must come from the understanding gained within everyday activities' and that a 'critique of the everyday production of natures is inseparable from this' (Loftus, 2009: 165).

Change that will bring about a new society in which humans interact with nature in ways which are not detrimental either to those humans or the natural environment will require action based on the understanding of present and potential forms of production and their relation to a 'way of life' fully considered. Contemporary consumerism reflects this narrow interpretation of the place of the individual in their society and in the world. To the possessive individualist, nature is even more of an irrelevance than others in society; it is 'not my concern'. However, if human beings are essentially productive, then of course it is my concern, both as an individual and as a human being. Let us echo how Sartre put the analogous situation: The expansion of our notion of production and economics reveals an existential 'burden' on human beings who are, by way of producing a way of life, creating an 'image' of the human.

This brings us back to the quotation from Gorz. Of particular significance is Gorz's mention of the foundations of existential autonomy. The concepts of species-being and alienation become very relevant in this respect. For the first Marx the species-being is produced by humans themselves. Once emancipated from exploitation the human will be able to reach the condition of flourishing in which the species-being will be realized. This can only happen when humans overcome alienation. The alienated human being is not an autonomous one. This is because that being accepts as normal a condition which has, perhaps over a period of generations, been manufactured. The human mind is conditioned and not allowed to recognize its true state, which is a state that flourishes in cooperation with other human beings and also in a way that respects the natural environment and resources by which humanity is sustained. An alienated human is not autonomous for several reasons relevant to Gorz's point: (i) because not in fact able to choose a different form of life; (ii) because distracted from this fact, and from genuine choices, by the illusion of choices and the illusion of individualism; (iii) because even the possibility of autonomy is withheld from me by the consumerist fracturing of any sense of unmediated responsibility even *for* myself; and (iv) because released from the *burden* of choice (i.e. the recognition of one's productive role towards a way of life and a state of nature) by that same illusion of individualism. Crudely put, such autonomy is gained not by cutting oneself off, but by recognizing that one is already a part of a way of life that is produced and thus can be changed.

If one considers Marx's theory of the species-being, existential autonomy might be conceived as being a condition one can realize by understanding and acting upon the place of humanity within nature. The word 'within' is significant. Nature is not the 'other' but, rather, that of which we as human beings are parts. If nature suffers or dies, then so do we. One may surmise that Marx's work is precisely the wrong sort of philosophy in this respect. After all, one of Marx's key points was that of the development of productive forces. Ecological crisis demands that humans hold those forces in check. However, as Eagleton (2011: 231–6) points out, Marx argued that productive forces develop under capitalism. He said very little about communism, and did not discuss the development of productive forces in communist society.

Of course, as Eagleton goes on to remind us, one may suggest that although Marx did not advocate boundless expansion of human powers over nature, he did underplay the natural limits on human development. If though we are correcting in thinking of the circular temporarily belonging to human flourishing, then the latter quite evidently puts such limits on human development, if only because it defines 'development' to include its effects.

Marx's works of the period can, as Loftus indicates in his analysis of the *Theses on Feuerbach*, provide a foundation for the exploration of answers to these problems of the world today – problems which may, if not resolved, become the final problems of humanity. As Bradley J. Macdonald (2006: 47–9) suggests, the radical ecotheorists who portray Marx as an 'anthropocentric Promethean' who saw 'nature as a senseless milieu for the development of human productive forces' have neglected aspects of Marx's early work that may be of some significance, even though it would be too much to say that Marx was an ecologist. The powers that capitalism has brought into being, as Eagleton (2011: 236) suggests, need to be brought under rational human control. Humans produce themselves and their world. To bring that world under rational control they need to change it by means of bringing about their own emancipation from alienation and thus from exploitation. As Marx clearly recognized in his early writings, the best way to preserve nature is to act together in cooperation. Sociality can help humans plan their future in a way which allows each to flourish and crucially in a way which preserves nature. Humans produce themselves and the broader nature. They need to continue to produce themselves and nature rather than act in ways which lead to their own demise as a result of the demise of nature. To work in cooperation requires the elimination of human exploitation. This in turn requires humans to free themselves from alienation. Those who benefit most from exploitation are unlikely to simply give way. Hence, the majority cannot simply wait for liberation. Indeed, liberation from exploitation and the opportunity to produce cooperatively require self-emancipation of the expanded working class of the contemporary world. Social change that will enable existential autonomy to become reality may thus be achieved.

Of course, we are not suggesting that one can find the answers to the problems of consumerism, helplessness and ecological crisis in the works of the first Marx or, were they there to be found, that in this brief last section of a chapter we could lay them out. Our concern is only to show that his political philosophy retains relevance to contemporary problems. One may not agree with what he said. Nevertheless, his ideas still warrant careful consideration and carry contemporary relevance. The first Marx does thus still provide both an internally coherent and distinctive, but also a valuable philosophy. Hopefully, the reconstruction on which this book has embarked will make a contribution in these respects.

REFERENCES

Abbey, R. (2002), 'Young Karl Does Headstands', *Political Theory*, 30 (1): 150–5.

Ackrill, J. L. (1978), 'Aristotle on Action', *Mind*, 87 (348): 595–601.

Allen, K. (2011), *Marx and the Alternative to Capitalism*, London: Pluto Press.

Althusser, L. (2006). *For Marx*, London: Verso.

Arblaster, A. (1984), *The Rise and Decline of Western Liberalism*, Oxford: Basil Blackwell.

Aristotle (1962), *The Politics*, Harmondsworth: Penguin.

Aristotle (1996), *The Nicomachean Ethics*, Ware: Wordsworth.

Arthur, C. J. (1974), 'Introduction', in K. Marx and F. Engels (eds), *The German Ideology*, 4–34, London: Lawrence and Wishart.

Avineri, S. (1972), *Hegel's Theory of the Modern State*, London: Cambridge University Press.

Babeuf, F.-N. and Marechal, S. (1997), 'The Manifesto of Equality', in L. P. Pojman and R. Westmoreland (eds), *Equality: Selected Readings*, 49–52, Oxford: Oxford University Press.

Ball, T. (1995), *Reappraising Political Theory: Revisionist Studies in the History of Political Thought*, Oxford: Oxford University Press.

Beiser, F. (2005), *Hegel*, London: Routledge.

Bernstein, E. (1993). *The Preconditions of Socialism*, Cambridge: Cambridge University Press.

Berry, C. J. (1986), *Human Nature*, Houndmills: Macmillan.

Berry, C. J. (1989), 'Need and Egoism in Marx's Early Writings', in M. Cowling and L. Wilde (eds), *Approaches to Marx*, 122–34, Milton Keynes: Open University Press.

Bevir, M. (2011), 'The Contextual Approach', in G. Klosko (ed.), *The Oxford Handbook of the History of Political Philosophy*, 11–23, Oxford: Oxford University Press.

Booth, W. J. (1989), 'Gone Fishing: Making Sense of Marx's Concept of Communism', *Political Theory*, 17 (2): 205–22.

Breckman, W. (1999), *Marx, the Young Hegelians, and the Origins of Radical Social Theory*, Cambridge: Cambridge University Press.

Breckman, W. (2001), 'Eduard Gans and the Crisis of Hegelianism', *Journal of the History of Ideas*, 62 (3): 543–64.

Brown, E. (2009), 'Politics and Society', in J. Warren (ed.), *The Cambridge Companion to Epicureanism*, 179–96, Cambridge: Cambridge University Press.

Brudney, D. (2001), 'Justifying a Conception of the Good Life: The Problem of the 1844 Marx', *Political Theory*, 29 (3): 364–94.

Brudney, D. (2002), 'Justification and Radicalism in the 1844 Marx', *Political Theory*, 30 (1): 156–63.

Buchanan, A. (1977), 'Exploitation, Alienation, and Injustice', *Canadian Journal of Philosophy*, 9 (1): 121–39.

Byron, C. (2014), 'A Critique of Sean Sayers' Marxian Theory of Human Nature', *Science and Society*, 78 (2): 241–8.

Callinicos, A. (1983), *Marxism and Philosophy*, Oxford: Oxford University Press.

Callinicos, A. (1995), *The Revolutionary Ideas of Karl Marx*, 2nd edn, London: Bookmarks.

Camus, A. (2005), *The Myth of Sisyphus*, London: Penguin.

Carver, T. (1983), *Marx and Engels: The Intellectual Relationship*, Brighton: Wheatsheaf.

Carver, T. (1998), *The Postmodern Marx*, Manchester: Manchester University Press.

Carver, T. (2010), 'The German Ideology Never Took Place', *History of Political Thought*, 32 (1): 107–27.

Chitty, A. (1997), 'First Person Plural Ontology and Praxis', *Proceedings of the Aristotelian Society*, 97 (1): 81–96.

Chitty, A. (2011), 'Hegel and Marx', in S. Houlgate and M. Baur (eds), *A Companion to Hegel*, 477–500, Chichester: Wiley-Blackwell.

Cohen, G. A. (1988), *History, Labour and Freedom: Themes from Marx*, Oxford: Oxford University Press.

Colletti, L. (1974), *From Rousseau to Lenin: Studies in Ideology and Society*, New York: Monthly Review Press.

Colletti, L. (1975), 'Introduction', in K. Marx, *Early Writings*, 7–56, London: Penguin.

Comninel, G. (2010), 'Emancipation in Marx's Early Work', *Socialism and Democracy*, 24 (3): 60–78.

Cowling, M. (1989), 'The Case for Two Marxes Restated', in M. Cowling and L. Wilde (eds), *Approaches to Marx*, 14–32, Milton Keynes: Open University Press.

Cullen, B. (1979), *Hegel's Social and Political Thought: An Introduction*, Dublin: Gill and Macmillan.

Delfgaauw, B. (1967), *The Young Marx*, London: Sheed and Ward.

Della Volpe, G. (1979), *Rousseau and Marx and Other Writings*, Atlantic Highlands, NJ: Humanities Press.

Draper, H. (1971), 'The Principle of Self-Emancipation in Marx and Engels', in R. Miliband and J. Saville (eds), *The Socialist Register 1971*, 81–109, New York: Monthly Review Press.

Dunn, J. (1993), *Western Political Theory in the Face of the Future*, Cambridge: Cambridge University Press.

Eagleton, T. (1997), *Marx and Freedom*, London: Phoenix.

Eagleton, T. (2011), *Why Marx Was Right*, New Haven: Yale University Press.

Easton, D. and Guddat, K. H. (1997), *Writings of the Young Marx on Philosophy and Society*, Indianapolis: Hackett.

Eccleshall, R. (1975), 'The Undivided Self', in B. Parekh (ed.), *The Concept of Socialism*, 95–119, London: Croom Helm.

Edwards, A. and Townshend, J. (2002), 'Introduction', in A. Edwards and J. Townshend (eds), *Interpreting Modern Political Philosophy: From Machiavelli to Marx*, 1–20, Houndmills: Palgrave Macmillan.

Elster, J. (1985), *Making Sense of Marx*, Cambridge: Cambridge University Press.

Elster, J. (1986), *An Introduction to Karl Marx*, Cambridge: Cambridge University Press.

Evans, M. (1975), *Karl Marx*, London: George Allen and Unwin.

Femia, J. (1993), *Marxism and Democracy*, Oxford: Oxford University Press.

Fenves, P. (1986), 'Marx's Doctoral Thesis on Two Greek Atomists and the Post-Kantian Interpretations', *Journal of the History of Ideas*, 47 (3): 433–52.

Ferrarin, A. (2000), 'Homo Faber, Homo Sapiens or Homo Politicus: Protagorus and the Myth of Prometheus', *The Review of Metaphysics*, 54 (2): 289–319.

Fetscher, E. B. (1980), 'Censorship and the Editorial: Baden's New Press Law of 1940 and the *Seeblätter* at Konstanz', *German Studies Review*, 3 (3): 377–94.

Feuerbach, L. (2012), *The Fiery Brook: Selected Writings*, London: Verso.

Fine, B. and Saad-Filho, A. (2010), *Marx's Capital*, 5th edn, London: Pluto Press.

Fraser, I. and Wilde, L. (2011), *The Marx Dictionary*, London: Bloomsbury.

George, S. (2004), *Another World is Possible If ...*, London: Verso.

Geras, N. (1983), *Marx and Human Nature: Refutation of A Legend*, London: Verso.

Gillis, J. R. (1968), 'Aristocracy and Bureaucracy in Nineteenth-Century Prussia', *Past and Present*, 41: 105–29.

Gorz, A. (1982), *Farewell to the Working Class: An Essay on Post-Industrial Socialism*, London: Pluto Press.

Gorz, A. (1994), *Capitalism, Socialism, Ecology*, London: Verso.

Green, A. (2001), 'Intervening in the Public Sphere: German Governments and the Press, 1815–1870', *The Historical Journal*, 44 (1): 155–75.

Guess, R. (1981), *The Idea of a Critical Theory: Habermas and the Frankfurt School*, Cambridge: Cambridge University Press.

Haddock, B. (1992), 'Saint Augustine: *The City of God*', in M. Forsyth and M. Keens-Soper (eds), *The Political Classics: A Guide to the Essential Texts from Plato to Rousseau*, 69–95, Oxford: Oxford University Press.

Hahn, E. J. C. (1977), 'The Junior Faculty in "Revolt": Reform Plans for Berlin University in 1848', *The American Historical Review*, 82 (4): 875–95.

Hammen, O. J. (1980), 'A Note on the Alienation Motif in Marx', *Political Theory*, 8 (2): 223–42.

Hands, G. (2010), *Marx: The Key Ideas*, London: Hodder.

Hanfi, Z. (2013), 'Introduction', in L. Feuerbach, *The Fiery Brook: Selected Writings*, 1–52, London: Verso.

Hardimon, M. O. (1992), 'The Project of Reconciliation: Hegel's Social Philosophy', *Philosophy and Public Affairs*, 21 (2): 165–95.

Hegel, G. W. F. (1991), *Elements of the Philosophy of Right*, Cambridge: Cambridge University Press.

Heidegger, M. (1962), *Being and Time*, New York: Harper and Row.

Herres, J. (2015), 'Rhineland Radicals and the "48ers"', in T. Carver and J. Farr (eds), *The Cambridge Guide to the Communist Manifesto*, 15–31, New York: Cambridge University Press.

Hess, M. (1845), *The Essence of Money*, in Marxists Internet Archive. Available online: https://www.marxists.org/archive/hess/1845/essence-money.htm (accessed 14 January 2018).

Hess, M. (1964), 'The Philosophy of the Act', in A. Fried and R. Sanders (eds), *Socialist Thought: A Documentary History*, 249–75, New York: Anchor Books.

Higonnet, P. L. R. (1998), *Goodness Beyond Virtue: Jacobins During the French Revolution*, Cambridge, MA: Harvard University Press.

Hobsbawm, E. (1962), *The Age of Revolution: 1789–1848*, London: Weidenfeld and Nicloson.

Hocutt, M. (1974), 'Aristotle's Four Becauses', *Philosophy*, 49 (190): 385–99.

Holmstrom, N. (1977), 'Exploitation', *Canadian Journal of Philosophy*, 7 (2): 353–69.

Hook, S. (1994), *From Hegel to Marx: Studies in the Intellectual Development of Karl Marx*, New York: Columbia University Press.

Hunt, T. (2010), *The Frock-Coated Communist: The Life and Times of the Original Champagne Socialist*, London: Penguin.

Jaffe, A. (2016), 'From Aristotle to Marx: A Critical Philosophical Anthropology', *Science and Society*, 80 (1): 56–77.

Jensen, G. E. (1974), 'Official Reform in *Vormärz* Prussia: The Ecclesiastical Dimension', *Central European History*, 7 (2): 137–58.

Kant, I. (1900), *Kant on Education*, Boston: D.C. Heath and Co.

Kant, I. (1993), *The Critique of Practical Reason*, trans. Beck, 3rd edn, New York: Macmillan.

Kant, I. (1996), *Critique of Pure Reason*, Indianapolis: Hackett.

Kant, I. (2002), *Grounding for the Metaphysics of Morals*, New Haven: Yale University Press.

Kelley, D. R. (1978), 'The Metaphysics of Law: An Essay on the Very Young Marx', *The American History Review*, 83 (2): 350–67.

Khilnani, S. (2003), 'French Marxism – Existentialism to Structuralism', in T. Ball and R. Bellamy (eds), *The Cambridge History of Twentieth-Century Political Thought*, 299–318, Cambridge: Cambridge University Press.

Kitching, G. (1988), *Karl Marx and the Philosophy of Praxis*, London: Routledge.

Klein, N. (2000), *No Logo*, London: Flamingo.

Knowles, D. (2001), *Political Philosophy*, London: Routledge.

Körner, S. (1955), *Kant*, Harmondsworth: Penguin.

Kroner, R. (1948), 'The Year 1800 in the Development of German Idealism', *The Review of Metaphysics*, 1 (4): 1–31.

Laclau, E. and Mouffe, C. (1985), *Hegemony and Socialist Strategy: Towards a Radical Democratic Politics*, London: Verso.

Lamb, P. (2010), 'Marx, Karl (1818–1883)', in M. Bevir (ed.), *Encyclopedia of Political Theory*, Vol. 2, 856–63, Thousand Oaks: Sage

Lamb, P. (2015), *Marx and Engels' Communist Manifesto: A Readers' Guide*, London: Bloomsbury.

Laski, H. J. (1925), *A Grammar of Politics*, London: George Allen and Unwin.

Laycock, H. (1999), 'Exploitation via Labour Power in Marx', *The Journal of Ethics*, 3 (2): 121–31.

Leopold, D. (2007), *Marx, the Young Hegelians, and the Origins of Radical Social Theory*, Cambridge: Cambridge University Press.

Leopold, D. (2015), 'Marx, Engels and Other Socialisms', in T. Carver and J. Farr (eds), *The Cambridge Companion to the Communist Manifesto*, 32–49, New York: Cambridge University Press.

Lessnoff, M. (1986), *Social Contract*, Houndmills: Macmillan.

Levin, M. (1998), '"The Hungry Forties": The Socio-economic Context of the
Communist Manifesto', in M. Cowling (ed.), *The Communist Manifesto: New
Interpretations*, 41–50, Edinburgh: Edinburgh University Press.

Levine, A. (1987), *The End of the State*, London: Verso.

Levine, A. (2002), *Engaging Political Philosophy from Hobbes to Rawls*,
Oxford: Blackwell.

Lichtheim, G. (1975), *A Short History of Socialism*, Glasgow: Fontana/Collins.

Loftus, A (2009), 'The *Theses of Feuerbach* as a Political Ecology of the Possible',
Area, 41 (2): 157–66.

Löwy, M. (2005), *The Theory of Revolution in the Young Marx*, Chicago:
Haymarket Books.

Lukes, S. (1987), *Marxism and Morality*, Oxford: Oxford University Press.

Macdonald, B. J. (2006), *Performing Marx: Contemporary Negotiations of a
Living Tradition*, Albany: State University of New York Press.

McCann, H. (1974), 'Volition and Basic Action', *The Philosophical Review*, 83
(4): 451–73.

McCarthy, G. (1985), 'Development of the Concept and Method of Critique in
Kant, Hegel, and Marx', *Studies in Soviet Thought*, 30 (1): 15–38.

McIvor, M. (2008), 'The Young Marx and German Idealism: Revisiting the
Doctoral Dissertation', *Journal of the History of Philosophy*, 46 (3): 395–420.

McLellan, D. (1969), *The Young Hegelians and Karl Marx*, London: Macmillan.

McLellan, D. (1972), *Marx Before Marxism*, Harmondsworth: Penguin.

McLellan, D. (2006), *Karl Marx: A Biography*, 4th edn, Houndmills: Palgrave
Macmillan.

Macpherson, C. B. (1962), *The Political Theory of Possessive Individualism*,
Oxford: Oxford University Press.

Maguire, J. (1972), *Marx's Paris Writings: An Analysis*, Dublin: Gill and
Macmillan.

Mah, H. (1990), 'The French Revolution and the Problem of Modernity: Hegel,
Heine and Marx', *New German Critique*, 50: 3–20.

Marcuse, H. (1969), 'Repressive Tolerance', in R. P. Wolff, B. Moore Jr. and Herbert
Marcuse, *A Critique of Pure Tolerance*, 81–123, Boston: Beacon Press.

Marcuse, H. (1986), *One Dimensional Man: Studies in the Ideology of Advanced
Industrial Society*, London: ARK Books.

Martin, K. (1962), *French Liberal Thought in the Eighteenth Century*, London:
Phoenix House.

Marx, K. and Engels, F. (1975–2004), *Collected Works*, 50 volumes, London:
Lawrence and Wishart.

Megill, A. (2002), *Karl Marx; The Burden of Reason (Why Marx Rejected Politics
and the Market)*, Lanham, MD: Rowman and Littlefield.

Mehring, F. (1962), *Karl Marx: The Story of His Life*, Ann Arbor: The University
of Michigan Press.

Mészáros, I. (2005), *Marx's Theory of Alienation*, 5th edn, London: Merlin.

Miliband, R. (1965), 'Marx and the State', in R. Miliband and J. Saville (eds), *The
Socialist Register 1965*, 278–96, London: Merlin.

Mill, J. S. (1924), *Autobiography*, London: Oxford University Press.

Mill, J. S. (1976), 'Chapters on Socialism', in G. L. Williams (ed.), *John Stuart Mill
on Politics and Society*, 335–58, Glasgow: Fontana.

Mill. J. S. (1991), 'On Liberty', in J. Gray (ed.), *On Liberty and Other Essays*, 1–128, Oxford: Oxford University Press.

Musto, M. (2009), 'Marx in Paris: Manuscripts and Notebooks of 1844', *Science and Society*, 73 (3): 386–402.

Olesen, T. A. (2007), 'Schelling: A Historical Introduction to Kierkegaard's Schelling', in J. Stewart (ed.), *Kierkegaard and His German Contemporaries, Tome I: Philosophy*, 229–75, Aldershot: Ashgate.

Ollman, B. (1976), *Alienation: Marx's Conception of Man in a Capitalist Society*, 2nd edn, Cambridge: Cambridge University Press.

Osborne, P. (2005), *How to Read Marx*, London: Granta.

Parekh, B. (1975), 'Marx's Theory of Man', in B. Parekh (ed.), *The Concept of Socialism*, 38–61, London: Croom Helm.

Parekh, B. (1982), *Marx's Theory of Ideology*, London: Croom Helm.

Pierson, C. (1996), *The Modern State*, London: Routledge.

Pippin, R. B. (1991), 'Idealism and Agency in Kant and Hegel', *The Journal of Philosophy*, 88 (10): 532–41.

Plant, R. (1983), *Hegel: An Introduction*, Oxford: Basil Blackwell.

Plato (1974), *The Republic*, Harmondsworth: Penguin.

Raphael, D. D. (1990), *Problems of Political Philosophy*, 2nd edn, Houndmills: Macmillan.

Redding, P. (2011), 'German Idealism', in G. Klosko (ed.), *The Oxford Handbook of The History of Political Philosophy*, 348–68, Oxford: Oxford University Press.

Rousseau, J.-J. (1993), 'The Social Contract', in G. D. H. Cole (ed.), *The Social Contract and Discourses*, 179–309, London: Everyman.

Sartre, J.-P. (1973), *Existentialism and Humanism*, London: Methuen.

Sartre, J.-P. (1992), *Being and Nothingness*, New York: Washington Square Press.

Saunders, P. (1995), *Capitalism: A Social Audit*, Buckingham: Open University Press.

Sayers, S. (2011), *Marx and Alienation: Essays on Hegelian Themes*, Houndmills: Palgrave Macmillan.

Schafer, P. M. (2006), 'Introduction', to P. M. Schafer (ed.), *The First Writings of Karl Marx*, 10–70, New York: Ig Publishing.

Seed, J. (2010), *Marx: A Guide for the Perplexed*, London: Continuum.

Seigel, J. E. (1973) 'Marx's Early Development: Vocation, Rebellion, and Realism', *The Journal of Interdisciplinary History*, 3 (3): 475–508.

Smaldone, W. (2014), *European Socialism: A Concise History with Documents*, Lanham: Rowman and Littlefield.

Speight, A. (2008), *The Philosophy of Hegel*. Stocksfield: Acumen,

Sperber, J. (2013), *Karl Marx: A Nineteenth-Century Life*, New York: Liveright.

Spies, A. (1996) 'Towards a Prosopography of Young Hegelians', *German Studies Review*, 19(2): 321–39.

Stanley, J. L. (1995), 'The Marxism of Marx's Doctoral Dissertation', *Journal of the History of Philosophy*, 33 (1): 133–58.

Stedman Jones, G. (2017), *Karl Marx: Greatness and Illusion*, London: Penguin.

Struhl, K. J. (2016), 'Marx and Human Nature: The Historical, the Trans-historical and Human Flourishing', *Science and Society*, 80 (1): 78–104.

Teeple, G. (1999), 'The Doctoral Dissertation of Karl Marx', in B. Jessop with R. Wheatley (eds), *Karl Marx's Social and Political Thought: Critical Assessments, Second Series*, Vol. 5, 62–103, London: Routledge.

Ten, C. L. (1980), *Mill on Liberty*, Oxford: Oxford University Press.

Thomas, P. (1980), *Karl Marx and the Anarchists*, London: Routledge and Kegan Paul.

Thomas, P. (2011), 'Max Stirner and Karl Marx: An Overlooked Contretemps', in S. Newman (ed.), *Max Stirner*, 113–42, Basingstoke: Palgrave Macmillan.

Thomas, P. (2012). *Karl Marx*, London: Reaktion.

Toews, J. E. (2004), *Becoming Historical: Cultural Reformation and Public Memory in Early Nineteenth-Century Berlin*, Cambridge: Cambridge University Press.

Townsend, T. (2007), 'Climate Change: A Marxist Analysis', in D. Holmes, T. Townsend and J. Bellamy Foster (eds), *Change the System Not the Climate!: A Socialist View of Global Warming*, Chippendale NSW: Resistance Books.

Turner, D. (1991), 'Religion: Illusions and Liberation', in T. Carver (ed.), *The Cambridge Companion to Marx*, 320–37, Cambridge: Cambridge University Press.

Turner, R. S. (1971), 'The Growth of Professorial Research in Prussia, 1818 to 1848 – Causes and Context', *Historical Studies in the Physical Sciences*, 3: 137–82.

Weldon, T. W. (1953), *The Vocabulary of Politics*, Harmondsworth: Penguin.

Weyher, L. F. (2012), 'Re-Reading Sociology Via the Emotions: Karl Marx's Theory of Human Nature and Estrangement', *Sociological Perspectives*, 55 (2): 341–63.

Wheen, F. (1999), *Karl Marx*, London: Fourth Estate.

Wilde, L. (1991), 'Logic: Dialectic and Contradiction', in T. Carver (ed.), *The Cambridge Companion to Marx*, 275–95, Cambridge: Cambridge University Press.

Wilde, L. (2003), 'The Early Marx', in D. Boucher and P. Kelly (eds), *Political Thinkers: From Socrates to the Present*, 404–18, Oxford: Oxford University Press.

Williams, H. (1983), *Kant's Political Philosophy*, Oxford: Basil Blackwell.

Williams, R. (1981), *Keywords: A Vocabulary of Culture and Society*, London: Fontana.

Wolff, J. (1999), 'Marx and Exploitation', *The Journal of Ethics*, 3 (2): 105–20.

Wolff, J. (2002), *Why Read Marx Today?* Oxford: Oxford University Press.

Wright, E. O. (1993), 'Class Analysis, History and Emancipation', *New Left Review*, I/202: 15–35.

Wright, E. O., Levine, A. and Sober, E. (2003), 'Marxism and Methodological Individualism', in D. Matravers and J. Pike (eds), *Debates in Contemporary Political Philosophy: An Anthology*, 54–66, London: Routledge.

Young, I. M. (1990), *Justice and the Politics of Difference*, Princeton, NJ: Princeton University Press.

INDEX